JUNE 2022
Volume 74, Number 2

Comparative Literature

FIRAT ORUC

Thalassological Worldmaking and Literary Circularities in the Indian Ocean

JUST BEFORE THIS special issue went to press, the Swedish Academy named Abdulrazak Gurnah as the winner of the 2021 Nobel Prize in Literature for his "uncompromising and compassionate penetration of the effects of colonialism and the fate of the refugee in the gulf between cultures and continents."[1] Consistent with its world-literary ideology, the academy clearly delocalized Gurnah's authorship, making sure that the citation's language was "purified of identifiable local content or topical references" (Damrosch 202). Curiously enough, nearly all the celebratory remarks in the aftermath of the announcement of the prize profiled Gurnah as an Anglophone postcolonial writer, while completely sidelining the fact that he has in fact been one of the most prominent narrators of the Indian Ocean (through a Joycean concentric cognitive mapping of Zanzibar, Tanzania, Africa, Britain, and the world). Gurnah himself has not forgotten the formative impact of the Indian Ocean on his writing journey:

When I first started writing, I was writing with the refugee issue very much at the center of my thinking. But overriding all that I'm describing were the monsoons. From as early as I could remember as a child, there are late months of the year from around November, December or so. So the arrival of dozens of ships of all sizes from different parts of the Indian Ocean. They would be from the Arabian Peninsula, from the Gulf, from India, and occasionally even further away—the huge ships that sometimes came from as far away as Thailand. And the sailors and the traders on these ships sprawled themselves and their wares among us, beside us, everywhere. It was impossible not to know that you were part of a wider world, a wider world with its own center of gravity, a cosmopolitan world if you like and that we were networked in a shared cultural and historical community. ("Discussion")

Gurnah fathoms the Indian Ocean as a network that produces "patterns" and "rhythms" in an ecological as well as imaginary space that constitutes a wide variety of "subjectivities" of people (Gupta 520). Gurnah's Indian Ocean world, moreover, is not only made by climate and trade cycles but also literary circularities.

---

[1] Nobel Prize Outreach AB, "The Nobel Prize in Literature 2021," October 9, 2021, www.nobelprize.org/prizes/literature/2021/summary/.

Comparative Literature 74:2
DOI 10.1215/00104124-9594787   © 2022 by University of Oregon

These circularities capture a dynamic cross-cultural traffic, exchange, and encounter across Asia, Africa, and the Middle East through a rich range of genres, including epics, story cycles, travelogues, memoirs, poems, and novels (Bose; Desai; Green; Hofmeyr; Ricci; Vierke).

Following the creative work of Gurnah and other writers, this special issue brings together articles on world literatures of the Indian Ocean as a site for studying mobile networks of capital and labor, diasporas generated by European imperial expansion and its aftermath, and cultures that bind together places and peoples. Literary scholars active in the field of Indian Ocean studies participate in tracking such circularities that urge us to "[move] away from relative immobile, essentializing 'trait geographies'—values, languages, material practices, ecological adaptations, marriage patterns, and the like—towards 'process geographies' with various kinds of action, interaction, and motion (travel, trade, marriage, pilgrimage, warfare, proselytization, colonization, exile, and so on), in which regions can be conceptualized as both dynamic and interconnected" (Vink 52).

Although the study of Indian Ocean literary circularities is a relatively new and dynamic field, it calls for alternative paradigms for global literary history in light of the nascent conversation between comparative world literature and oceanic studies. Although it is self-evident that continents and languages have been shaped by "oceanic routes" (Bystrom and Hofmeyr) for millennia, both old and new comparative literature has been remarkably territorial. The polysemic nature of the Indian Ocean invites the following question: what would world literature look like if we unsettled terracentric biases of the field? In other words, how does the thalassological poetics of the Indian Ocean also remap approaches to literary categories themselves? The Indian Ocean's literary waves and the generic wateriness they create offer a set of analytical categories as they rescale narrative as a living, moving, recombining, recycling practice of memory, connection, and connectivity. As such, the historically connective capacities of the Indian Ocean and the process geographies of oceanic flows not only "enable different ways of seeing and writing the world" but also track "movement across national and linguistic boundaries, taking in experiences and ideas from diverse latitudes and longitudes" (Bystrom and Hofmeyr 2). The essays in this issue critique the privileging of the North Atlantic in the world-literary canon and in the critical discourses of oceanic studies by attending to literatures of the Indian Ocean and the routes and circulations that they narrativize without exceptionalizing them.

Possibly the most distinctive feature of Indian Ocean literary circularities is the extent to which they operate through an aesthetic sensorium of objects from distant "elsewheres." Clarissa Vierke's semiotic and topographic reading of the fifteenth- to eighteenth-century Swahili poems attributed to the master poet Fumo Liyongo foregrounds these intimate aesthetic sensory experiences with cultural objects and luxury goods arriving on the Swahili coast. Traditionally performed through *gungu* dances on special occasions, the Liyongo poems feature objects evocative of transoceanic connections and interregional circularities across the Indian Ocean world such as the betel plant. The fluid aestheticization of the betel quid—an Indian Ocean plant par excellence—in those poems illustrate the various kinds of economic circulation that have historically animated the Indian Ocean (Sheriff) and the confluence of material culture and sensuous aesthetics along the Swahili coast. Vierke argues that a study of literary production on the precolonial Swahili coast—a space defined by liminality and in-betweenness—will allow us to appreciate the physical manifestations of cosmopolitanism and move beyond what one simply *imagines* cosmopolitanism to be. The self-fashioning role of these objects for a rising merchant class—especially in culturally and religiously sensitive matters—is a case in point. At the heart of Vierke's close readings of the Liyongo poems is a keen understanding of the role of circulation in the formation of Creole cosmopolitanism as a practice of active construction of cultural semantics through mobile things from multiple elsewheres (Lionnet). To say that a given artifact or plant is "native" or "indigenous" to a region is to dismiss millennia of cross-pollination across a very heterogeneous littoral space. Royal ornaments, porcelain or glazed ware, and furniture on the Swahili coast have historically been formed within a shared ecology of circulating cultures, languages, and artistic forms (Meier). The object-oriented, sensuous imaginaries of the Liyongo poems, then, are quintessentially cosmopolitan as they draw on exterior forms to produce an iterative intimate aesthetic that forms layered, sensational seascapes.

Through a "liquid reading" of Gurnah's *By the Sea*, Vilashini Cooppan takes Indian Ocean circularities to the theoretical waters of object-oriented ontology, genre theory, narrative spatiotemporality, and phenomenological relationality. Cooppan's looking back, out, and in to circularity as an Indian Ocean method is embedded in language—in words that are evocative of the intimacies of subject-object relationships. *By the Sea*'s object-words become carriers of subject histories, connectivities, and memories. Cooppan's orientation toward object-words is accompanied by a discussion of the chronotopes of the Indian Ocean, as the latter require us to move beyond our preoccupation with trade-related links across the littoral and instead look to the narrative forms that have taken shape at the intersection of many regional, overlapping Indian Ocean worlds. While there are multiple layers of unity in the Indian Ocean, emic imaginations of its space are in flux. Indian Ocean historians' preoccupation with elements of "deep structure" (Pearson) posits rainfall distribution, monsoons, and climate changes; north and north-westerly winds; and ocean currents, tidal flows, and tumultuous waves as the primary ecological and structural factors that governed how, where, and why people traveled across the Indian Ocean. Yet these elements of deep structure vary dramatically according to both the region and time of the year, thus creating a certain rhythm of movement and interaction across the oceanic space. As historian Jeremy Prestholdt argues, a closer look at the social worlds of the Indian Ocean reveals the role of emic (intraregional) and etic (extraregional) actors in historically producing regional "affinities"—perceived forms of continuity across littoral societies. Prestholdt emphasizes that disaggregated cultural hybridity in the Indian Ocean was an essential feature of the precolonial era, while conceptions of "unity" have, since the nineteenth century, been colonial or etic impositions on littoral societies to, for instance, transport bonded slaves from East Africa across a seamlessly colonized space. As such, Prestholdt urges us to understand contemporary ideas of unity and cohesion as layered and fraught with tension vis-à-vis longer standing, albeit marginalized, histories of racial, religious, and cultural difference. By the same token, Cooppan pushes back against the structuralist study of the Indian Ocean as an integrated totality or as what Prestholdt calls a "meta-culture" (26).

Cooppan responds to the structuralist problem of relationality by repurposing Franco Moretti's account of the "trees and waves" that respectively explain patterns of literary distribution and circulation. Gurnah's *By the Sea* provides a model for literary studies by its very grafting and intermeshing of spoken languages, family histories, individual lives, and goods (rhizomatic trees) in the larger palimpsestic histories of migration, slavery, indenture, trade, empire, and globalization (waves). For Cooppan, the metaphoric work of trees and waves also explains the circulatory economies of Indian Ocean literatures, as in the case of the relationality between *The Arabian Nights* and *By the Sea*, where the latter simultaneously develops a branching tree of its own *and* opens itself to the figurative waves of stories of the former.

Moretti's world-systems thinking views waves as "uniformity, engulfing an initial diversity" (60): but waves drift. If the homogenizing impulse of the colonial archives in the histories of the Indian Ocean was geared toward presenting monolithic narratives of the complex multilingual communities and toward some form of domesticated translation, contemporary novelists of the Indian Ocean world such as Amitav Ghosh and Abdulrazak Gurnah attempt to drift narrative away from such presumed authority. Kritish Rajbhandari names this acting of snatching the past from colonial structures of power as anarchival drift, and analyzes how Ghosh's *Sea of Poppies* and Abdulrazak Gurnah's *Paradise* not only critically rewrite the past differently from colonial genres of dictionaries and travelogues but also imaginatively create and translate new historical documentary material to give voice to the various subaltern subjectivities silenced by the normative archive. Drifting anarchically away from colonial texts, these novels circle their readers back to the multivalent, multilingual, translative worlds of the Indian Ocean by showing circularity in how words gain new definitions and are absorbed into other languages and cultures. At the same time, they do not assume absolute authority and allow for continuous reinterpretation. From this perspective, Ghosh and Gurnah illustrate what it entails to be a writer of the Indian Ocean by taking on multiple intersecting roles of chronicler, translator, archivist, editor, and publisher.

Another name for what Rajbhandari identifies as the multiplicity of linguistic registers and the translative processes that are subject to transoceanic historical forces is Creolization. Theorizing Creolity as a matter of (un)translatability, Françoise Vergès and Carapin Marimoutou write: "There is no creolization without loss, just as it cannot happen without inequality because creolization demands or requires room to manoeuvre where tensions and conflicts are resolved without being dissolved" (15–16). Rejecting the placing of the subjects of Creole Indias on the negative, deficit end of the continuum of cultural hybridity and mobility (as subjects defined by cultural and historical loss and subjugation), Ananya Jahanara Kabir reads Franco-Tamil novelist Ari Gautier's *Le thinnai* as a creative work that is able to capture the many Creole ways in which we can speak of and study the porosity and heterogeneity of the Indian Ocean littoral. In Gautier's novel, the space of a *thinnai*—the veranda on the ground floor of Tamil homes—is *a world* in which people of many races, ethnicities, and religions meet and mesh together, allowing for perpetual Creolization. Not only do the novel and the architectural space host these togethernesses in an archipelagic form, but so does Pondicherry, which acts as India's *thinnai* due to its situatedness as a contact zone where foreign and native encounters begin. In narrating the *thinnai* as a Creole space, Gautier aims to free it from language, caste, and gender-based hierarchies. It is rather conceived as a heterotopia, a place, in other words, of difference and otherness. The trespassing figure is the novel's only speaking female character, Lourdes, who accesses the *thinnai*, while also fashioning a complex social identity. Lourdes enters the *thinnai*, traditionally limited to males and high castes, as a Bas Créole servant only to release dormant memories of Pondicherry's Creole history as it is embodied in her lineage, cuisine, language, and conduct. This is not history in the usual sense of the term but what Kabir calls "archipelago of fragments," an affective epistemology and sensorium of Creole lived experiences at the intersections of transoceanic and littoral circuits.

Even so, the Creole archipelagos and littoral enclaves of the Indian Ocean have been seriously tested by the contemporary effects of postcolonial migration crises. In particular, the forced and voluntary movements across the ocean have directed the thematic orientation of the contemporary Indian Ocean novel toward human and ecological loss, trauma, and violation (Poddar). In invoking global empathy toward the lesser-known, ultraperipheral Mayotte's Mahoran migrant crisis, Mauritian author Nathacha Appanah's *Tropique de la violence* draws on a comparative reference to the Mediterranean refugee crisis, a presumably familiar case. But what are the stakes of such comparisons? asks Nikhita Obeegadoo in her contribution to this issue. In employing ironic comparison to make a statement about the invisibility of clandestine migration from the Comoros to the French island-territory of Mayotte in the global media, argues Obeegadoo, Nathacha Appanah's novel runs the risk of reproducing the very ironic situation that she criticizes: "Should the novel be lauded for drawing attention to an invisibilized part of the world, or criticized for turning human suffering into literary raw material?" As the current precarities and volatilities facing Indian Ocean littoral societies enter the narrative domain, the ethics of "relational comparison" (Shih)—of bringing into relation seemingly distant entities, issues, terms, or (con)texts for comparison—becomes a more pressing methodological issue. Appanah's use of "comparable" crises to invoke empathy and her presentation of migration as essential to humanity's story comes with the ironic risk of producing "literary violence" toward the refugees themselves.

The appeal to comparative ethics, moreover, straddles the line between opposing and inviting the foreign gaze. Appanah's novel centers on a rarely acknowledged issue but does not give a voice to the voiceless; that is, Mayotte's refugees. Different from the Rabelaisian polyglossia that Rajbhandari and Kabir trace in the novels of Ghosh, Gurnah, and Gautier, Obeegadoo characterizes Appanah's migrant narrative with "incomplete polyphony," observed in the difference between French-speaking characters who express themselves vocally and the subalterns who struggle with French to the extent that other characters (and readers) do not understand them or "hear" their lived experience. Similarly, in its invocation of the ironic relationship between Mayotte and France (namely, Mayotte is French in name, but not French in everything else), Appanah's novel offers a critique of the metropolitan silence over the Mahoran refugee crisis but only, as Obeegadoo aptly remarks, vocalizes it through French characters expressing their shock at the bad state of

France-Mayotte, laying bare the ironies of underdevelopment as well as class difference along the center-periphery axis.

In response to the entanglements of Indian Ocean migratory circularities in
irony, comparison, and silence, Weihsin Gui directs us to the alternative trajectory
of "small narratives" in "the global creative economy" (Lionnet and Jean-François).
Shifting the focus from single-author novels to literary anthologies of the Indian
Ocean, Gui makes a compelling case for collections of multiple narratives by multiple authors as a more fluid and diverse form of reading. Different from the terracentric cartographies of mainstream anthologies, the anthologies of Perth's
Centre for Stories— *Ways of Being Here* and *Wave After Wave*—embrace the ocean
as form. Like a vast body of water, they flow, ripple, move, and reach to the shore,
bringing with them stories from distant shores. Gui adopts Barbadian poet and
historian Kamau Braithwaite's tidalectics to refer to the anthological iterations of
back-and-forth exchanges between coast and sea. The tidalectical aesthetics and
polyphonic form of Indian Ocean literary anthologies generate hybrid, syncretic,
archipelagic circulations of narratives, tropes, and interweaved experiences, while
enabling authors, readers, and stories to move across time and space.

Produced by Australians of Indian Ocean heritage, *Ways of Being Here* and *Wave
After Wave* also deconstruct the singular nation-state discourse of a white Australia,
presenting an intermixed, transnational story of a multicolored Australia. Through
this narrative shift to Afro-Asian Australia, they highlight the issues of diaspora,
race, and migration as well as questions of belonging, assimilation, exclusion, and
inclusion. The two anthologies weave Australia and the Indian Ocean through circular writing and interconnected themes that address Indian Ocean heritage and
the complexity of belonging to a new space bound by nation-state lines.

While migration is a major mode of contemporary Indian Ocean circularities, an
oft-overlooked aspect of postcoloniality is the resurgence of new, specifically Asian,
hegemonic powers. As critical geographer Sharad Chari cautions, postcolonial
infrastructures of capitalism and resource extraction systematically disadvantage
African societies, turning them into extractive enclaves for a so-called rising Asia:
"If the 'gatekeeper state' was an institutional form forged in the wake of Africa's
incomplete decolonization from European colonialisms," writes Chari, "we do
not yet have a vocabulary for Asian corporate-imperial power and influence in
Africa or in the Afro-Indian Ocean" (97). Neelofer Qadir's essay aims precisely to
construct a critical lexicon by tracing a narrative genealogy of the present in "the
long space" (Hitchcock) of the trilogy form. Through a paratactical reading of
Amitav Ghosh's *Ibis* trilogy and Kevin Kwan's *Rich* trilogy as Indian Ocean narratives, Qadir dismantles Orientalist notions about Asian wealth as a "miracle" of
some recent decades and shows how it is in fact a manifestation of a prolonged circular relationship between racial capitalism, colonialism, and accumulation. These
multigenerational sagas are haunted by the specters of colonial capitalist structures
and trade networks into which Asian elite classes adapted themselves, laying the
groundwork for today's wealth in the interregional space of the Indian Ocean.
The inheritance romance that undergirds these narratives, Qadir states, becomes
the symptom of the intimate "desire for wealth" and "practices of ensuring its accumulation across generations of their families." The political unconscious of these
novels gives itself away in the moments of heightened anxieties of the elite classes

losing their inherited economic status due to world-historical events in the Indian Ocean such as the Opium Wars. While this narrative practice enables the emplotment of Asian wealth accumulation on the Indian Ocean's *longue durée*, the romance of "commerce with the universe" (Desai) reifies into what Qadir calls "a desire for dominant position, not one that seeks to interrupt the machinations of an already robust global capitalism."

This oscillation between romance and reification (Jameson) is a long siren call from Joseph Conrad, arguably the first *novelist* of the Indian Ocean. In circling back to Conrad past Gurnah and Ghosh, one becomes alarmed with the extent to which the comparative ground of Anglocentric world literature has been based on the binaries of modern/premodern, value/nonvalue, reason/faith, individual heroism / group action, goal orientation / submission all along. This dualist perspective informs the narrative techniques, figurative strategies, and imaginative horizons of the twentieth-century novel as a teleological narrative of the destruction of traditional cultures and a symbolic form of absorbing the violence that modernization and imperialism have caused on earth. In that regard, the mode of reading world literature as an archaeology of lost worlds, historical remnants, and archaic marvels remains within the aforementioned teleological framework. In this framework, world literature functions merely as the mourning house of the violently and tragically destroyed social forms and practices, or the cultural enclave of a heterogeneous and different universe whose anachronisms could be dramatized only in fiction.

If we were to revisit *Lord Jim*, one of Conrad's Indian Ocean narratives, Jim's quest for a world away from rational capitalist Europe in the "great circular solitude" of the Indian Ocean ultimately leaves us with the scandal of the Conradian *plot*. If, as Fredric Jameson observes, "Jim's crisis requires him to have put lives in danger" (246), those lives are portrayed as entirely *unaware* of the plot into which they are inserted, not even more aware of it than the "screw-pile lighthouse, planted by unbelievers on a treacherous shoal, [which] seemed to wink at [the pilgrim ship] its eye of flame, as if in derision of her errand of faith" (Conrad 12). This setting offers a convenient ground for Jim's pseudosublime:

He stood on the starboard side of the bridge, as far as he could get from the struggle for the boat, which went on with the agitation of madness and *the stealthiness of a conspiracy*. The two Malays had meantime remained holding to the wheel. *Just picture to yourselves the actors* in that, thank God! unique, episode of the sea, four beside themselves with fierce and secret exertions, and three looking on in complete immobility, above the awnings covering *the profound ignorance of hundreds of human beings, with their weariness, with their dreams, with their hopes, arrested, held by an invisible hand on the brink of annihilation.* (70; emphasis mine)

Jim experiences great aesthetic ecstasy at this moment of the possible annihilation of the pilgrims. He does not even pay attention to them—not even "one single glance." Being "a gifted poor devil with the faculty of swift and forestalling vision," he takes pleasure in the idea of "the suspended menace discovered in the midst of the most perfect security" (70). But Conrad's vision of the sublime can no longer afford the comfortably detached vantage point of the Kantian aesthetic paradigm—not in the new geopolitical situation of the imperial age. In Natalie Melas's astute observation, Conrad's sublime becomes "the sublime incomprehensibility of catastrophic turns" (50). The specter of *Patna*, I would argue, haunts our times in the many ships filled with the dispossessed and disenfranchised immigrants, asylum seekers, refugees who are abandoned and left to vanish in the middle of the seas and oceans of the world.

And yet, at the heart of almost all Kojèvean narratives of the twentieth century such as Conrad's is the spectral presence of plebeian agencies who perpetually refashion their being-in-the-world *not* "in a geopolitical space that conjures up a tabula rasa or the utopias associated with desert islands" (Lionnet 26). Rather, they assert themselves into the flow of the objectivist history and operational logic of capital to interrupt its totalizing thrusts and expose its *failure* in mediating the multiplicity and heterogeneity of the world's times and spaces (Chakrabarty; Arava-mudan). Françoise Lionnet's afterword to this special issue assures us that although the Indian Ocean has been increasingly challenged by the ecological, geopolitical, military, and economic furies of our times, its writers and artists continue to stand and fight against them by imaginatively and creatively incarnating the watery and airy spirit of Ariel.

Georgetown University in Qatar

Works Cited

Aravamudan, Srinivas. "The Return of Anachronism." *Modern Language Quarterly* 62, no. 4 (2001): 331–53.

Bose, Sugata. *A Hundred Horizons: The Indian Ocean in an Age of Global Imperialism*. Cambridge, MA: Harvard University Press, 2005.

Bystrom, Kerry, and Isabel Hofmeyr. "Oceanic Routes: (Post-It) Notes on Hydro-colonialism." *Comparative Literature* 69, no. 1 (2017): 1–6.

Chakrabarty, Dipesh. "Universalism and Belonging in the Logic of Capital." *Public Culture* 12, no. 3 (2000): 653–78.

Chari, Sharad. "Africa Extraction, Indian Ocean Critique." *South Atlantic Quarterly* 114, no. 1 (2015): 83–100.

Conrad, Joseph. *Lord Jim*. Oxford: Oxford University Press, 2002.

Damrosch, David. *What Is World Literature?* Princeton, NJ: Princeton University Press, 2003.

Desai, Gaurav. *Commerce with the Universe: Africa, India, and the Afrasian Imagination*. New York: Columbia University Press, 2013.

Green, Nile. "The Waves of Heterotopia: Toward a Vernacular Intellectual History of the Indian Ocean." *American Historical Review* 123, no. 1 (2018): 846–74.

Gupta, Pamila. "Monsoon Fever." *Social Dynamics* 38, no. 3 (2012): 516–27.

Gurnah, Abdulrazak. "A Discussion on *By the Sea*, with Abdulrazak Gurnah." Discussion with Cóillín Parsons and Rogaia Mustafa Abusharaf, November 20, 2020. Uploaded by Georgetown University Qatar, March 31, 2021. YouTube video, 56:23. www.youtube.com/watch?v=fJInO5EfSjE.

Hitchcock, Peter. *The Long Space: Transnationalism and Postcolonial Form*. Redwood City, CA: Stanford University Press, 2010.

Hofmeyr, Isabel. "Indian Ocean Lives and Letters." *English in Africa* 35, no. 1 (2008): 11–25.

Jameson, Fredric. *The Political Unconscious: Narrative as a Socially Symbolic Act*. London: Routledge, 1983.

Lionnet, Françoise. "Cosmopolitan or Creole Lives? Globalized Oceans and Insular Identities." *Profession* 1, no. 1 (2011): 23–43.

Lionnet, Françoise, and Emmanuel Bruno Jean-François. "Literary Routes: Migration, Islands, and the Creative Economy." *PMLA* 131, no. 5 (2016): 1222–38.

Meier, Prita. "Unmoored: On Oceanic Objects in Coastal Eastern Africa, circa 1700–1900." *Comparative Studies of South Asia, Africa, and the Middle East* 37, no. 2 (2017): 355–67.

Melas, Natalie. *All the Difference in the World: Postcoloniality and the Ends of Comparison*. Redwood City, CA: Stanford University Press, 2007.

Moretti, Franco. *Distant Reading*. New York: Verso Books, 2013.

Pearson, Michael. *The Indian Ocean*. London: Routledge, 2003.

Poddar, Prem. "The Indian Ocean Novel." In *The Novel in South and South East Asia since 1945*, edited by Alex Tickell, 550–63. Oxford: Oxford University Press, 2019.

Prestholdt, Jeremy. "The Ends of the Indian Ocean: Notes on Boundaries and Affinities across Time." In *Reimagining Indian Ocean Worlds*, edited by Smriti Srinivas, Bettina Ng'weno, and Neelima Jeychandran, 25–41. New York: Routledge, 2020.

Ricci, Ronit. "Islamic Literary Networks in South and Southeast Asia." *Journal of Islamic Studies* 21, no. 1 (2010): 1–28.

Sheriff, Abdul. *Dhow Cultures of the Indian Ocean: Cosmopolitanism, Commerce, and Islam*. Oxford: Oxford University Press, 2010.

Shih, Shu-Mei. "World Studies and Relational Comparison." *PMLA* 130, no. 2 (2015): 430–38.

Vergès, Françoise, and Carapin Marimoutou. "Moorings: Indian Ocean Creolizations." *PORTAL: Journal of Multidisciplinary International Studies* 9, no. 1 (2012). https://doi.org/10.5130/portal.v9i1.2568.

Vierke, Clarissa. "Poetic Links across the Ocean: On Poetic Translation as Mimetic Practice at the Swahili Coast." *Comparative Studies of South Asia, Africa, and the Middle East* 37, no. 2 (2017): 321–35.

Vink, Markus P. M. "Indian Ocean Studies and the 'New Thalassology.'" *Journal of Global History* 2, no. 1 (2007): 41–62.

CLARISSA VIERKE

An Intimate "Range of Elsewhere": Sensuous Imaginaries of the Indian Ocean in Precolonial Swahili Poetry

Indian Ocean Studies, African-Language Literature, and Aesthetic Theory

Indian Ocean studies has been paradigmatically reassessed in the last two decades to question the "container thinking" of fixed identities tied to neatly defined national geographies. Exploring "the Indian Ocean as a method" (Hofmeyr 584), instead of hewing to bounded areas, the field has cast a light on network relations and redoubled its emphasis on topics that highlight mobilities across the region, like migration and diaspora memories. However, despite its emphasis on cultural contact and its history of *longue durée*, and although the European presence was of even more marginal importance than in other oceanic regions, like the Atlantic and the Mediterranean (Pearson 3), non-European-language cultures and literatures in the Indian Ocean have been rather sidelined. With respect to East African Indian Ocean literary imaginations, it has been mainly literature in the former colonial languages of English, French, and Portuguese—from Kenya, Tanzania, the Comoros, and Mozambique—that has gained attention for its alternative Indian Ocean imaginary, which cuts through national and continental boundaries (Brugioni 87–91). Ironically, their use of former colonial languages carries the risk of reinforcing linguistic boundaries as well as shallow temporal frames rooted in colonialism.

The "Swahili map" offers a historically longer and different transnational perspective of the Indian Ocean: since at least the end of the first millennium, the East African Bantu language Swahili has been a first language to many people on the coast, and a second or third language to even more. It has connected port

---

I am grateful to the late Ahmed Sheikh Nabhany, and also to Amira Msellem, Ustadh Mahmoud Mau, Zoë Goodman, and Kristen de Joseph. The research for this article was carried out within the framework of the research project "Multiple Artworks—Multiple Indian Ocean," funded by the German Research Foundation (DFG) under Germany's Excellence Strategy (EXC 2052/1–390713894).

Comparative Literature 74:2
DOI 10.1215/00104124-9594800   © 2022 by University of Oregon

cities on the coast and on nearby islands, roughly from Mogadishu (in what is now Somalia) to Sofala (in Mozambique), each home to Muslim sailors and merchants who not only had far-reaching connections across the Indian Ocean, but also strong local linguistic and cultural identities, which they have chiefly expressed in poetry.

In this contribution, I will take the reader to the affluent port cities of the Lamu archipelago on the northern Swahili coast, in what is now Kenya, to consider the Indian Ocean connections evidenced in the most ancient Swahili poetry we have, which dates to roughly between the fifteenth and eighteenth centuries. I focus on the earliest poems in this corpus, not only because they are the oldest historical sources on Indian Ocean connections in any African language (which in fact they are!), but because, as I will show, they offer a unique way of relating to the Indian Ocean through sensorially perceptible figurations that largely disappear from later periods of Swahili poetry. Further, more than just representing moments of Swahili literary history, the poems suggest a distinctive and productive perspective on the Indian Ocean, which I call an aesthetic one. I take inspiration mostly from more recent studies by anthropologists and historians emphasizing aesthetic *practices*, like dance or music, and the shared material culture of the Indian Ocean to counter the emphasis on economic, political, and religious *structures* in Indian Ocean studies.

Relying on aesthetics in its etymological sense of "sensual perception," which the philosophical discipline also draws on, Julia and Markus Verne, for instance, argue for the Indian Ocean as a translocal aesthetic space. They outline—with reference to Kant and Baumgarten—such aesthetic experience as a form of "knowledge," comparable to reason, in that it offers palpable revelations about the Indian Ocean world. Such a sensual experience of the wider Indian Ocean is "triggered substantially by sounds and images, stories and narratives, tastes or smells" (316), as Verne and Verne highlight in thinking about the Indian Ocean as a "translocal aesthetic space" (315). In also taking inspiration from Paolo Ivanov's concept of the Indian Ocean as an "aesthetic seascape" of "shared material and aesthetic expression" ("Aesthetic" 369), I will show how the poems do not represent the Indian Ocean, but rather elicit it through concrete imageries that make the abundance of the Swahili material world—implicated as it is in the Indian Ocean space—perceptible. The poems are important cultural nodes that refract flexible oceanic relations and identities. They are thus an important part of a dynamic Swahili Indian Ocean intellectual history (see also Alpers).

The Baroque Tableaux of the Liyongo Poems

Many of the most ancient Swahili poems have been attributed to the mystical hero and master poet Fumo Liyongo. He is believed to have been a historical figure, hailing from the mainland's Tana Delta, just opposite the Lamu archipelago, which was implicated in an old Indian Ocean trade network between the fifteenth and eighteenth centuries, the period when the city-state of Pate rose to power (Vernet 167–80). The historical shift ushered in by the affluent new elite of Pate is echoed in many Liyongo poems and narratives: he has to prove himself in an enduring struggle for succession to the throne of Pate. And though the dating of his life as well as the many compositions ascribed to him have frequently been points of intense discussion, a number of historians situate him between the fifteenth and eighteenth centuries (e.g., Pouwels 407; Shariff 153–67). What further complicates the dating is the fact that the Liyongo compositions do not comprise one fixed and definable text. Besides the many episodes of his adventures that continue to be retold, there is a cycle of poetry—only loosely thematically linked—whose verses were most probably interspersed between the episodes, and formed part of the so-called *gungu* dances performed on occasions such as weddings.

We have only a vague idea of how the poems were performed, since the oral poems survived only because they were written down in Arabic script in the nineteenth century. At that time, the Indian Ocean networks had shifted, and the world emerging from the ancient Liyongo songs came to an end: the close of the eighteenth century brought not only a change in trade constellations, but also the rise of Islamic reform movements, mostly run by well-educated members of Sufi brotherhoods of Hadhrami descent, who had settled on the East African coast but also partook in far-reaching Indian Ocean networks (Vierke 226–30). Questioning the elite's monopoly on Islamic knowledge passed on in Arabic, the most erudite Sufi scholars adapted Muslim hagiographies into Swahili verse to reach wider audiences all along the coast, from northern Kenya to northern Mozambique (Vierke 228). A manuscript culture of prominently religious Swahili poetry in Arabic script flourished, partly parallel to the oral traditions, but also increasingly overriding dance poetry, like the serene Liyongo songs. In the late nineteenth century, local scribes, who felt the poems would soon die out, preserved these too by writing them down in Arabic script.

The "Utumbuizo wa Mwana Mnazi" ("Utumbuizo of Lady Coconut") is a good example of the vanishing poems written down at that time, so different from the Islamic epics depicting the victories of the Prophet over the unbelievers that become fashionable in the nineteenth century. The poem presents a scene in a richly decorated mansion in—as the Swahili variety of the poem suggests—Pate or Lamu. A lady receives her long-awaited husband (probably Liyongo) at home and urges the servant, Time, to attend to his needs, as depicted in the following bipartite verses (Miehe et al. 66–69, verses 22–31):

> Nitiyani hoyo Time aye, ♦ naanguse, ate masindizi.
> Apakuwe pilau ya Hindi, ♦ mzababu isiyo mtuzi.
> Ete kiti chema cha Ulaya ♦ na siniya njema ya Shirazi.
> Mnakashi inakishiweyo ♦ na sahani hung'ara ja mwezi.
> Kaamuru hudama na waja, ♦ ai, ninyi, hamtumbuizi?
> Basi, hapo akamwandikiya, ♦ naye Time yushishiye kuzi,
> Yapijeto mayi ya inabu ♦ kimnosha kama mnwa shizi.
> Kimlisha akimpa hiba ♦ kimuonya yakeye maozi,
> Kimlisha tambuu ya Siyu ♦ yi laini laini ya Ozi.
> Kiukuta k'ono kimwakiza, ♦ kwa iliki pamwe na jauzi.

> Call Time, let her come ♦ quickly and let her not tarry.
> Let her serve up a dish of Indian *pilau* ♦ cooked with raisins without curry.
> Bring a fine European chair ♦ and a good Persian tray
> Engraved with fine designs ♦ and a plate shining like the moon.
> And she ordered the servants and slaves ♦ "You, why are you not entertaining (us)?"
> Immediately she served him, ♦ while Time held the jug
> Full of grape juice. ♦ She made him drink it like a drinker of wine.
> She fed him lovingly ♦ and gave him a meaningful gaze,
> Offering him the special *tambuu* of Siyu, ♦ as soft as the one from Ozi.
> She folded it and put it into his mouth ♦ together with cardamom and betel nut.[1]

---

[1] Unless otherwise noted, translations are my own.

The poem highlights the cosmopolitan air of the couple's house. The servant has to bring the husband a *kiti cha Ulaya* (European chair), a widespread piece of furniture in the Indian Ocean space: more a throne than a chair, an "Indo-Portuguese design" from the era of Portuguese rule, fabricated of "flat pieces of plainsawn hardwood" (Meier 363) with an inlay of mother of pearl and ivory (Ivanov, "Aesthetic" 372). The food, wine, and the betel quid at the end—which foreshadows a love scene, as the audience is meant to imagine—as well as precious goods like the engraved tray, the shining plate, and the earthen jug add to the depiction of an exquisite, bohemian, and sophisticated cosmopolitan lifestyle of cultural distinction.

Historically, the poem reflects the rise of the northern Swahili city-states between the fifteenth and eighteenth centuries; these profited from trade opportunities in the era of the "first pan-Indian Ocean Portuguese imperial reign" (Prestholdt 29). Affluent Swahili patricians sent their ships to the Comoros and Madagascar as well as to India and South Arabia (Vernet 167–202). But the poem does not merely *reflect* a historical epoch; rather, its baroque tableau also offers a particular way to *reflect on* it: it makes the various Indian Ocean links sensuously perceptible through a pregnant moment at a Swahili house, with its furniture, accessories, tastes, and scents. In her consideration of the particularly opulent interior decoration of nineteenth-century Zanzibar, Prita Meier highlights the intended "intimate, multisensorial experiences of a range of 'elsewheres'" (364) that also dominate the Liyongo poems.

The senses play a prominent role, first in the repertoire of shared embodied practices, like the drinking of wine, eating of rice dishes, and chewing of betel, common all along the rim of the Indian Ocean, and second, in the shared experience of images, tastes, scents, and sounds. A particular kind of aesthetic "knowledge" of the Indian Ocean is produced: "These imaginations," as Verne and Verne describe such an aesthetic view of the Indian Ocean, "are often elusive and less well defined, fluid, situative, and uncritical in nature" (316). In his *Critique of Judgment*, Kant describes what he calls an "aesthetic idea" (in contrast to a "rational idea") as "a representation of the imagination that occasions much thinking, though without it being possible for any determinate thought, i.e., concept, to be adequate to it; it consequently cannot be completely compassed and made intelligible by language" (314, sec. 49). The way in which an aesthetic idea differs from a concept or argument lies in the concrete figurations the poem works with. The poet renders things palpable in its concrete gestalt—here, the mansion—and sticks to the "abundance of characteristics" of the material world (Grünbein 89) rather than subsuming it under an argument. The aim is not precision, but salience.

In the poem, the Indian Ocean's embeddedness in various "elsewheres" acquires concrete form in the *hic et nunc* of the house, its interior, the Indian pilau, and the wine from Shiraz. Yet it is the sensuous immediacy of the concrete figurations in the poem, which does not characterize the Indian Ocean in terms of definite logical attributes or clear confines, but gives way, in Kant's words, to "an illimitable field of kindred representations" (318). For the German poet Durs Grünbein, this is the paradox of an insurgent "palpability," on the one hand, and a "blurred view" on the other (84–94). There is the vast imaginative "field" of, for instance, the taste and the scent of the rice, the meat or fish, and the variety of spices of the Indian pilau, which evokes festivity and more particularly weddings, emphasizing the love scene; it thus forms part of the "entertainment" that the lady of the house calls for in line 5, but also, through the epithet *ya Hindi*, gestures across the ocean. The wine, characterized as "from Shiraz," not only adds another transoceanic link, but also underlines the sense of intimacy, which reaches its conclusion in the betel quid.

Taking into account philosopher Hans Blumenberg's concern with the role of metaphors (not concepts) in the history of ideas and knowledge production, one can understand why such a poetic view might be particularly productive for the Indian Ocean, which itself is a vast "field of kindred representations." For Blumenberg, what he calls the "total metaphor" particularly plays a role: "the more we move away from the short distance of fulfillable intentionality and refer to total horizons that our experience can no longer grasp or delimit, the more pervasive the use of metaphors becomes" (90). These metaphors—in our case, the Swahili mansion— do not illustrate, but rather open a view onto a complex totality that typically gives form to an emergent lived world. For Swahili patricians of the fifteenth to eighteenth centuries, the mansion spelled out the "unfathomable, unobservable totality" (Blumenberg 93) of the wider horizon of the Indian Ocean, which they found themselves taking part in.

An aesthetic emphasis on the figurations that evoke the Indian Ocean can also help to overcome two dichotomies: first, the relation between local and cosmopolitan—so troublesome for Indian Ocean studies—and second, that between subject and object. With regard to the former, in Indian Ocean discourse, cosmopolitan relations have often been emphasized at the expense of processes of adaptation, as Jeremy Prestholdt has recently warned, reflecting on the "layered maps" of the Indian Ocean and reminding us that "Indian Ocean relationships have been highly localized" (26) and are ever-changing. From an aesthetic angle, this binary dissolves, since perception is essentially locally situated, tied to concrete materiality or figuration, which nonetheless echoes the "wider world."[2] The poem concretely features the "oceanic" elsewhere amid the intimacy of the Swahili scene, thus creating a sensuous bridge between local and cosmopolitan. To me, this calls for a reconsideration of the dichotomy between localized (highlighting the adaptation to a smaller world) and cosmopolitan readings (projecting a larger oceanic elsewhere), since such a dichotomy precludes a more multifaceted and processual reading of figurations and their dynamic range of elsewheres in concrete contexts.

Further, the dichotomy of human being and material world or subject and object dissolves. In the "Utumbuizo wa Mwana Mnazi," the material culture, scents, and tastes, are not only accessories to the scene, but interact with and define its characters: the *kiti cha ezi*, the "European chair," spells out the man's cosmopolitan sophistication, his social standing and affluence, and thus embodies his attributes— much as the seductiveness of the woman is characterized in terms of wine and betel quid (the latter, as we shall see, can even symbolize the female body). In the

---

[2] In a similar way, Andrew Eisenberg analyzes musical references in East African *taarab* by one of the most renowned Swahili musicians from Mombasa, known for cultivating a distinctive Swahili "Indian style"; he underlines the creative process of appropriation, which results in the seemingly paradoxical presentation of Indian sounds as Swahili expressions (317).

lyric poetry of the time, attributes from social status to sensuality needed to find concrete form. This is also why the material world is so prominent in Liyongo poems: the inside-outside dichotomy is suspended. As the anthropologist Paola Ivanov finds, making a case for an aesthetic reading of Zanzibari worlds, "person" and "object" are not separate from each other as absolute categories; rather, as she underscores, it is their relation that defines them: "human beings do not define themselves in opposition to objects, but by the delegating, mixing, and putting-into-relation of form" (*Verkörperung* 70).

The simulacra of here and there, on the one hand, and of person and object, on the other, are also related: because personhood and objects co-constitute each other, and objects oscillate through a range of elsewheres, identities too can range from specifically East African Swahili to cosmopolitan. It is the "European chair," for instance, that emblematically evokes Swahili culture, power, and (in the poem) virility, but also evokes the cosmopolitan air, sophistication, and affluence (based on transoceanic trade) of its owner. As Farouk Topan notes in his "Swahili Aesthetics: Some Observations," some cultural objects—in his case study, the incense burner (*chetezo*) and the fly whisk (*usinga*)—"are not only multifunctional" in the Swahili context, but are dynamic "nodes of cultural meaning" that provide "entry points into people's conceptual worlds" (90).

While the chair and the mansion itself are certainly such important "cultural nodes" of flexible range and engrained in embodied practices, in the following, I will zero in on another prominent "cultural object": the betel quid with which the "Utumbuizo wa Mwana Mnazi" ends. The betel quid, a widespread Indian Ocean practice, has become a highly productive Swahili cultural object and poetic topos that has allowed Swahili cultural identities to be imagined and reimagined. Drawing on Roland Barthes's notion of "mythological substance," I will first examine its multiple cultural ascriptions. Afterward, I will continue the aesthetic exploration of the betel quid as a poetic topos open to a "wide field" of mental images.

Betel: A "Mythological Substance"

A betel quid consists of the leaf of the betel plant, *tambuu*, into which, as the "Utumbuizo wa Mwana Mnazi" tells us, the *jauzi* ("betel nut," also called "areca nut") and some *iliki* ("cardamom") are folded, together with other spices, tobacco, and lime. The areca palm tree and the betel vine, not to mention the cultural practice of chewing betel, are widespread in the greater Indian Ocean, from the tropical regions of Southeast Asia (like Papua New Guinea) to Indonesia, Malaysia, and Taiwan, and from India and westward to the coastal regions and islands of Arabia and Africa (Beaujard 199–200, 204; Lichtenberk 340; Vaughan and Geissler 128).[3] They probably arrived in East Africa from the east, via India and Madagascar, by the sixteenth century, roughly at the same time that the Liyongo poems were being

---

[3] The wider oceanic connections are echoed in the etymology. In Sanskrit, betel is *tāmbūla*, Hindi *tambol*, Arabic *tanbūl*, and Swahili *tambuu* (Beaujard 199–200). The areca nut, referred to with the Arabic loanword *jauzi* (nut) in the poem, is more commonly called *popoo* in Swahili (Gujarati *phophal*, Arabic *fawfal*, Persian *popal*, from the Sanskrit compound *pūgaphala*; *phala*, "fruit" [Beaujard 204]; a link to the reconstructed Proto-Oceanic **buaq* [Lichtenberk 343] is not unlikely).

composed, when they seemingly evolved into markers of Swahiliness, as I will show in the following.[4]

Though rarely found any longer, in the nineteenth century, its consumption was still widespread all along the coast, and much of Swahili poetry sang the betel quid's praises: poems like the "Sifa za mtambuu" ("The Benefits of Betel"), of which stanzas 7 and 8 are presented below.

> Utafunapo hutoka ♦ hamu moyoni na ghamu
> hutakata kama shuka ♦ kalibi hutabasamu
> Ukawa mwenye kuteka ♦ na kusema na hirimu.
> Siati kwenda dawamu ♦ kuuzuru mtambuu
>
> Ukisha kula chakula, ♦ ndruza, niwape khabari,
> msipateni ghafula ♦ itake iwe tayari,
> huja mangi masiala ♦ maneno mazuri-zuri
> ndripo nisitafakhari ♦ haupenda mtambuu

(Vierke, "Plants" 72, stanzas 7 and 8)[5]

> When you chew it, ♦ anxiety and worries leave your heart.
> You become pure like a loincloth ♦ and your heart smiles.
> You become someone who laughs, ♦ chatting with your peers.
> I can never stop ♦ visiting the betel pepper.
>
> When you have finished your food, ♦ I am telling you, my friends,
> Don't be unprepared: ♦ (the betel quid) must be ready.
> Many topics arise, ♦ various nice words.
> I do not boast of myself; ♦ I enjoy the betel pepper.

Singing the betel bite's praises, the poem attributes cultural importance to the betel quid, as it creates a communal moment of self-forgetting removed from the everyday *hamu na ghamu* (anxiety and worries), underscoring and constructing a certain bohemian Swahili lifestyle. The poem transforms the quid and its physiological effects, which are said to range from the suppression of tiredness to an exhilarating effect, into a quasi-"mythological substance"—as Roland Barthes describes wine, which also exceeds its physical reality as a drink in the French context.[6] Similarly to the betel quid, wine has a culturally ascribed meaning of nearly "alchemical heredity"—with the power of "reversing situations," like making the "silent one talkative" (Barthes 58). Besides its power as a "converting substance" (58), wine offers a locus of manifold but also contradictory cultural self-understandings, like conviviality, virility, and Frenchness. Betel too is tied to varied, sometimes ambivalent cultural ascriptions, like sociality and conversation, imagination as well as intimacy; its use as an aphrodisiac is referred to in stanza 9, quoted below. Furthermore, the poem also showcases betel as emblematically Swahili, in

---

[4] Betel is mentioned as a translocally traded good coming to India "from the East" (McCrindle 137). In the fourteenth century, Ibn Battutah commented on the orchards of "betel trees" in Zafar (Yemen), citing the high esteem—"more valuable than . . . gold and silver"—betel leaves enjoyed in India (92).

[5] I published a first translation of this poem and the following ones in this article, together with a commentary on their variations in the Arabic manuscripts. While I am quoting from this publication, some of the translations in this article have also been revised.

[6] Such effects of the betel quid can be explained physiologically: supported by the lime, the areca nut produces alkaloids, substances also found in hashish, tobacco, and coffee, which stimulates the neurological system (Kupfer 314).

contrast to Arabic coffee—also frequently consumed in East African contexts—which remains *mgeni* (a "stranger" or "guest").

> Kahawa nda wa Arabu ♦ wa Hejazi na Yamani
> kwethu ni kithu gharibu ♦ thaipendani mgeni?
> na twambe ni mahabubu ♦ tusiitowe funguni,
> tungiapo faraghani ♦ ifaayo ni tambuu
> (Vierke, "Plants" 73, stanza 9)

> Coffee belongs to the Arabs ♦ from Hijaz and Yemen.
> For us, it is a foreign thing; ♦ how am I supposed to love a stranger?
> And if it is love-making, ♦ we should not dismiss it.
> When we become intimate, ♦ betel is the best.

The narrator is aware of the wider "Arabic" connections with "Hejazi na Yamani"; thus this poem too evokes a wider Indian Ocean map, but deliberately removes betel from the category of "stranger" from across the ocean. Returning to the notion of the flexible range of elsewheres that poems dynamically construct—as I have highlighted above, questioning the fixed dichotomy of local and cosmopolitan—in this poem, it is the "here" of the Swahili coast that is highlighted against the backdrop of an "Arab world."[7] One can read the poem as deliberately delineating a Swahili lifestyle from an Arab one in a historical context where dichotomies of "Arab" verses local "Swahili" identity became enhanced, namely at the end of the nineteenth century (Abdulaziz 7–28). At that time, both the arrival of new "strangers"—particularly from Hadramawt—with a new religious and moral agenda, as outlined above, as well as the economic and political suppression of city-states like Pemba, Mombasa, and Pate under "Arab" Omani rule kindled notions of a distinct Swahili group identity. Here the betel quid is put forward as cultural mythology, opening up a view onto a Swahili lifestyle of sensuality, intimacy, and enjoyment in contrast to Arab "coffee-drinking" rather associated with social gatherings which, as a cultural ascription itself, does not connote intimacy. The poem contrasts coffee, highlighting its alien nature, with the "alchemical" substance betel, which has the further power to create intimacy. Earlier, in stanza 6—which reads like a metaphor of the cultural adaptation of betel—the poem describes the plant as locally cultivated in "well-prepared" East African soil, carefully cultivated by a gardener, the narrator of the poem:

> Nipete nti tayibu ♦ ardhi imetengeya
> nalekeza hitharibu ♦ kuilimia-limia
> N'na yangu matulubu ♦ n'liyoyaazimia
> nataka kuutulia ♦ ukono wa mtambuu
> (Vierke, "Plants" 72, stanza 6)

> I got good land; ♦ the soil had been well prepared.
> I plowed and tilled it, ♦ cultivating it.
> I have a plan ♦ that I have decided on:
> I want to plant ♦ the offshoot of a betel pepper.

The narrative that opens the "Sifa za mtambuu"—that of a gardener planting a betel plant, impatiently waiting for it to grow—is older than the work itself, and recurs in a series of poems loosely attributed to Fumo Liyongo. In the following,

---

[7] The "Utumbuizo wa Mwana Mnazi" likewise seems to highlight the "Swahiliness" of betel: it boasts of the *Indian* rice dish, the *European* chair, and the *Persian* tray; the "best betel," however, which completes the list, is characterized as coming from the Swahili heartland, namely Siyu, Pate island, and Ozi, in the Tana delta, the mystical homeland of Fumo Liyongo, the geographic core of the Swahili sagas of origin.

I will proceed to examine the various reexplorations and reinterpretations of the betel plant. My aim is to explore how the plant has served as a poetic "figure of thought" with a view to flexible ranges of Indian Ocean worlds. To better depict how poetic reformulations in the serialized Swahili poetry of the time worked, I will recur to the *terminus technicus* "topos."

The Betel Quid as a Poetic Topos

I use the term *topos*, derived from Greek rhetorical terminology, with regard to the *tambuu* here since, more than the terms *stock image* or *leitmotif*, it underlines the thought-provoking capacity of imagery: it is the topos, literally the "place," that one may "think" and "compose" from and "imagine with." The figuration of the betel plant lends itself to flexible poetic reexploration precisely because—as I observe above with regard to the aesthetic idea—it is not subsumable under a concept, but provides the salience of a palpable image. The *tambuu* as a topos does not give form to some predefined concept of the poet, but rather provides the poet's initial inspiration and is part of the process of composition. Thus, the topos does not *represent* but *presents* numerous ideas to the poet; it is through and with this topos that the poet gradually composes the poem. Similarly, Lila Abu-Lughod describes the composition of formulaic Bedouin love poetry (238–40), in which the poet does not spontaneously give expression to his feelings, but formulates his experience by recurring to ritualized, cloaked means of depiction and recurring figurations. For Swahili poetry too, particularly before the twentieth century, it is not novelty of imagery that is the poetic ideal, but the creative exploration of metaphorical topoi like the betel.

The "Shairi la mtambuu" ("Poem of the Betel Plant"), for instance—a poem in the shorter *shairi* meter, dating to the time of Portuguese rule—likewise starts with the topos of the gardening narrative, which we have seen above.

> Nipete nti kiwambo ♦ unyika usiyameya
> khafungata masombo ♦ mno khaipotoleya
> khatimba kwa mitimbo ♦ hata yaliporegeya
> mti mwema khatuliya ♦ ukono wa mtambuu
>
> Shughuli ikanipata ♦ sikuwa nao usono
> nisi ndaa nisi nyota ♦ kwa mahaba khenda mno
> nisikulala khaota ♦ kupelekwa mikono
> nisikufinika meno ♦ kwa hawaa ya mtambuu
> (Vierke, "Plants" 64–68, stanzas 1–2)

> I got a strip of wasteland ♦ where the bush had not yet grown.
> I girded my belt, ♦ tightened it well.
> I dug with a spade ♦ until the soil loosened.
> I planted a good plant, ♦ the offshoot of a betel plant.
>
> Restlessness took hold of me; ♦ I could not relax.
> I had neither hunger nor thirst; ♦ love had driven me to such a state.
> I did not sleep, but dreamed: ♦ I was given the offshoots;
> I could not but smile ♦ out of desire for the betel plant.

The "Shairi la mtambuu" takes a different course than the praise poem "Sifa za mtambuu," discussed above, where the successfully harvested plant is praised. There is growing tension in the poem: the gardener is so anxious about the plant that he even stops eating and sleeping, lost in his dreams of the plant. And though the gardener takes good care of the plant, even constructing supports for the vine, he ultimately discovers a monster sitting in its roots (see below). He furiously curses the enemy:

> Khautiya na zipoya ♦ nafasi ya kutambaa
> hata siku zichongeya ♦ khauwakiya na taa
> siku moya khatembeya ♦ khalimatiya khakaa
> khiya mbwene mnyangaa ♦ si mnani mwa mtambuu
> ....
> Mwizi alongiya kwangu ♦ kafasidi mtambuu
> ngwampa fumo la Mungu ♦ nalo ndrilo fumo kuu
> afe nti za wazungu ♦ ya Diu na Damao
> afufuwe na chepeo ♦ ufito mkononi
>   (Vierke, "Plants" 67, 68, stanzas 8 and 12)
>
> I even put up supports, ♦ for the plant to climb.
> After a few days had passed, ♦ I even put up a trellis.
> One day, I took a walk, ♦ tarrying along the way.
> When I arrived, I saw a monster: ♦ "Could there be someone in my betel pepper?"
> ....
> The thief, who intruded into my place, ♦ violated the betel pepper.
> May God throw his spear at him! ♦ it is an enormous spear!
> May he die in the lands of the whites, ♦ in Diu und Damão.
> May he be resurrected with a hat [on his head] ♦ and a walking stick in his hand.

Both his love for the betel plant as well as the curse at the end would seem over-exaggerated if *tambuu* merely referred to the literal plant, which grows easily in gardens on the northern Swahili coast. For the Swahili audience of the time, versed in poetic topoi—where plants, particularly betel, often refer to women—the poem depicted the familiar story of a mature man full of desire—the impatient gardener—who has to wait until the woman of his choosing is old enough to get married, only to see her snatched up by someone else. The metaphorical topos of the deceived gardener is also a socially acceptable narrative of desire. As Abu-Lughod describes for Bedouin love poetry, which stages sentiments (not individual emotions), topoi provide the poet with a template that allows him to gain vantage points on his own experiences and emotions, namely by formulating them in the light of the existing form and without violating the norms of modesty and honor that guide everyday speech (Abu-Lughod 240). Similarly, in the Swahili lyrical poem, the vicissitudes of love are conveyed through the narrative of the sudden theft of the beloved plant—a trope that persists even in popular music nowadays. The topoi that the poet explores are *mafumbo*, often translated as "metaphors," or better, "riddles" or "enigmas": literally, "knots" into which the poet ties his thoughts so that he or she can always retreat behind the literal meaning. It is the tension of such veiled language, based on topoi, both intimate and expressive, that accounts for much of the poem's lyrical quality.

Given their concrete figurations, double readings, multiple interpretations, and reinterpretations of topoi are not only possible, but a poetic ideal (Vierke, "Ocean" 226–34). While in the "Sifa za mtambuu," the reference to the betel plant has been reduced to praise of the literal plant, without its metaphorical implications (which, however, shine through in the "Utumbuizo wa Mnazi"), the "Shairi la mtambuu" uses the *mafumbo* of the gardener waiting for the nighttime tryst—which, in this poem, never happens. Additionally, in light of the curse in the poem, where the narrator wishes that the rival die overseas in the *nti za wazungu* (land of the whites), "Diu and Damão," one can also read the *tambuu*—whose importance as cultural metaphor I have already highlighted—as standing in for Swahili culture being "devoured" by the Portuguese, thereby voicing resistance against cultural oppression. The poem thus reveals a wider imaginary of the Indian Ocean map, on which it plots the boundaries of the betel garden of the Swahili coast. The two readings of the poem, as resistance or love poetry, do not exclude each other; the betel as an aesthetic idea is fundamentally open to many readings and reemphases, as the following "plant poem," with the same garden narrative, also shows. The poem evokes a particularly blended map of the Indian Ocean. In the "Utumbuizo wa mjemje" ("Poem of the Lotus"), the gardener reappears, taking care of the *mjemje*—probably referring to the lotus, another aphrodisiac, which replaces the betel in this love poem:[8]

> Mjemje mte wali wangu ♦ thuliyeo kwa mani uwani
> Thuliyeo kwa embe la chuma ♦ na mtanga mwema wa ziwani
> Mjemje ukisa kumeya ♦ tumo simo shirikani
> (Vierke, "Plants" 36, stanzas 1–3)

> *Mjemje*, the seedling, was mine. ♦ I planted it in the yard with a heavy hoe.
> I planted it with an iron hoe ♦ and fine sand from the lake.
> When the *mjemje* had matured [to bear fruit], ♦ I did not have a share in the harvest.

While the gardener's efforts are disappointed early on in this poem, instead of cursing his rival as in the previous poem, the narrator loses himself in his memory or imagination of the love scenes. The temporal frame of the subsequent verses is vague: "no longer" and "not yet" blur into each other. In his reverie, a crossing of representational spheres takes place: the narrator leaves the depiction of the woman as *mjemje* but, turning to a third-person narrative, depicts a love scene in which the woman is characterized in relation to various fruits, plants, tastes, and scents: The shape of her body is *hinzirani* (reed), her vulva a blossoming *ua* (flower) concealing a *kito dond'oni* (a pearl in a shell). In the last lines, the pleasures of love are described with similar attributes as the stimulating betel above—capable of "reversing situations" and leading to a loss of everyday *hamu na huzuni* (anxiety and sadness):

> Ivumapo ya mande ♦ hunemka kama hinzirani
> Na maniye nda zabarijudi ♦ ahdhari isiyo kifani
> Uwa lake landapo kutoka ♦ jauhari huwa kito dond'oni
> Ling'aa kama nyota ya makungu ♦ ya zuhura iwapo kutwani
> Na tund'ra liliwapo kutosha ♦ hupendeza kwangaliyani
> Si kuu si toto kamuono ♦ lingine katika wizani
> Na gand'rale ni kama sulami ♦ na maniye nguo ya nyuni
> Arufuye nda uwale ♦ si misiki si zaafarani
> Kalibusu mwenye kulitunda ♦ kiifunga hungiya shioni
> Alilapo mwenye kulipata ♦ humwepuka hamu na huzuni
> Kalishumu muiliwe kitwa ♦ huwambuza la majinuni
> Ladha yake hupita haluwa ♦ yaliyoetwa Yamani
> Hufadhili sukari nabati ♦ ya Mswiri kuburudishani
> (Vierke, "Plants" 39–42, verses 22–34)

---

[8] Whether *mjemje* really refers to lotus is doubtful. The plant is unknown nowadays; only the late local scholar Ahmed Sheikh Nabhany mentions the plant in the dictionary he compiled. Without describing it, he merely refers to its use as potency remedy (83). Knappert translates *mjemje* as "lotus" in the version of the poem that forms part of his anthology (*Four Centuries*, 95–97).

When the morning breeze blows, ♦ she sways like a reed.
Her leaves are peridot green, ♦ an incomparable green.
When her flower blossoms ♦ her jewel becomes a pearl in a shell.
It shines like the morning star, ♦ the star of Venus, when it sets.
Once the fruit has been amply enjoyed, ♦ it pleases the eye to look at it.
It is neither big nor small: you could not find ♦ another that is of the same weight,
And her fruit's peel is as soft as a fine, green plant, ♦ and her leaves like a bird's plumage.
Her scent is that of her flower, ♦ better than musk and saffron.
He kissed it carefully; ♦ tying it, he entered in great silence.
When the one who reaches it eats it, ♦ he evades worries and sorrow.
He kissed her body and head; ♦ she made him crazy.
Her taste is better than *haluwa* ♦ brought from Yemen;
It spoils the senses like sweet syrup, ♦ the pleasant taste of Egypt.

In the poem above, like in the "Shairi la mtambuu," the topos not only proves itself ripe for reformulation, but exemplifies blurring the boundary between subject and object, inside and outside. It is the plant, the *mjemje*, that oscillates between the woman, her body, and the shape and effects of the plant: her sensuality extends to the plant, and the plant with its aphrodisiac properties extends its seductive powers to her. In his anthology of Swahili love poetry, Jan Knappert considers the similarly used *tini* (fig), referred to as *tunda la tamasha* (fruit of pleasure),[9] as a "double entendre," which also holds for the many other fruits—like grapes, apples, and lemons—found in love poems: "The poet is discussing three subjects under one name, i.e. by one metaphor: the fig, i,e, love and love-making, woman and a particular woman" (*Choice* 41). In the "Utumbuizo wa mjemje," the sudden crossing of spheres of depiction reveals the same fluidity: while it is first the figuration of the "garden scene" that guides him in reflecting upon her body, it is later the gestalt of her body that guides the third-person male narrator's imagination, leading him to compare the shape of her sex to flowers and fruits, its softness to "bird feathers," its scent to saffron, and its taste to *haluwa*, switching between sensory spheres.[10]

The relationship to the Indian Ocean also plays out in a particular way. Similarly to the "Utumbuizo wa Mwana Mnazi" (earlier in this essay), where oceanic material culture furnishes the house and also extends to the owners of the house, the personhood of the woman seeps into the plants and accessories of her environment, and vice versa. However, more than that, in the "Utumbuizo wa mjemje," the woman's body is not only likened to a range of objects, but the narrator also projects a specific littoral landscape onto her: the reeds swaying in the *mande*, the early morning breeze blowing in from the sea, at the moment when the morning star, Venus, is setting; this evokes both the amorous tête-à-tête at nighttime, depicted in many love poems, as well as the natural environment of the coast. The image of the "pearl in its shell" sustains both the imaginary of the coast as well as the anatomy of the female body. The "incomparable" "green leaves" of the reed can refer to her elegant attire or, particularly in combination with the following verses, the delicacy of her sex. It is

---

[9] Knappert translates *tini la tamasha* as "fruit of love," but notes himself that *tamasha* "means love, pleasure and a precious present" (41).

[10] Similes of scents and taste play a prominent role in Swahili poetry, echoing the cultural importance attributed to an "olfactory rich environment" both as a "sign of sophistication and refinement" and that of a distinctive coastal culture eager to emphasize "historical transoceanic connections with Arabia" (Hillewaert 51).

described with the Arabic loanword *adhahari*, green, the color of paradise, promising paradisiac pleasures; the "fabulous shade of green" is likened to *zabarijudi*, peridot, the famous gemstone found on the island of Zabarjad in the Red Sea, thereby also revealing the scene's oceanic milieu: peridot, also referred to as topaz, was widely traded in the Indian Ocean, and called *chrysolithon* in the *Periplus of the Erythraean Sea* (McCrindle 109). The double reading, as both an exquisite color and a gemstone tied to a specific oceanic map, is enhanced by the reference to *jauhari* (jewel) in the subsequent verse, which foregrounds the meaning of the gemstone as well as its metaphorical relation to the female sex. The exquisite scent of saffron (*zafarani*) and the expensive musk of the civet, both widely traded in the Indian Ocean, as well as the final reference to *haluwa* from Yemen and sweet syrup from Egypt, conclude the blended bodily and oceanic map. Through the male gaze of desire, the coastal image of the reeds swaying at night gives way to a wider and at the same time increasingly sensuous seascape the more intimate the poem becomes. The dichotomy not only between subject and object, but also between "here" and "there," bodyscape and oceanic world (both as landscape and ensemble of traveling objects), dissolves.

Conclusion

This article brings ancient Swahili poetry to the debate about Indian Ocean literary imaginations, which urges us, as I argue, to expand our views on how to conceptualize the Indian Ocean. The poetry suggests that we think about the Indian Ocean not merely in terms of networks and traveling ships, but as emerging in "mythological" topoi or Swahili *mafumbo*, "knots" of veiled meaning, like the betel plant itself, which provides a flexible lens for thinking about cultural identity and spelling out a variety of experiences. To explain how betel quids and mansions evade representing a neatly defined idea—as they stick to the abundance and concreteness of their gestalt, and thus are open to multiple meanings and inspire reexploration—I have referred to aesthetic theories that underline the revealing nature of sensorially perceptible form.

Why is an aesthetic perspective productive for Indian Ocean studies? First, aesthetic experiences of a various "range of elsewheres," sometimes near, sometimes far—through scents, tastes, and imagery; sound, poetry, and music; and bodily practices like betel chewing, but also dance and recitation—play a fundamental role in most Indian Ocean communities. In the culturally and linguistically diverse Indian Ocean, far less influenced by "Euro-American Christian culture" and education than, for instance, the Caribbean—which has produced important theorists of Creolization like Aimé Césaire—it is not testimonies or essays, as Edward Alpers has argued, but embodied practices, like music, folklore and religious rituals, and formulaic language, that have persisted over the centuries, but have received too little attention (Alpers 86). In this contribution, I have added figurations, which can act as poetic topoi and play an essential role in imagining a varied range of oceanic maps. I have shown how powerfully thought-provoking these topoi can be, functioning as aesthetic ideas that can open up a view onto the totality of a wide oceanic horizon, or reject it in favor of a more local coastal map. The openness of the aesthetic idea helps us to suspend the boundary-drawing between far and near, and thus to avoid a preconceived and inert dichotomy of local and cosmopolitan, instead urging us to consider how the betel quid or other plants flexibly evoke maps of various scopes in each poem. These maps can also become embodied, as the last poem in particular reminds us, illustrating the suspension of the subject/object dichotomy. Under the male's gaze, the woman extends into the oceanic scape, and the oceanic world is projected onto the woman's body. Desire is spelled out as a journey into the sensuous abundance of the oceanic and coastal world, and a "range of elsewheres" are brought into the intimate present of the poem.

Bayreuth University

Works Cited

Abdulaziz, Mohamed. *Nineteenth Century Swahili Popular Poetry.* Nairobi: Kenya Literature Bureau, 1979.

Abu-Lughod, Lila. *Veiled Sentiments: Honor and Poetry in a Bedouin Society.* Oakland: University of California Press, 1986.

Alpers, Edward "Recollecting Africa: Diasporic Memory in the Indian Ocean World." *African Studies Review* 43, no. 1 (2002): 83–99.

Barthes, Roland. "Wine and Milk." In *Mythologies*, 58–61. New York: Noonday, 1972.

Battutah, Ibn. *The Travels of Ibn Battutah*, translated by Tim Mackintosh-Smith. London: Picador, 2003.

Beaujard, Philippe. *Histoire et voyages des plantes cultivées à Madagascar avant le XVI siècle.* Paris: Karthala, 2017.

Blumenberg, Hans. *Schiffbruch mit Zuschauer: Paradigma einer Daseinsmetapher.* 1979; repr., Frankfurt am Main: Suhrkamp, 2012.

Brugioni, Elena. "Literaturas Africanas e o Oceano Índico." In *Literaturas Africanas Comparadas: Paradigmas Críticos e Representaçoes em Contrapunto*, edited by Elena Brugioni, 87–112. Campinas, Brazil: Editora da Unicamp, 2019.

Eisenberg, Andrew. "The Swahili Art of Indian Taarab: A Poetics of Vocality and Ethnicity on the Kenyan Coast." *Comparative Studies of South Asia, Africa, and the Middle East* 37, no. 2 (2017): 336–54.

Grünbein, Durs. *Gedicht und Geheimnis: Aufsätze 1990–2006.* Frankfurt am Main: Suhrkamp, 2007.

Hillewaert, Sarah. *Morality at the Margins: Youth, Language, and Islam in Coastal Kenya.* New York: Fordham University Press, 2020.

Hofmeyr, Isabel "The Complicating Sea: The Indian Ocean as Method." *Comparative Studies of South Asia, Africa, and the Middle East* 32, no. 3 (2012): 584–90.

Ivanov, Paola. "The Aesthetic Constitution of Space: Mimetic Appropriation of Foreign 'Styles' and the Creation of Transoceanic Connections on the Swahili Coast." *Comparative Studies of South Asia, Africa, and the Middle East* 37, no. 2 (2017): 368–90.

Ivanov, Paola. *Verkörperung der Welt: Ästhetik, Raum und Gesellschaft im islamischen Sansibar.* Berlin: Reimer, 2020.

Kant, Immanuel. *Critique of Judgement*, translated by John Henry Bernard. New York: Barnes and Noble, 2005.

Knappert, Jan. *A Choice of Flowers: Chaguo la Maua; An Anthology of Swahili Love Poetry.* Nairobi: Heinemann, 1981.

Knappert, Jan. *Four Centuries of Swahili Verse: A Literary History and Anthology.* Nairobi: Heinemann, 1979.

Kupfer, Alexander. *Göttliche Gifte: Kleine Kulturgeschichte des Rausches seit dem Garten Eden.* Stuttgart: Metzler, 1996.

Lichtenberk, Frantisek. "Did Speakers of Proto Oceanic Chew Betel?" *Journal of the Polynesian Society* 107, no. 4 (1998): 335–63.

McCrindle, John. *The Commerce and Navigation of the Erythraean Sea.* Calcutta: Thacker, Spink, 1879.

Meier, Prita. "Unmoored: On Oceanic Objects in Coastal Eastern Africa, circa 1700–1900." *Comparative Studies of South Asia, Africa, and the Middle East* 37, no. 2 (2017): 355–67.

Miehe, Gudrun, Abdilatif Abdalla, Ahmad Nassir Juma Bhalo, Ahmed Nabahany, Angelica Baschiera, Clarissa Dittemer, Farouk Topan, Mohamed Abdulaziz, Said. A. M Khamis, Yahya Ali Omar and Zainab Mahmoud Fadhil al-Bakary, eds. *Liyongo Songs: Poems Attributed to Fumo Liyongo*. Cologne: Köppe, 2004.

Nabhany, Ahmed. *Kandi ya Kiswahili*. Dar es Salaam, Tanzania: Kiswahili Researched Products, 2012.

Pearson, Michael. "Introduction: Maritime History and the Indian Ocean World." In *Trade, Circulation, and Flow in the Indian Ocean World*, edited by Michael Pearson, 1–14. New York: Palgrave Macmillan, 2015.

Pouwels, Randall. "Eastern Africa and the Indian Ocean to 1800: Reviewing Relations in Historical Perspective." *International Journal of African Historical Studies* 35, no. 2–3 (2002): 285–425.

Presthold, Jeremy. "The Ends of the Indian Ocean: Notes on Boundaries and Affinities across Time." In *Reimagining Indian Ocean Worlds*, edited by Smriti Srinivas, Bettina Ng'weno, and Neelima Jeychandran, 25–41. London: Routledge, 2020.

Shariff, Ibrahim Noor. "The Liyongo Conundrum: Re-examining the Historicity of Swahili's National Poet-Hero." *Research in African Literatures* 22, no. 2 (1991): 153–67.

Topan, Farouk. "Swahili Aesthetics: Some Observations." In *Art in Eastern Africa*, edited by Marion Arnold, 85–94. Dar es Salaam, Tanzania: Mkuki na Nyota, 2008.

Vaughan, John, and Catherine Geissler. *The New Oxford Book of Food Plants*. Oxford: Oxford University Press, 2009.

Verne, Julia, and Markus Verne. "Introduction: The Indian Ocean as Aesthetic Space." *Comparative Studies of South Asia, Africa, and the Middle East* 37, no. 2 (2017): 314–20.

Vernet, Thomas. "East African Travelers and Traders in the Indian Ocean: Swahili Ships, Swahili Mobilities ca. 1500–1800." In *Trade, Circulation, and Flow in the Indian Ocean World*, edited by Michael Pearson, 167–202. New York: Palgrave Macmillan, 2015.

Vierke, Clarissa. "From across the Ocean: Considering Travelling Literary Figurations as Part of Swahili Intellectual History." *Journal of African Cultural Studies* 28, no. 2 (2016): 225–40.

Vierke, Clarissa. "Of Plants and Women: A Working Edition of Two Swahili Plant Poems." *Swahili Forum*, no. 14 (2007): 69–73.

VILASHINI COOPPAN

Object Orientations and Circulatory Form in Abdulrazak Gurnah's *By the Sea*

> Circulation. Noun. 1. Movement to and fro or around something, especially that of fluid in a closed system ... *similar*: flow, motion, movement, course, passage.
>
> —*Oxford Languages*, s.v. "circulation"

THE NOUN INVITES verbs: *flowing* in a closed circle or circuit, like blood in the body or sap through a plant or goods in an economy built on them; *encircling*, as a frame or border might if the unity it contained was also porosity; *pouring*, as in something that exceeds the containers that would catch it, like holds that spill forth and things that come in waves—slaves, merchant ships, migrants, cultures, epistemes, histories, memories. Stacks and sacks of pearls, cowrie shells, cloves, cinnamon, sugar, tea, opium, rice, cloth; bulk goods and luxury objects. Circulation speaks to material stuff, the trade routes and traffics long taken as the decisive referent of the Indian Ocean world. Considering the civilizational worlds of Islam, India, Southeast Asia, and East Asia from the seventh-century Islamic world to the mid-eighteenth century, K. N. Chauduri foregrounded a "basic underlying structure, the ground floor of material life, which remained invariant while displaying variations within certain limits" ("Unity" 7). As Alan Villiers, Abdul Sheriff, Engseng Ho, Edward Alpers, Devleena Ghosh, Stephen Muecke, and numerous others have shown, the Indian Ocean comes into focus through the circulation not only of commodities but of all that puts them in motion: monsoons, trade winds, lingua francas, common religions, lateen sails, the pluralist sensibilities of littoral societies, long histories of migrant peoples, all freighted and weighted by the systems of slavery, indenture, multiple empires, and long globalizations.

Imagine the Indian Ocean world from a series of interlocked standpoints, looking out, looking back, and looking in. Looking out scans the horizons for the large and small elements of transverse networks and relational enmeshments over long

Comparative Literature 74:2
DOI 10.1215/00104124-9594813   © 2022 by University of Oregon

centuries. Looking back unfolds through Indian Ocean scholarship's engagement of Fernand Braudel's different levels of time: the short-term and rapid-motion movements of events and individuals that are "mere crests of foam on the tides of history" (*History* 3–4), the slower accrual of social time that arises from accumulated human-environment interactions, and the *longue durée* that stretches deep into geographic time and brings to light "a history of constant repetition, ever-recurring cycles" (*History* 11). Watery figures of evanescence, duration, and repetition—the very rhythms of the sea—highlight multiple temporal movements, levels, and processes through which it is possible to look back both at "that conspicuous history which holds our attention by its continual and dramatic changes" and "that other, submerged history almost silent and always discreet, virtually unsuspected by either its observers or its participants" (*Mediterranean* 16). Multiplying and thickening both time and space, Braudel's looking back approach intercuts the fast and the slow, the particular and the large, the near and the far, the visible and the hidden, urging perspectival oscillation. If looking back to regional space-time is the warp of Indian Ocean studies and looking out to networked relationality the weft, looking in is this critical fabric's fold, an invitation to find the points—rustling touch, pleated proximity—where history and memory, materiality and figurality, objects and affects, converge. Looking in is oriented to identifications, desires, longings, and doings that pulse like heartbeats and flow like blood, the sensory records of Indian Ocean lives and cultures, what Tanzanian anthropologist May Joseph indexes as the "mnemonic traces," "shards of exchange," and "striated spaces of the senses" whose "violent repositories" generate "intuitive ripples into tactile knowing" (62–63). Such memories are a necessary supplement to history, given that the history of the Indian Ocean is told not only in things traded but also in things not seen, things blown out on a breeze, submerged beneath the surface, held in sensuous materialities, raised like treasure, the pearls and bones of a field formation.

This essay surfaces that field through a reading of Abdulrazak Gurnah's 2001 novel *By the Sea*. Entwining commodity objects, migrant memories, oceanic networks, and narrative relationality, the novel, in Meg Samuelson's astute and comprehensive reading, "crafts a poetics of passage while reflecting on the enthralling nature of things" (78).[1] I take a deeper dive into the ontological and phenomenological status of objects in order to illuminate: 1) *By the Sea*'s object world; 2) the Indian Ocean world as object; and 3) the reading of both via a recombinant relationality, an elemental fluidity. While one novel is a mere drop in a polyglot, multigeneric, spatiotemporally vast ocean, I turn to it as an anchor, a point where various methodological currents can be momentarily stilled into one line of inquiry. Bringing together world literature, genre theory, and the philosophy of things, I explore *By the Sea*'s circulatory poetics: a language that surges and flows, histories and memories that accumulate, descriptive droplets clinging to the surface of things, including persons treated as things, the thickly viscous materiality of a hydropoetical imaginary, a waterworld. The novel's ability to fold together distant points in space and time, from the reconnection of two Zanzibari migrants in England at the

---

[1] See also, on the materialities of things, trades, and tellings in *By the Sea*, Lavery; Kohler; and especially Cooper. On human migration, see Ocita. On rhizomatic relationality, see Steiner.

turn of the last century to Indian Ocean trade networks going back a thousand years, and to saturate its many objects with circulatory meaning, are formal responses to regional connectivity, the "sedimentation" of history into form described by Fredric Jameson extended into watery irrigation, coursing flow, and dense viscosity (71). Viscosity is a thickness that resists flow, produced by internal molecular friction as well as external forces of temperature, pressure, and velocity. The viscous is what stills within what flows, a sticky, cumulative density that is equally a part of flow economies. *By the Sea* approaches the past, both that of its two narrators and that of the region, as distant horizons brought near and momentarily stilled into objects thick with the history of their bartering, selling, taking, and mourning. If the novel thus recalls the world of trade practically synonymous with Indian Ocean circulations, it also invites us to consider what else is carried in those object-heavy flows, adrift in space and time, chronotopically vast and intimately keyed, dense with memory and feeling.

"I want to look forward, but I always find myself looking back, poking about in times so long ago and so diminished by other events since then, tyrant events that loom large over me and dictate every ordinary action. Yet when I look back I find some objects still gleam with a bright malevolence and every memory draws blood" (Gurnah 86). So says Latif Mahmud, a University of London lecturer recalling the events that bind him to *By the Sea*'s other narrator, Saleh Omar, a one-time seller of "beautiful, intricate things" to British colonials and European tourists eager to "take them home and possess them" (Gurnah 20). Latif and Saleh are linked by two generations of property dealings encompassing houses and their contents, deathbed quests and collateral loans, deeds sold and possessions repossessed, grudges held and losses mourned—a tale that recalls the intricate plot machinery of *Bleak House* but also, in the frame tale of Latif and Saleh's conversation in England thirty years after those long-ago events, the slipperiness and liquidity of storytelling's exchanges. In one of the many scenes of narrative exchange that form *By the Sea*'s narrative backbone, one character tells another "stories are always slipping through our fingers, changing shape, wriggling to get away" (130). Like the fish that the fisherman in the *Tales of the Arabian Nights* thinks he has caught only to haul up a jar containing a djinn, the novel's form also eludes capture, offering in lieu of fixity a form best described as circulatory.

Objects in *By the Sea* go around and come around. Some objects are story-catalysts, some are bit players—narrative flotsam and jetsam in a novel as dense with descriptive enumeration as any nineteenth-century realist tale. And some objects, like those recalled by Latif, are live-wired to memory, be it the personal history of betrayal embedded in the "beautiful table" (19) Saleh repossesses from Latif's family, or the regional history distilled into the fragrant *ud-al-qamari* (aloe wood resin) whose scent, conjuring centuries-old merchant routes and the storied world of the *Nights*, seduces Saleh into selling the table in the first place to an itinerant trader who gives it to Latif's father in unspoken exchange for Latif's "beautiful" brother (22, 30). If Latif's effort to look forward is always waylaid by looking back, what surfaces in that circulatory movement are objects themselves, thickly charged both with the flowing history of exchange and the bright gleam and pulsing throb of an almost animate life, a life both thingly and narrative. This essay links the lives of *By the Sea*'s objects to the forms of a region. The capacity of *By the*

Sea's objects to condense large-scale and small-scale histories, to hold and catalyze memories, to occasionally reverse the flow of time and the scale of distance, and to consistently traverse geographic, categorical, and conceptual borders, in turn reveal the Indian Ocean as *itself* such an object, equally thick with meaning. In what follows, I do not offer a comprehensive reading of either the novel's or the Indian Ocean's form. Instead I practice a form of catch-and-release, taking up and then letting go descriptive fragments of novel and region, allowing their similarly dense chronotopes and interlocking circulatory forms to flow into one another, a critical waterworld of liquid reading.

Object Forms

The "beautiful table" with "three delicately bowed legs, made of ebony so highly polished that it glowed tremulously even from a distance" occupies the center of *By the Sea* (22). It is sold by Saleh under the spell of another thing also nested within a narrative. What is in the *ud* that the canny merchant Hussein brings to Saleh's shop is more than the *ud*. A microregional history voiced by Saleh precedes it, tracing the long deep of oceanic routes and the thick materiality of their yield, in Saleh's childhood, "ghee and gum, cloths and crudely hammered trinkets, livestock and salted fish, dates, tobacco, perfume, rosewater, incense and handfuls of all manner of wondrous things" (16); and half a century before that, "the opium, the rubber, the tin, the timber, the spices" (23); the symbiotic rhythms of human and natural cycles bringing Hussein, "who had come to our part of the world with the musim, the winds of the monsoons, he and thousands of other traders from Arabia, the Gulf, India and Sind, and the Horn of Africa . . . every year for at least a thousand years," bearing "their goods and their God . . . their stories and their songs . . . their hungers and greeds, their fantasies and lies and hatreds, leaving some among their numbers behind for whole life-times and taking what they could buy, trade or snatch away with them, including people they bought or kidnapped or sold" (15). The enumerative, accumulative syntax in which these stories of exchange are told, all lists and layers, is itself a materiality through which both things and the Indian Ocean world come into being as the product of trade diasporas, Muslim networks, slave systems, indenture economies, and multiple empires. Alongside this materiality lies an affective circuit that captures Saleh's imagination, an era of intimate circulatory bonds when "someone borrowed money from you here, went to trade somewhere else, then repaid the loan to an associate of yours at yet another place" (33). Enchanted by proxy proximity to this vast, fabled world, so distant "now that everyone is scrambling for the merest coppers" (32), Saleh agrees to discount the beautiful table in exchange for a quantity of *ud*, and later to lend Hussein a large amount in exchange for Hussein's unscrupulously acquired claim to the deed to Latif's family home. These are acts conducted in currency but operating as current, bearing back one time, place, and networked culture to another, and carrying not only personal tragedy but regional history and memory forward in their wake.

The *ud* is one thing and one story in this flow but, like the beautiful table, it multiplies its appearances across the novel. Just as the *ud* initially short-circuits spatiotemporal distance for Saleh ("I thought I could catch the odour of the fantasy of those distant places in the dense body of that perfume" [30]), so too does it return to conjure memory's reach for the other narrator. *Ud* swirls through Latif's recollections of the perfumed clothing of a mother, incense filling a home, stories of djinn exiting vessels in the *Nights*, and himself as a boy climbing into a clay jar in a courtyard and hoping to awake elsewhere. The *ud*'s animation of the economies of trade and narration, like the life it breathes into regional history and its sensuous materiality and affective resonances, renders it a lively thing. Spilling forth in wonder-tales and reveries of regional-familial-personal memory, it condenses into itself the vaster circulations of places, times, stories, and feelings—as if the *ud* were itself caught in the nested infinities of the *Nights*. Similarly nested is the "beautiful table" in a shop filled with "beautiful things" that is bartered and sold for a "beautiful boy" only to eventually return to Saleh, along with all of Latif's family's other possessions and home, after Saleh collects on the collateral loan offered to him by Hussein (22, 20, 30). When Latif visits a few years later to futilely ask for the ebony table, linked for his mother to the lost son who left to follow Hussein, the scene of Saleh's refusal is a sad one, filled with the pathos of the commodity fetishism that turns relations between people into relations between things, and even (beautiful) people into (beautiful) things. Beauty capitalizes itself, as the proliferation of the adjective underscores. Yet beyond the metonymic proximity of the beautiful boy and beautiful table is the intimacy of the stories they reveal, the networked alignments, convergences, and collusions that make one thing almost infinite. In this the table further doubles the *Nights*' frame tale structure, that multiplication table proliferating stories by a "narrative structure by which one tale contains another tale that in turn contains a third" (Naddaff 41). Outside and inside entangle, as do essences and actions, a thing's thingliness and a thing's expansion or movement beyond itself.

A table within a shop within a house within a trade network stretching back and out as far as the Indian Ocean of a thousand years ago and the postcolonial England of now, where in Latif's and Saleh's exchanges the lost table is one of those "objects [that] still gleam with a bright malevolence" (86). If the table flows across time, it also freezes or viscously thickens time, its loss remaining raw decades later. Spatially, the table is both networked and nodal, a point through which connections happen and associations saturate. The events it sets in motion spiral out to a lawsuit brought by Latif's family that results in Saleh's eight-year imprisonment in the murky system of a state nationalism that denies its own syncretic and connective regional history by expelling the Omani Muslim population and prohibiting the musim trade and coastal cities' cosmopolitan networks in favor of new alliances with the German Democratic Republic, Russia, and China. Saleh returns from prison to spend fifteen years selling basic goods in his old furniture shop before fleeing yet another court case brought by Latif's family for England, which has recently declared Zanzibar's government a credible danger to its citizens, and where he will reencounter Latif for the exchange of narratives about their tragically entwined pasts. As they talk, Saleh confesses "I should've given that table back. Such a small thing. . . . I was too angry" (209). Small things can have big circuits. "Philosophy is full of tables," Sara Ahmed observes, inviting the question of what this particular table is full of, and how the theory of the object's life might help us read it (*Queer* 2). Ahmed considers how phenomenological orientations to objects "align body and space," thus shaping how we are in the world as well as how objects are in the world, how they carry emotions and histories into intimate relation (both proximate and distant) with subjects and their bodies (7).

What is in the object is more than the object. At its greatest extent, this is the world "out there": brought in, nested, or accordioned; held in the object along with its worldly movements; everything simultaneously stilled and animate, like the table that Marx says dances on its head thanks to the magic of commodity fetishism or the ebony table that "glowed tremulously" (Gurnah 22) in Saleh's narrative and "gleam[ed] with bright malevolence" (89) in Latif's. Like the *ud*, the beautiful table not only indexes the Indian Ocean's circulatory system, trade as lifeblood, but echoes the phenomenon that Ahmed calls affective "stickiness," the object's gathering of the contexts it passes through onto its surface, into its gleam. For Ahmed, "what sticks 'shows us' where the object has traveled through what it has gathered onto its surface, gatherings that become a part of the object, and call into question its integrity as an object" (*Cultural* 91). The object's lack of integrity corresponds to its ineluctable relationality, the fact that objects, subjects, and signs all circulate and "the more [they] circulate, the more affective they become" (8). Such stickiness or viscosity (a state of thick semifluidity due to internal friction) is a passageway to liquid reading of both the Indian Ocean and its objects. The notion of an object that cannot be thought apart from its circulations and sedimentations, flows and densities, differs from Jane Bennett's sense of the capacity of things "to act as quasi agents or forces with trajectories, propensities, or tendencies of their own" (viii), that "strange ability of ordinary, man-made items to exceed their status as objects and to manifest traces of independence or aliveness" (xvi). *By the Sea*'s things gleam across time less because of the inherent vitality of "Thing-Power," the force Bennett says is "not transpersonal or intersubjective but impersonal, an affect intrinsic to forms" (xii), than because these things are dense with circulatory form, the layered accumulations of histories, memories, and meanings. Seen thus, the beautiful table is bright with the past's aura and deep with a relational structure intrinsic to regional form. The table is an object-correlative to the Indian Ocean, which similarly asks to be understood by looking out to networks of exchange, looking back to the palimpsestic thickening of the past, and looking in to what is caught and held in objects and memories. *By the Sea*'s sedimentation of large and small histories into its objects' circulatory yet stilled forms, like its folding together of distant points in space and time, can furthermore reorient us to think differently about flows at the scales of both region and world.

Flows of Form and Figure

Flow dynamics have been central to world literature's mapping of various literary scales, forms, spreads, and movements. So Franco Moretti adopts Immanuel Wallerstein's model of a capitalist world system divided into cores, peripheries, and semiperipheries (a world "simultaneously *one*, and *unequal*") in order to posit a "one-and-unequal literary system [that] is not just an external network outside; it's embedded well into its form" (Moretti 58–59). The notion that flows might be perceived both by looking out and looking in suggests one route for reading Indian Ocean world literature, in whose descriptive and diegetic worlds circulatory economies are indeed deeply embedded. Movement, migration, travel, and trade are veritable engines of narration, proliferating such microgenres as travelers' tales and shipboard sagas and producing the thick thingliness that renders so many narratives into descriptive storehouses of a lost world. But for Indian Ocean literature it might be less important to identify, as Moretti does, "form as a struggle . . . between the story that comes from the core, and the viewpoint that comes from the core, and the viewpoint that 'receives' it in the periphery"—a formulation still bearing the traces of Eurocentrism—and more urgent to account for how formal mixtures and textures attest to the region's own mixed, plural, syncretic sensibility, as well as to the liquid *processes* of those connections (134).

Such processes include the viscous, sticky circuits that yoke subjects, objects, worlds, and feelings. They also entail what Lisa Lowe terms "intimacies" or "the circuits, connections, associations, and mixings of differentially laboring peoples [African slaves, peoples of Indigenous descent in the Americas, and colonized laborers from India and China] eclipsed by the operations that universalize the Anglo-American liberal individual" (17). Intimacies' relations of connection, proximity, alliance, and affinity surface hidden relations, "forgotten" processes, and "braided" histories (71). Lowe takes literature to mediate these historical circulations "not by literally reflecting them in fixed, transparent fashion" but by registering them symptomatically, "portray[ing] that such conditions were more often grasped as isolated effects, glimpsed in particular objects in the social fabric, rather than seized totally or framed systemically" (81). So the Sedleys' India-patterned chintz bed-curtains and Becky Sharp's pink silk gown and the tiny silk-stockinged foot in Thackeray's *Vanity Fair* metaphorically substitute and displace the imperial flows of Indian textiles, Chinese silk, and the labor that produced them against the backdrop of the British East India Company's transition from mercantile monopoly to catalyzing agent of a free trade imperialism. This is an important brief for approaching large-scale connectivities at small-object closeness, with a keen sense for the materiality of literary figuration, particularly metaphor, that "process that both evokes through equivalence and occludes through exchange . . . [and] offers us an instruction in how to read for the presence of colonial goods and the absence of colonial labor and imperial trade in the history, politics, and economics of the modern world" (97). Lowe's intimacy is also a kind of looking in, an orientation to circulatory connections that can be surfaced or intuited in the descriptive language around things, as well as found in historical records or modeled in historical explanations. Such critical reorientation is another version of the approach I advocate for world literature, a multiperspectival attunement experienced as a perpetual oscillation between the close and the distant, the big and the small, the old and the new, the material and the figurative, the systemic and the textual, the world-historical and the affective-intimate, the regional and the personal.

With this kind of looking in mind, and an object-intensive grasp close at hand, we might consider again the trees and waves that Moretti's world-systems thinking adopts as metaphors for the flows of literary form. Trees, which describe "the passage from unity to diversity: one tree, with many branches," are "what nation states cling to" (Moretti 60). A wave, "uniformity engulfing an initial diversity," is "what markets do." Trees need geographical discontinuity, separation, and borders, while waves "thrive on geographical continuity." Both metaphors, Moretti adds, work for cultural history made of both processes. In Indian Ocean world literature, trees are more than organizing principles rooted in differentiation; they are the tangled genealogies of family sagas, the plantation scenes and economies of rubber, tea, teak, and mahogany cultivation over the span of Dutch, British, German, and French control, and the philological and intertextual graftings of polyglot narratives. Gurnah's novel crafts its syncretic form not through the multilingualized English of, say, Ghosh's *Ibis Trilogy* but through migrant circulations of multiple things and a recombinant storytelling inflected with the regional specificity of the *Nights*, from Latif's Sindbadesque clay jar, to the way when Hussein enters Saleh's story "my head filled with words: Persia, Bahrain, Basra, Harun al-Rashid, Sindbad and more" (23), to the relational economy that ultimately binds Saleh and Latif, two narrators telling their tales so they might escape the iron grip of past grudges. In this, *By the Sea*'s uptake of the seductive story economy of the *Nights*, with its "arabesque structures ramify[ing] in infinite recession, offering numerous repeats and recurrent motifs," offers a branching tree of a different kind, not Moretti's protonational passage "from unity to diversity" but a proliferating spread and recursive time that casts its shadow over a regional whole (Warner 8, 6).[2]

And waves, in the *Nights* into *Beyond the Sea* and the larger waterworld of Indian Ocean literature, are more than flow analytics tracking the uniformity of a literary form's global spread. Waves are the surge of a liquid literature animated by the circling, cycling rhythms of the sea, in which plots, stories, figures, and histories are subjected to use and reuse; raw material within literature's circulatory system. Waves are also the liquid forms of oceanic cultures, echoing Braudel's formulation of the migrations of Mediterranean civilization as "great waves that are balanced by continual returns," a marine metaphor for a cultural process of change and absorption (*Mediterranean* 168). Michael Pearson's regional elaboration recalls Claude Penrad's connection of "ressac, the threefold violent movement of the waves, turning back on themselves as they crash against the shore" to "the way in which the to-and-fro movements of the Indian Ocean mirror coastal and inland influences that keep coming back at each other just as do waves" (Pearson, "Littoral" 359).[3] The undertow of waves here does not conjure Moretti's protonational market uniformity, or merely the agglutinative commonalities of culture, language, and maritime occupations that Pearson says link littoral societies more to one another than to their inland counterparts, but also a broader, distinctively oceanic process of syncreticism figured as recursivity, the deep waters of deep time turning back on itself. This cycling back of a form and its return bearing new elements is not unlike *By the Sea*'s fluid and repetitive mix of the wonder of trader's tales, the ur-text of the *Nights*, the high realism of countless stories about houses and things (Austen, Dickens, Balzac, James, Wharton, V. S. Naipaul), the gothic of family histories filled with twice-told tales and haunted histories, and the postcolonial migrant novel.

As stories and the genres that contain them seep, pour, flow, eddy, and cycle into one another, a porous narrativity reflects a sea's worth of relations, linking spaces

---

[2] For excellent discussions of the *Nights*' place and effect on *By the Sea*'s thingly imaginary, see Samuelson; Cooper.

[3] In an illuminating essay Rila Mukherjee argues that "the littoral's spatial model becomes a chart on which Pearson projects social reality, a template for the different movements of time—the three-way movement of *ressac*—and for all categories of social life," thereby "becoming deterministic" ("Revisiting" 20).

and times, histories and memories, persons and things. If *By the Sea* cuts against that style of genre theory in which taxonomy, classification, and location within boundaries—period, language, nation—dominate, it further invites us to consider generic practice as circulation, a recombinant flow or recursive recycling. Wai-Chee Dimock frames this as a world-literature method, urging us to put "fluidity front and center in our study of genres," to see them not as individual unities, "familiar and stable-seeming," but rather "afloat in the same pool, with generic particles released by cross-currents, filtering into one another and coalescing in different ways" (1381, 1379). "Generic wateriness" names the compositional process by which monadic parts enter fluid combinatrics, further described as "*regenreing*, to highlight the activity here as cumulative reuse, an alluvial process, sedimentary as well as migratory" (1379–80). Genre is no fixed substance but one that regularly passes between surface and depth, what settles and what moves. "Genre is best seen not flatly, as the enactment of one set of legislative norms, but as an alternation between dimensions, mediated by vectors of up and down, front and back in and out" (1380). The Indian Ocean itself recalls this wateriness of form as it solicits looking out, back, and in; as it stretches across space and time; as it folds and layers multiple histories, trades, stories, and memories into a regional flow; and as it emerges as both a unified object and a morphing one, whose boundaries expand and contract. Regenreing in this sense does the work of reregioning, capturing the multidimensional chronotopes of the Indian Ocean and paradoxically offering, in its wateriness, something to hold onto in making sense of the category itself.

The Form of the Object and the Indian Ocean as Object

What is the Indian Ocean? The category has had to be *made*, produced, as Pearson says, as "something which we call the Indian Ocean and which can be studied, analysed, treated as a coherent object" (*Indian* 6). I begin not with what the Indian Ocean is but what it isn't, focusing on the object-oriented philosopher Graham Harman's account of one historical Indian Ocean entity, the Dutch East India Company, or the Vereenigde Oostindische Compagnie (VOC). In contrast to the investment of Bennett and other new materialists in the hidden life and animate potentiality of things, Harman's object-oriented ontology insists with a sober empiricism that an object must be understood to exist in itself, as "an entity that cannot be paraphrased in terms of either its components or its effects" (2). Whereas Harman understands new materialism to believe "what a thing *does* is more interesting than what it is," that "everything occurs along continuous gradients rather than with distinct boundaries and cut-off points"; and that "everything is constantly changing" (13–14), his own "axioms of immaterialism" hold that "what a thing *is* turns out to be more interesting than what it does," that "everything is split up according to definite boundaries and cut-off points rather than along continuous gradients," and that "change is intermittent and stability the norm" (15). Such relative fixity in terms of historical change, bordered definition, and categorical essence is at odds with the Indian Ocean as object. Indeed, the Indian Ocean world—that set of mobile and morphing connections over Sugata Bose's "hundred horizons" of space and time, each criss-crossed by vectors of trade, sovereignty, labor, climate, and culture, and further swelled by figurative description drawn from its component medium, its wateriness—is the very opposite of what Harman declares an object to be, an autonomous thing that exists purely in itself, "a surplus exceeding its relations, qualities, and actions" (3). Harman argues that when "we substitute a loose paraphrase of the thing for the thing itself" we are precisely not dealing with the thing (7). Descriptive nomination runs the dangers of what he calls "duomining": 1) the reduction of the object to what it is made of (undermining); and 2) the extension of the object to what it does, how it acts, relates, connects, cathects (overmining). The metaphors in which my essay has already trafficked— fluidity, wateriness, circulation, cycling, ebbs, flows, viscous clinging, accretions— would seem prime candidates for both variants of object-obscurantism. So too does my concern with the thick descriptive circuitry within which Indian Ocean relationality is ensnared, both in field-shaping models and Gurnah's novel, contradict such an "axiom of immaterialism" as "what a thing *is* turns out to be more interesting than what it does" (or how it is described) (15). In contrast to the nominative probity Harman urges over "loose paraphrase of the thing," Indian Ocean circulations lead precisely into the descriptive waters of a connectivity that is historical, material, and figurative. Description can serve as method allowing an object to come into focus more rather than less clearly. Metaphor is a circulation of a kind, literally the "carrying across" of a term from one realm of signification to another in order to produce the equivalences or similar charges that allow us to speak of a regional water-world or a generic wateriness. Literary language is particularly dense with the thing-making possibility of description, as *By the Sea* reminds us in its depiction of objects like the *ud* that bring to mind the larger spatiotemporal contours, interscalar oscillations, and dense historicities of the Indian Ocean.

Certainly the Indian Ocean and the VOC that is the central example of Harman's *Immaterialism* are different kinds of objects. One is a regional formation, the other a mercantile corporation that dominated Southeast Asia between 1602 and 1795, in the period between Portuguese control and British imperial rule; the former precedes and exceeds the lifespan of the other. What concerns me is the logic of Harman's argument, and its misfit with the thing that the Indian Ocean is. Inspired by the monadic philosopher Leibniz's citation of the VOC as an example of an artificial aggregate compound rather than a natural substance, Harman sets out to prove that the VOC is in fact a substance in Leibniz's terms and an object in his own, "an entity that cannot be paraphrased in terms of either its components or its effects" (2). He explores the VOC as something that exists neither in its components (ships, fleets, depots, soldiers, merchants, governor generals) nor in its effects (deforestation, enslavement, and monopoly trade that eroded long-standing networks with Arab, Chinese, and Indian merchants) but simply in itself, as it *is*. Philosophical readers like Andrew Ball have seen the example as bizarre, opaque, and irrelevant, but I take it up as a provocation, a "how not to look" at the Indian Ocean. In a lengthy review of the VOC's history Harman notes some of its most spectacular "doings," including the arsenal of imperial tactics deployed by its notoriously brutal first, two-term Governor General Jan Pieterszoon Coen and the larger litany of "ceremonies, battles, weddings, treaties, massacres, annexations, and discoveries" that are the stuff of historical accounts of the company (39). Harman's study, however, is not a history but an "ontology" of the VOC, animated by the immaterialist conviction that "if we misinterpret the VOC as consisting of 'what it can do' rather than 'what it is,' we will tend to overreact to the most histrionic incidents during its lifespan, since these are the most vivid examples of 'doing' that a thing can provide" (52). Equally dangerous for Harman is the tendency to isolate certain doings to elaborate the essence of an object, be it the villainous Coen's ruthless style of discipline-and-punish in achieving economic stranglehold, or the VOC's initial closure and rapid reopening of extant trade networks in the company's first decade. While the latter fact enabled the early survival of the VOC prior to its monopoly control, Harman observes that it cannot be "overmined" into a description of the VOC's essentially link-based nature. Tracing what he claims are a mere handful of moments when the VOC consolidated the thing it was, Harman observes that "relational theories of objects often go wrong [because] they overemphasize the links and alliances made by objects while neglecting to consider the ways that symbiosis *protects* an object from links, and thus further solidifies its autonomy" (92).[4] Here Harman's argument about the VOC's relatively fixed ontology, its nonrelational or autonomous being, meets its Indian Ocean limit, or, better, the uncertain edges of a field whose conceptual parameters urge its mapmakers to see it as link-based, *relational*, both a unified whole and a heterogeneous composite, whose boundaries shift across sea and land, space and time, cognition and imagination.

Harman's unchanging, nonrelational object is precisely *not* what the Indian Ocean world is, either in itself or as we can critically know it, think it, and describe it. To capture the Indian Ocean's "unity amid diversity" (12), Bose adopts "nonlinear narratives" characterized by the "weaving of broad patterns of interregional networks" and "unraveling of individual tales" at the level of persons ("proconsuls and pirates, capitalists and laborers, soldiers and sailors") and things (pearls, cloves, rubber, rice) (23). If the imperial focus of *A Hundred Horizons*, as Rila Mukherjee notes, narrows a long history of layered temporalities and "multi level and multi local spaces" to posit the Indian Ocean as "a harbinger of globalization" ("Indian" 293), it nonetheless foregrounds this world's constitutive relationality and the deep connectivity of its materialities. Citing "elasticity," "porosity," and "mutability" as region-defining characteristics, Jeremy Prestholdt attributes the "dynamism of the Indian Ocean as a social concept" to "pliant" boundaries and "multifocal, layered affinities" that unfold in both intra- and extra-regional connections (25). If post–Cold War "metageographical imaginaries" (25) and postcolonial nation-states' affiliative investments have yielded an increasingly "unified concept of the Indian Ocean" (27), Prestholdt also notes that "while *longue durée* patterns of interface often inform historical memory and nostalgia, they have also been discarded in re-imaginings of the region" (25). However, this is not a progress narrative, a march toward definitional consolidation of a "unified concept," but a process narrative unfolding through spatiotemporal flux and flow and further yoking regional change to the histories, memories, affinities, attachments, and objects that cling to the thing of the Indian Ocean. Considering how the Indian Ocean coheres across space and through time, and informed by mathematical set theory, the philosophy of language, and Braudel's Mediterranean history, Chauduri

---

4 Harman's account of VOC's relatively slow, steady, and stable growth based on a mere six defining moments is drawn from the biologist Lynn Margulis's account of "symbiosis," or the process whereby independent organelles become subordinate components of a unified cell, undergoing a handful of decisive changes rather than a steady current of transformation.

emphasizes the Indian Ocean's "unity and disunity, continuity and discontinuity, ruptures and thresholds" (*Asia* 9). He further foregrounds the Indian Ocean's perception not as "a matter of objective truth" but rather "a question of mental constructs" ("Unity" 17) while Mukherjee specifies a "cognitive space" that "possesses various levels of place, space, structures, boundaries, time and memory" ("Indian" 297). To see the Indian ocean thus is to see (unlike Harman) a profoundly relational and changing object.

Here we might also recall Iain Chambers's suggestion that the sea issues "an ontological challenge" in the form of "historical configurations that precede and exceed the shape we believe we are bestowing on them," a history that "commences not from the eye but from the external light of the world that strikes it" (682, 683). While Chambers shares with Harman a sense that the gaze does not determine the object, Chambers is more oriented to his object's distinctive qualities, that light which is the shimmer of the sea's substance, "its liquidity, its seemingly anonymous materiality . . . an anchorless image loaded with time" (679). Looking is only the beginning: the challenge is to get beyond ourselves and our categories, to think with watery fluidity, and, reversing Harman, to surface from the thing the sea *is* to what the sea *does*, namely "lead to rethinking ideas of time, space, and change" (679). In this, the flowing, circulatory form and thick descriptive object-worlds of *By the Sea* can perhaps serve as a guide, a reminder that the doctrine of an object's existence cannot exist apart from its relationality, and its relating (telling). In the final section I briefly take up the work of words as things in *By the Sea*. Words in the novel are thingly in the sense that they "do" as much as they "are," and what they do is charm, seduce, wound, repair, recycle, expand out, and contract down, offering the spatiotemporal expanse of whole oceans of story but also regularly "sticking," as circulations are wont to do.

Word Links

Like objects, words in *By the Sea* are a means by which to relate relation within a narrative whose compass is not strictly regional but extends the ends of the Indian Ocean all the way to cold English waters. Upon Saleh's arrival at Gatwick airport, moments before Saleh utters the magic words "Refugee, Asylum" (9), the customs official takes up the *ud* he carries in his meager suitcase and, sniffing it, posits "Mahogany?" Then, opening the casket, "'What's this?' . . . 'Incense,' he said. 'It is, isn't it?'" (8). Where the revolving orbits and thickly embroidered circuits of Saleh's subsequent reverie about the *ud* unfold circuits of trade and the fluid chronotopes of regional space-time, the *ud* as caught in the official's minimalist, one-sided definition anticipates the sticky circuits that catch the racial thing, that subject-turned-object, in long national-historical nets of descriptive differentiation. The *ud* is easy for the official to name and pocket, and easier still to dismiss (like Saleh himself) as a foreign thing, something about which it's possible to say simply "it is" or "you are." Calling Saleh by the name on his passport (taken like so many other possessions from Latif's father), the official remonstrates, "Mr. Shaaban, look at yourself, and look at these things you've brought with you. . . . This is all you'll have if you stay here. . . . You don't belong here, you don't value any of the things we value, you haven't paid for them through generations, and we don't want you here" (12). Things enact the slicing cut between "you people" and the national-racial "us"; for Saleh to have "these things" in his suitcase is to be one kind of thing forever distant from other, English things. In a subsequent internal monologue Saleh invites the official to "think of me as one of those objects that Europe took away with her" (12). The ironic assumption of objecthood that indicts British imperialism is shadowed by subsequent accounts of Saleh's own complicity with this extractive economy, from his initial trade with the Europeans who wanted "to acquire the world's beautiful things" (20) to the home he repossesses, filled as Latif recalls with "objects which had beauty and purpose, but which stood like refugees in that room . . . looking like objects in a gallery or a museum . . . looking like plunder" (102). "Things" and "objects" double one another and layer together, thick with meanings as vast as entire imperial systems and as small as the repetitive loops of personal betrayal. The more charges such words accumulate, the more they loosen the borders separating distinct times, places, histories, things, objects, and persons in what is a hallmark of *By the Sea*'s relational form.

Similar densities and passages cluster around the thingifying word with which Latif's half of the narrative commences, "a grinning blackamoor" (71). Spoken to him on an English street, the word sends him to the dictionaries, first an intolerable index, a "torrent of vituperation" reading "blackhearted, blackbrowed, blacklist, blackguard, blackmail, Black Maria, blackmarket, black sheep . . . so much black black black on a page," and then, in the *Oxford English Dictionary*, a list of the English pedigree of its usage by Sidney, Shakespeare, Pepys, and the like dating back to 1501 (72). Although Latif confesses relief at the latter's suggestion that "I had been present in all those strenuous ages, not forgotten," he is haunted by the notion that the "black black black" index is "the house I live in, I thought, a language which barks and scorns at me" (73). The rendering of language as house—in a novel centrally concerned with how possessions possess us—evokes words' capacity to enact thingly life and social death. For all that Latif tries to conjure, conjugate some agency ("*I* am a grinning blackamoor, *You* are a grinning blackamoor, *He* is a grinning blackamoor" [76]), the word as noun, as thing seems steeped in its own staying power, the endlessly recyclable material of racist fabrication and the slow accrual of racist signification making long-ago histories circulating through multiple usages suddenly skin-tight, as close as one's own body. Here is a version of what Ahmed describes as migration's activation of a racially inflected phenomenology of the body in which the skin, the subject world-object world's contact point, is saturated with all that is *in* the object, its past histories, its emotional resonances, the structures of feeling it catalyzes, all of which "surface as impressions on the skin" (*Queer* 20). The relationality of Ahmed's object "orientations" and the sticky circuits through which objects, subjects, and signs acquire the density of historical meanings and affective charges, in contrast to object-oriented ontology's creed of autonomy, allow us to see skin, things, and the skin-thing of "blackamoor" as both fixed and fluid. The movements of such thingly entities can also be changes, as when toward the end of their conversation Latif calls Saleh "you grinning blackamoor" and promises to return—"after all, we're related it seems" (Gurnah 194). Beyond Saleh's adoption of Latif's father's name, the tangled family trees, and the contested possessions held fiercely in each man's memory, it is also relation that relates them, an exchange of story that, as Shahrazad's does to Shahriyar, brings about a final peace, the end of a rage sustained through long years (195).

This settling is also in its way the fruit of a perpetual circulation: the eddying of story forms, generic wateriness filtering one narrative world into another and endlessly making good on Latif's German host mother's observation that stories are "always slipping through our fingers, changing shape, wriggling to get away" (130). The same might be said of words or of the watery concept of the Indian Ocean itself, so incapable of having its boundaries drawn once and for all or its nature autonomously fixed. At a scale sometimes as minute as individual words and things, *By the Sea*'s thickly connective, agglutinative, viscous textuality creates link after link in a literary equivalent to the region-making relationalities of space, time, history, and memory. If some word-things capture resolutely racial nationalist ways of looking at migrant things and persons, their flowing repetitions through the narrative and their sticky accumulations of distinct histories, memories, and charges are also reminders of what I have wanted to read as regional form. Here the novel's ability to saturate both its things and words with circulatory meaning offers a formal response to connectivity, a registering in language of what passes in, and as, history. Lingering on only a few moments in *By the Sea*, I have tried to surface the multiple temporalities eddying through them, the sensate lives they distill, the sociohistorical currents they traverse, and the memories coursing through them. It is as a further form of wateriness that we might consider the novel's interscalar oscillation between large and small histories, the circulatory flows of regional pasts into and out of personal ones, and the thick descriptive circuits around objects. These waters in turn reflect the relationality of the Indian Ocean, its status as a thing made by spatiotemporal connectivities but also made in part by how we imagine it, the words we describe it with, and the metaphors we attach to it. To see the Indian Ocean in *By the Sea* is not only to see it from an English afar and a modern day, and not only from a national-territorialism that counters its regional translocalities, but from the close up of the intimacies and animacies of things and words, another kind of stuff that regional dreams are made on.

University of California, Santa Cruz

Works Cited

Ahmed, Sara. *The Cultural Politics of Emotion*. New York: Routledge, 2004.

Ahmed, Sara. *Queer Phenomenology: Orientations, Objects, Others*. Durham, NC: Duke University Press, 2006.

Alpers, Edward. *The Indian Ocean in World History*. Oxford: Oxford University Press, 2013.

Ball, Andrew. Review of *Immaterialism: Objects and Social Theory*, by Graham Harman. *Philosophy in Review* 37, no. 3 (2017): 111–13.

Bennett, Jane. *Vibrant Matter: A Political Ecology of Things*. Durham, NC: Duke University Press, 2010.

Bose, Sugata. *A Hundred Horizons: The Indian Ocean in the Age of Empire*. Cambridge, MA: Harvard University Press, 2006.

Braudel, Fernand. *The Mediterranean and the Mediterranean World in the Age of Philip II*, translated by Sian Reynolds. Vol. 1. New York: Harper, 1972.

Braudel, Fernand. *On History*, translated by Sara Matthews. Chicago: University of Chicago Press, 1980.

Chambers, Iain. "Maritime Criticism and Theoretical Shipwrecks." *PMLA* 125, no. 3 (2010): 678–84.

Chauduri, K. N. *Asia before Europe: Economy and Civilization of the Indian Ocean from the Rise of Islam to 1750*. New York: Cambridge University Press, 1990.

Chauduri, K. N. "The Unity and Disunity of Indian Ocean History from the Rise of Islam to 1750: The Outline of a Theory and Historical Discourse." *Journal of World History* 4, no. 1 (1993): 1–21.

Cooper, Brenda. "Returning the Jinns to the Jar: Material Culture, Stories, and Migration in Abdulrazak Gurnah's *By the Sea*." *Kunapipi* 30, no. 1 (2008): 79–96.

Dimock, Wai-Chee. "Introduction: Genres as Fields of Knowledge." *PMLA* 122, no. 5 (2007): 1377–88.

Ghosh, Devleena, and Stephen Muecke, eds. *Cultures of Trade: Indian Ocean Exchanges*. Cambridge: Cambridge Scholars, 2007.

Gurnah, Abdulrazak. *By the Sea*. London: Bloomsbury, 2002.

Harman, Graham. *Immaterialism*. Cambridge: Polity, 2016.

Ho, Engseng. *The Graves of Tarim: Genealogy and Mobility across the Indian Ocean*. Berkeley: University of California Press, 2006.

Jameson, Fredric. *The Political Unconscious: Narrative as a Socially Symbolic Act*. Ithaca, NY: Cornell University Press, 1981.

Joseph, May. "Old Routes, Mnemonic Traces." In Ghosh and Muecke, 62–75.

Kohler, Sophy. "'The Spice of Life': Trade, Storytelling and Movement in *Paradise* and *By the Sea* by Abdulrazak Gurnah." *Social Dynamics* 43, no. 2 (2017): 274–85.

Lavery, Charne. "White-Washed Minarets and Slimy Gutters: Abdulrazak Gurnah, Narrative Form, and Indian Ocean Space." *English Studies in Africa* 56, no. 2 (2013): 117–27.

Lowe, Lisa. *The Intimacies of Four Continents*. Durham, NC: Duke University Press, 2015.

Moretti, Franco. *Distant Reading*. New York: Verso Books, 2013.

Mukherjee Rila. "The Indian Ocean in the 'New Thalassology.'" Review of *A Hundred Horizons: The Indian Ocean in the Age of Global Empire*, by Sugata Bose. *Archipel*, no. 76 (2008): 291–306.

Mukherjee, Rila. "Revisiting Michael Pearson's Indian Ocean Littoral." *Asian Review of World Histories* 5, no. 1 (2017): 9–30.

Naddaff, Sandra. *Arabesque: Narrative Structure and the Aesthetics of Repetition in the 1001 Nights*. Evanston, IL: Northwestern University Press, 1991.

Ocita, James. "Travel, Marginality, and Migrant Subjectivities in Abdulrazak Gurnah's *By the Sea* and Caryl Phillips's *The Atlantic Sound*." *Social Dynamics* 43, no. 2 (2017): 298–311.

Pearson, Michael. *The Indian Ocean*. New York: Routledge, 2003.

Pearson, Michael. "Littoral Society: The Concept and the Problems." *Journal of World History* 17, no. 4 (2006): 353–73.

Prestholdt, Jeremy. "The Ends of the Indian Ocean: Notes on Boundaries and Affinities across Time." In *Reimagining Indian Ocean Worlds*, edited by Smriti Srinivas, Bettina Ng'weno, and Neelima Jeychandran, 25–41. New York: Routledge, 2020.

Samuelson, Meg. "Narrative Cartographies, 'Beautiful Things,' and Littoral States in Abdulrazak Gurnah's *By the Sea*." *English Studies in Africa* 56, no. 1 (2013): 78–90.

Sheriff, Abdul. *Dhow Cultures of the Indian Ocean: Cosmopolitanism, Commerce, and Islam before the Coming of the Europeans*. London: Hurst, 2010.

Sheriff, Abdul. *Slaves, Spices, and Ivory in Zanzibar: Integration of an East African Commercial Empire into the World Economy, 1770–1873*. London: James Currey, 1987.

Steiner, Tina. "Writing 'Wider Worlds': The Role of Relation in Abdulrazak Gurnah's Fiction." *Research in African Literatures* 41, no. 3 (2010): 124–35.

Villier, Alan. *Monsoon Seas: The Story of the Indian Ocean*. New York: McGraw-Hill, 1952.

Warner, Marina. *Stranger Magic: Charmed States and the Arabian Nights*. London: Chatto and Windus, 2012.

KRITISH RAJBHANDARI

Fugitive Archives: Translation, Sea, and History in Indian Ocean Fiction

> There is nothing solid about the way languages interact with each other. Their movement is more like that of liquids; they mingle and flow not just between groups but often within individuals.
>
> —Amitav Ghosh, "Speaking of Babel"

AMITAV GHOSH'S *SEA of Poppies* opens with a vision of a ship sailing on the Indian Ocean, which appears to Deeti, a Bhojpuri woman living in a village far inland in the northern part of India. Anticipating her journey across the sea, Deeti's vision disrupts the linearity of the narrative and warps space and geography. This seemingly fantastical vision that brings the sea into land, conflating the center and the periphery, nonetheless aligns with the colonial reality of the Indian village in the middle of the nineteenth century. Signs of the empire built on the sea assume a powerful presence in this village located in the periphery of the periphery: Deeti is surrounded by poppy fields, an opium factory with a British flag flying on top, and a church. The vision, which one might read as a reflection of this colonial condition, fills Deeti with apprehension. The problem posed by the vision strikes her as a problem of language: "Deeti knew that the vision was not materially present in front of her—as for example, was the barge moored near the factory. She had never seen the sea, never left the district, *never spoken any language but her native Bhojpuri,* yet not for a moment did she doubt that the ship existed somewhere and was heading in her direction" (8; emphasis added). The barge and the factory, "materially present," interpellates Deeti as a colonized subject in nineteenth-century British India, containing her in the periphery of the global colonial order of production. Recognizing this colonial difference, Deeti conflates the condition of being autochthonous with her monolingualism. However, her confidence in the vision of the ship as already part of her destiny pulls her out of her monolingual provinciality. Her vision places Deeti in the temporality of the future anterior, casting the ship as already contained in her past. If the ship is a site of plurilingual cosmopolitanism,

Comparative Literature 74:2
DOI 10.1215/00104124-9594826 © 2022 by University of Oregon

or "a babel of language," as Ghosh puts it elsewhere, her vision reveals Deeti as already inhabiting multiple languages, not just her native Bhojpuri ("Fanás" 20). Despite having lived an autochthonous existence, Deeti's monolingualism is imbricated in the fluid cosmopolitanism of the sea.

Deeti's problem of responding to the ship's cosmopolitan interpellation from her provincialized monolingual position mirrors the challenge that Ghosh (or for that matter, any contemporary fiction writer) faces in writing about the Indian Ocean past.[1] How does one represent a multilingual past using a single language that speaks to the present (Ghosh, "Speaking" 292)? My analysis here focuses on two novels, Ghosh's *Sea of Poppies* (2008) and Abdulrazak Gurnah's *Paradise* (1994), which engage with the linguistic and translational challenges of writing historical fiction. Set in the colonial era, on the opposite shores the Indian Ocean, one in India and the other in East Africa, both narratives are driven by historical forces linked to the ocean, primarily, colonial expansion, migration, and trade. *Sea of Poppies* tells the intertwined stories of a diverse set of characters including Indian indentured laborers, convicts, sailors, and stowaways as they travel from inland India toward and across the ocean during the mid-nineteenth century. Similarly, *Paradise* follows young Yusuf, forced into bondage, as he travels with a trading caravan from the Swahili coast toward the African interior at the onset of European colonialism in East Africa in the early twentieth century. Both novels draw on multilingual nineteenth-century sources to recreate a colonial Indian Ocean world for a twenty-first-century audience in a predominantly monolingual medium of the novel. Ghosh uses colonial dictionaries to reconstruct the linguistic heterogeneity of colonial India, and Gurnah, likewise, reworks nineteenth-century travelogues written in Swahili, commissioned by German colonial administrators, to tell the story of trading expeditions in East Africa. The impulse to renarrate history in these novels can be understood as "the postcolonial desire to re-translate" the past, which means that the archival work of recuperating multilingual pasts is inseparable from the work of translation (Niranjana 172). For Indian Ocean fiction, the task of translation is twofold: first, constructing linguistic difference in cross-cultural interactions made possible by Indian Ocean routes of circulation; and second, adapting this linguistically heterogeneous past for contemporary readers of fiction. Examining these fictional works alongside their historical sources, I ask: what role do language and translation play in the process of narrativizing communities of the past for the present? And how does the turn to linguistically plural archives transform the form of the novel as a genre of fiction?

Critical discussions of postcolonial historical fiction tend to retain the Eurocentric binary in which the critical form of novels from the "periphery" is shaped in response to the totalizing ambitions of colonial or global capital (Baucom; Forter; Kent). Greg Forter, for instance, locates the postcolonial historical novel's critical impulse in "a dialectical understanding of colonial capital and resistance to it" (35). Eddy Kent similarly suggests that the "neo-Victorian" aesthetic of novels like *Sea of*

---

[1] The ambivalence between the colonial and the cosmopolitan interpellation of the ship is also reflected in the language of the novel. While Deeti's Bhojpuri is transcribed in English, Ghosh's English is infiltrated by Bhojpuri and several other languages of the Indian Ocean.

Poppies "[articulates] a tactics of resistance to the hegemonic mode of global capital" (108). While these insights illuminate how historically oriented novels reject the notion of the past as a totality, emphasizing the interdependence of the past and the present, such a generalized approach to the postcolonial as a global condition overlooks local and regional variations in power structures and forms of relations. Therefore, I propose the concept of "anarchival drift" that takes the ocean as a framework to see how novels from the region engage with the entanglements of global, regional, and local forms of relation that the dialectical model passes over. Anarchival drift, as I show in the following pages, highlights the simultaneous turn to the past and the ocean in contemporary Indian Ocean fiction. I argue that the turn to the past in these novels is not meant to retrieve alternative visions of the past or future that contest dominant imperial, nationalist, or globalist historical forces; instead, the intertextual references to the past take a metafictional form that opens up the past to the multipolarity of the Indian Ocean world where the colonial structure is one among many overlapping, incongruous power structures that shape the shifting categories of race, religion, ethnicity, gender, and language. Following Gaurav Desai's call to read Africa's history of encounter "not only with the West but also with the East" as a way to decenter Europe in the studies of the Global South, I argue that the encounters depicted in these novels ask for a different spatial and temporal imagination where the local is always already infiltrated by translocal, transoceanic forces (*Commerce* 6).

My argument follows Linda Hutcheon's discussion of "historiographic metafiction" from the late twentieth century as "intensely self-reflexive" in her treatment of both history and fiction (275). In opening up history and fiction to each other, such historical fiction unsettles both the formal autonomy of the literary text on the one hand and the epistemological grounding of historical representation on the other. Even in formally realist novels like *Sea of Poppies* and *Paradise*, the use of historical realism is accompanied by a self-reflexivity about the epistemological limitations of the realist mode to accurately mediate historical reality. I argue that the self-reflexivity in these texts results from the multiplicity of linguistic registers on which they operate, making visible the translative processes subject to transoceanic historical forces. Through a parody of the colonial dictionary in "The Ibis Chrestomathy," Ghosh reveals the poetic potentialities in the errancy of words within and across languages, reflecting the mobilities of migrants across the ocean; meanwhile, rewriting colonial Swahili travelogues, Gurnah's *Paradise* represents the pitfalls of cross-cultural exchange where translatability is subordinate to uneven economic relations in the Indian Ocean world. In both cases, the sematic drift between languages is inseparable from the slippage between history and fiction, between the sociohistorical processes that shaped the nineteenth-century Indian Ocean world and the fictional narratives that translate these processes for the twenty-first-century readers.[2] The self-reflexive incorporation of the past, that I call anarchival drift, turns the archive fugitive, making it slip through the multivalent linguistic play and oceanic drifts.

---

[2] Here I refer to the concept of history as both "what happened" and "that which is said to have happened" (Trouillot 13).

The Archive and the Drift

Scholars across disciplines have grappled with the limitations of the archive. Following the Foucauldian insight that archives are "monuments for particular configurations of power," Antoinette Burton has argued for the necessity to question the "apparently self-evidentiary nature of 'historical' documents" (Burton 9, 20). Saidiya Hartman, likewise, calls for an approach that uncovers archival sources, particularly the archives of slavery, as "fictions of history" constituting what Gayatri Spivak would call the epistemic violence of colonial/imperialist/nationalist projects (Hartman 11; Spivak, *Critique* 250). Both *Sea of Poppies* and *Paradise* affirm a self-reflexivity that accentuates the instability and fallibility of the archive. Their archival references take a metafictional form offering a means to "defamiliarize and consequently demystify" the construction of history as narrative and/or knowledge (Mwangi 15). The past emerges as "a competing babble" marked by differential and shifting power relations within the geohistorical site of the ocean (Gurnah, "Idea" 7). Through a "heightened mode of historical self-reflection" (characteristic of contemporary fiction, according to Theodore Martin), Ghosh and Gurnah reformat the form of the novel as a critical space for assessing transoceanic pasts (Martin 228).

I call this this self-reflexive mode of historical fiction "anarchival drift," a practice of rewriting the past that incorporates without assimilating the archival sources, reintroducing historical context—that is, the historical, cultural, and geographical specificity of the Indian Ocean—to undermine the transparency of the archives and question the translatability of the past. If the "archive" is understood as the intersection of the place and the law, "anarchival drift" implies both the subversion of law as well as the lack of a stable ground (Derrida 10; Mbembe 19). The "anarchive," as Lia Brozgal suggests, is "an epistemological system in oppositional relationship to an official archive" (Brozgal, "Absence" 50).[3] Although oppositional, it is also intrinsic to the archive. As Jacques Derrida notes, the anarchic component is itself not foreign to the archive, which means that the archival impulse to preserve is inseparable from the impulse to destroy, since the existence of the archive as a substitution depends on the loss of the origin that it replaces.[4] By reproducing an event, the archival trace, selective and systematized, also signals its disappearance. Anarchival drift, thus, highlights the anarchy beneath the order and authority vested in the archive, official or otherwise, suspending the epistemological and ontological grounds that renders the past knowable. Both *Sea of Poppies* and *Paradise* emphasize this contradiction through the rewritings of Indian Ocean archives, opening them up to complex networks of inter- and intralinguistic routes specific to the Indian Ocean world.

---

[3] Brozgal's use of the term *anarchive* implies the epistemological production that happens outside the jurisdiction of the state (see Brozgal, *Absent* 26). My use of the adjectival form, "anarchival," follows Derrida's emphasis of the instability of the archive as both an authoritative record and a place of authority.

[4] This destructive impulse or "the death drive" of the archive "destroys in advance its own archive, as if that were in truth the very motivation of its most proper movement. It works to destroy the archive: on the condition of effacing but also with a view to effacing its own 'proper' traces—which consequently cannot be properly called 'proper.' . . . This drive, from then on, seems not only to be anarchic, anarchontic . . . : the death drive is above all *anarchivic*" (Derrida 14).

The analytic of "anarchival drift" shifts the critical frame for theorizing the archive from land to ocean. It builds upon the attempts by oceanic studies scholars to incorporate "actual, lived experiences of the ocean into the studies of maritime regions" and to be "attentive to the material conditions and praxis of the maritime world" (Steinberg 161; Blum 671). Drawing on Lagrangian fluid dynamics, Phillip Steinberg argues that the ocean is not just a space over which movement happens, but it is a space "constituted by and constitutive of movement" (165). "Drift" evokes this "fluid alterity" of the ocean that shapes different forms of human and nonhuman relations but which cannot be fully determined or known (DeLoughrey 35). "Drift" is a slow movement, a diversion or digression, with more or less direction, but also a state of vacillation or indecision; it figures the oceanic space as irreducible alterity that "remains underived from us" (Spivak, *Death* 73). It connotes planetary force beyond one's control and allows us to trace connectivities as well as closures. Jeremy Prestholdt reminds us that "rather than flows alone, it is the shifting apertures, closures, and frictions that define the contours of the Indian Ocean" (442). In the precolonial Indian Ocean world, the seasonal monsoon winds that change directions twice a year enabled and restricted travel across the ocean, determining the nature and depth of interaction between the migrants and the locals (Sheriff 1). Similarly, the reconstitution of the geopolitical space under colonial and postcolonial states opened new movement patterns reinforcing certain precolonial channels while restricting others. This has given rise to complex social and cultural formations that complicate the categories of race, ethnicity, religion, or nation. Desai notes that the binary "Manichean" model based on the opposition between the colonizer and the colonized is inadequate for the understanding of cultural and identity politics in the colonial and postcolonial Indian Ocean worlds ("Oceans" 717). Gurnah's novels set in East Africa show how the meanings of categories such as "Native," "non-Native," "Indian," "Swahili," "African," and "Arab" were constantly changing even within a single historical moment. Such emphasis on fluidity offers "rhizomatic alternatives to the dystopic narratives of 'root identity'" (Steiner 127). In *Sea of Poppies*, the characters, similarly, shift identities across race, gender, caste, and class, as they find their way to the ship *Ibis* and sail across the ocean. The analytic of the drift ties such fluidity of relations to the materiality and the historicity of the ocean.

This mutual imbrication between sea and history is nowhere more apparent than in the opening scene of *Sea of Poppies* discussed above, where Deeti's vision complicates the history of a colonized land by foregrounding its connections to the sea. Critics have expounded on the ways in which Gurnah's engagement with perspective, similarly, accentuates the ambivalence of Indian Ocean spaces and discloses "submerged" histories of "global connections and power structures" preceding European colonialism (Lavery 120; Olaussen 66). This play with spatial perspectives takes on a linguistic significance in *Paradise*. Like *Sea of Poppies*, *Paradise* announces the linguistic pluralism of its setting toward the beginning, after Yusuf is displaced from his home inland to work for the merchant Aziz at his mansion on the coast as a *rehani*, a bonded servant, alongside Khalil. Unlike Yusuf, Khalil, originally from the islands, is a native speaker of Arabic. The narrator describes Khalil's way of speaking as having "the pronounced accent of the Arabic-speaker although his Kiswahili was fluent. He managed to make liberties he took with the syntax seem inspired as well as eccentric. In exasperation and anxiety, he burst into a powerful torrent of Arabic which forced the customers into silent but tolerant retreat" (23). Linguistically marked among the community of Swahili speakers, Khalil speaks from the interspace between Arabic and Swahili. Given its significance in Islam and the hierarchy of languages in the Indian Ocean world, Arabic gives Khalil an upper hand, which he uses at times of crisis. Khalil talks to Aziz in Arabic and Yusuf is excluded from these conversations. Since the narrative is mediated through Yusuf's Swahili translated into English, the reader is consequently twice removed from the Arabic already impenetrable to Yusuf. Although the English "translations" level out the differences in the dialogues of the characters, Gurnah consistently alerts the reader of the linguistic landscape that becomes increasingly uneven and heterogeneous as the narrative follows Yusuf through different villages in the interior.

Ghosh and Gurnah refigure the site of Indian Ocean encounters, not as a "contact zone" between separate cultures, but as what Francesca Orisini calls a "multilingual local" where different languages were always already in contact, infected and inflected by each other (352). Both novels demonstrate that the "amphibian visions" that Meg Samuelson locates in the Indian Ocean littoral can be extended to inland locations that "ceaselessly overlap [with] and draw apart [from]" the forces of the sea (Samuelson 17). They rewrite colonial archives in the mode of anarchival drift, turning the gaze into the past sideways, making visible sites of Indian Ocean relations that exist simultaneously *outside and alongside* colonial paradigms.[5] This takes place through a self-conscious turning toward the translation and movements of words and their meanings from one language to another, from the past to the present, and from archival documents to the fictional narrative. Attending to such linguistic processes specific to the Indian Ocean world, I read these novels as an instance of what Françoise Lionnet calls "*littérature mondialisante* rather than *littérature-monde*—that is, as world-forming literature rather than world literature" that foregrounds "the mobilities within the texts and . . . the circulation of these texts into contexts where some original meanings are inevitably untranslatable" ("World" 288). While both writers appeal to the linguistic aspects of the crosscultural exchange, in the following sections, I show the divergent ways in which the semantic drift among languages stage the materiality and historicity of transoceanic encounters.

Itinerant Words in Ghosh's "*Ibis* Chrestomathy"

Sea of Poppies intersperses its narrative with numerous non-English expressions in Bhojpuri, Bengali, French, Mauritian Kreol, and Hindustani among others, signifying its characters' diverse linguistic backgrounds. While Ghosh transforms

---

[5] In her study of the representation of Islam and slavery in the South African Cape, Gabeba Baderoon uses the trope of "sideways glance" as a method of historical inquiry to "render visible previously overlooked experiences in postcolonial writing" (4–5). This sideways glance does not negate vertical structures of power, colonial or otherwise. Driven by a postcolonial nostalgia for a precolonial past imagined to be free from the forms of domination and divisions attributed to colonialism, Indian Ocean writings have sometimes veered toward idealized visions of community and solidarity that pay insufficient attention to multiscalar structural inequalities. See Gaurav Desai's critique of Ghosh in Desai, *Commerce* 12, 50; Moorthy and Jamal 3.

English itself into a "language of intimacy and connection" among the characters, the multilingual prose reveals an "interpretive dynamic that generates, communicates, and withholds meaning" depending on the reader's linguistic competence in various languages (Han 299; Kertzer 188). Several critics have commented on Ghosh's linguistic experimentation, whether as a reflection of "the kaleidoscopic multiplicity of its characters' mutable identities" or as a "vernacular cosmopolitanism," revealing the capacity of language to "both unite and divide, betray and empower" (Rollason 8; Luo 390). Existing scholarship has focused more on linguistic hybridity within the text rather than on "The *Ibis* Chrestomathy," which appears as an appendix after the end of the novel. The chrestomathy, I argue, treats linguistic hybridity at a metafictional level: it stages the movement of words between different linguistic registers revealing the link between language and history, specifically the history of mobilities in the Indian Ocean.

The chrestomathy exemplifies Ghosh's fascination with lists. As Anupama Mohan notes, "The list as archive is a central device for Ghosh in assembling vast but provisional unities among the multiple languages spoken by the characters" (12). In the "*Ibis* Chrestomathy," Ghosh adopts the glossary, an Orientalist tool for enumerating "things Oriental into manageable parts," in order to undermine its stability as a compendium of knowledge (Said 72). Glossaries were common features in early postcolonial novels, but they disappear in later Anglophone novels, mainly because of their association with Western constructions of the non-West as exotic and in need to be translated into a Western idiom. Glossaries were widely used to facilitate the colonial administration by making local meaning available to colonial officials. As Ari Singh Anand argues in his reading of Henry Yule and Arthur Coke Burnell's *Hobson-Jobson* (1886), a major source for the Anglo-Indian words used in *Sea of Poppies*, the dictionary played an important role in the production and legitimation of the Anglo-Indian imperial subject through language, allowing this imagined consumer of the dictionary, the Anglo-Indians, to claim authority over local knowledge and peoples.

The "*Ibis* Chrestomathy" problematizes such ideological function of the glossary by performing a parody of the genre. This "glossary" is not exterior to the novel but part of its fictional world, integrated into its narrative space and time. It is prefaced with a narrator's note, explaining that it was originally compiled by Neel, a major character in the novel who ends up on the *Ibis* as a convict. The narrator reveals himself as a descendant of Neel and indicates that the document emerges out of Neel's interests in words, specifically those non-English words that entered the English language through journeys around the Indian Ocean. The formatting of the text with two columns and footnotes, distinct from the rest of the novel, simulates the pages of a dictionary. Furthermore, the chrestomathy prolifically invokes the authority of several major dictionaries from the colonial era including Thomas Roebuck's *Laskari Dictionary*, the *Hobson-Jobson*, and the *Oxford English Dictionary* (*OED*), mimicking Orientalist texts mired in a "system for citing works and authors" (Said 23). While through its form, the chrestomathy points to a continuity between the colonial past and the postcolonial present, its function as parody suggests a rupture that renders the past elusive.

The preface insists that the chrestomathy is a process rather than a finished product. Unlike colonial dictionaries that render foreign words transparent to colonial agents, the "*Ibis* Chrestomathy" treats words not as objects of knowledge but as "people . . . , endowed with lives and destinies of their own" (501). It rejects the idea that language can be contained and challenges the colonial knowledge production deployed in the service of power:

The Chrestomathy is a work that cannot, in principle, ever be considered finished. One reason for this is that new and previously unknown word-chits in Neel's hand have continued to turn up in places where he once resided—these unearthings have been regular enough, and frequent enough, to confound the idea of ever bringing the work to completion. But the Chrestomathy is also, in its very nature, a continuing dialogue . . . (502)

As a "continuing exchange of words between generations," the chrestomathy eschews finality and insists on the temporality and historicity of words, rendering the past of the words as fluid and undetermined as their future (503). In addition to being citational in the Orientalist sense, the chrestomathy is also an archival and genealogical project tied to Neel's family and lineage. The knowledge compiled therein is subject to the vagaries of the archive, the "unearthings" of "new and previously unknown word-chits," and cannot be dissociated from the personal whims and beliefs of the archivist.

By juxtaposing Neel's voice alongside colonial dictionaries, this document performs a rewriting of the oceanic past woven with a linguistic web of words, recontextualizing not just the words but the dictionary itself as an epistemological site. The chrestomathy reinserts the disembodied and apoliticized genre of the dictionary into the political and historicized perspective of the embodied colonial subject Neel. The materiality of this embodiment is recognized in the "word-chits in Neel's hand," which are the sources for the entries. Initially from a landowning family in Calcutta, Neel is later convicted for fraud and condemned to hard labor in Mauritius. So, coming from a fugitive, an outlaw, this (an)archive is literally located outside the law. Moreover, in several entries, the narrator's voice interjects quotes from Neel's "word-chits," bringing the novel's heteroglossia into the glossary. This blurring of the line between the fictional text and the paratext urges the reader to question the authority of this glossary, or any such document, and its capacity to make transparent the meaning and origin of words. In fact, this glossary does little to shed light on the many untranslated expressions throughout the text. Every entry in the chrestomathy cites an English dictionary but adds commentary by Neel. Instead of providing different meanings of the words, Neel's metacommentary animates each word, concocting narratives that trace their trajectories as they travel from one language to another. The attitude toward other sources is largely satiric, at times critical and even irreverent.

Take for instance, Neel's mildly dismissive note on the word *achar*, which, as he indicates, has secured a place in the *OED*:

+**achar**: "There are those who would gloss this as 'pickle,'" writes Neel, "although that word is better applied to the definition than the thing defined." (504)

Here, *pickle* refers to the definition given by the *OED*, which glosses *achar* as "a type of pickle or relish made from fruit or vegetables preserved in spiced oil or vinegar."[6] Neel turns the English definition of the word over and onto itself, exploiting the double meaning associated with the word *pickle* to produce a "self-erasing definition worthy of Lewis Carroll" (Kertzer 195). On the one hand, *pickle* denotes

---

6 *Oxford English Dictionary*, s.v. "achar," www.oed.com/view/Entry/1448 (accessed June 11, 2021).

preserved food, usually vegetables preserved in liquid such as vinegar or brine. This definition is closest to the meaning of *achar*, a component of South Asian meals made up of vegetables preserved in oil and spices. On the other hand, in its collo-quial use, *pickle* also means a difficult situation, or, as the *OED* puts it, "a plight or predicament."[7] Neel's comment, first, points to this double meaning and hence, the ambiguity and instability inherent in the English language even without the intro-duction of foreign words such as *achar*. Second, the elusiveness of Neel's definition highlights a failure of translation: the opacity of the word *achar* persists despite its importation into the *OED*.

In the chrestomathy, "the vessel of migration," if words like "achar" resist migra-tion into English, there are other words that travel, transform, and adapt to their new linguistic environment, leaving behind their old meanings. Take the entry for the word *shampoo*, which has entered into common usage in English. Here too, Neel is interested less in determining its root than in mapping its routes as it travels from *chāpo/chāpna* in Hindustani to "shampoo" in English. He takes interest in the meaning of the Hindi verb, which relates to "massaging" or "pressing," only because he sees in the migration of this word an allegory for British colonialism in India. He asks, "Is it not a commentary on the relationship of England and India that most of the Hind. candidates for the Peerage of the English Verb per-tain to grappling, grasping, binding, tying and whipping?" (540).

Conversely, there are some words that not only fail to survive the odysseys across languages whether due to corruption, misuse, or competition with other words, but also transform their meaning in the original language as a result of contact between languages. The Hindi word *karcanna*, now commonly translated into English as *factory*, is the case in point:

carcanna/karcanna: (* **The Glossary**); Already in Neel's lifetime this long-pedigreed English word (from Hind. *kar-khana*, "work-place" or "work-shop") was slowly yielding to the term "factory"—a lexi-cal scandal in Neel's ears, which were still accustomed to hearing that word used to designate the resi-dence of a "factor" or "agent." But it was not for nostalgic reasons alone that he mourned the passing of **carcanna/karcanna**: he foresaw that its wreckage would also carry into oblivion many of those who had once worked in these places of manufacture—for example the factory-clerks known as **carcoons**. It was in mourning the fate of this word that the unknown wordy-wallah penned his comments on logocide. (517)

This entry shows again that the chrestomathy does not serve the utilitarian function of a glossary. Here Neel is concerned with the demise of this word and its altered usage within its language of "origin." The death of a word dramatized as "logocide" and animated in a nautical metaphor as "wreckage" has implications far beyond its immediate usage. *Carcanna* becomes a synecdoche for a waning world, for a partic-ular workplace associated with a precapitalist mode of working. The loss of this word implies an end to the community of people who worked in such places, and its acquisition of a new meaning signals a changing world order. Neel presents *car-canna* as an allegory of loss in the wake of colonial and capitalist incursions in the Indian Ocean world. What is central to this entry is not the "knowledge" regarding the word or its meaning, but rather the memory of a particular form of community associated with the usage of the word. Neel displaces the function of the dictionary from cognition to affect.

---

7 *Oxford English Dictionary*, s.v. "pickle," II.4.a., www.oed.com/view/Entry/143416 (accessed June 11, 2021).

The chrestomathy repurposes historical linguistics through poetic invention, revealing the multiple potentialities of words as they travel across the uneven field of multiple languages (Guilhamon 71). Ghosh adapts the dictionary into a poetic idiom that encodes both imperial histories from above, as in the entry for "shampoo," as well as migration histories from below, as in the entry for "carcanna." Throughout the chrestomathy, words travel or resist traveling across languages and through space and time, they make friendships and rivalries, some are elusive, some contradict themselves, some stray from their meanings, some are celebrated for their poetic soundness and resilience across languages, while some die, caught in a shipwreck, and are mourned for. In this sense, these words mirror the lives of the characters in the novel, the migrants, lascars, sailors, and prisoners, who move across geographies and languages as they sail across the ocean. The errancy and ambiguities inherent in the words and their resistance to translation as they straddle the space between languages defy the transparency that dictionaries impose over local idioms. The chrestomathy as *anarchive* reveals that as words traverse the Indian Ocean along with their speakers, subject to its forces, their meanings and usages drift in different directions through the occlusions and passageways, diversions and returns at the intersections of languages.

Errant Translations in *Paradise*

Like *Sea of Poppies*, Gurnah's *Paradise* presents us with a cosmopolitan cast of characters enmeshed in an intercultural, multireligious, and multilingual web of the Indian Ocean littoral. However, as Shanti Moorthy has argued, the diverse East African society that Gurnah portrays is not an example of a peaceful coexistence in difference but of one "riven by fissures, with factions that divide society along the lines of ethnic loyalties and communal grievances even before the advent of European colonialism" (89). The society composed of cultural, religious, ethnic, and linguistic hierarchies is held together not by Islam or other shared beliefs or values but by the economic ties of the caravan trade (Berman 56). In this portrait of a society, where "everything, whether goods or human beings is commodified," Gurnah reveals the fragility of the economic ties as linked to the precarity of translation and linguistic difference in cross-cultural interactions (Nasta 314).

Comparing the treatment of language in *Paradise* with Gurnah's Swahili sources illuminates the function of translation in the historical records of the East African caravan trade. Gurnah's account of Yusuf's journey borrows various elements from primarily two Swahili texts, namely, the Zanzibari slave trader Tippu Tipp's autobiography *Maisha ya Hamid bin Muhammed el Murjebi* and Selemani bin Mwenye Chande's "Safari Yangu ya Bara Afrika" ("My Journey Up-Country in Africa"). While these sources provide a rare glimpse into colonial and precolonial East Africa from the Swahili perspective, it is important to note that their production was still tied to the prerogatives of European colonialism. Both texts were transcribed and published by Europeans and owe their existence to European linguists and ethnographers. Tippu Tip's autobiography was written under the directive of Dr. Heinrich Brode, an employee of the German consulate at Zanzibar, who transcribed, translated, and published the text in an Orientalist journal in Germany in 1902 (in Kiswahili and German). Similarly, Chande worked as a chief informant to the German collector Carl Velten, who transcribed and collected his account along with other accounts by Swahili informants. As part of the colonial repertoire, these Swahili accounts do not provide unmediated access to the Swahili point of view. The production of the original texts is already conditioned by their colonial destination, traveling "a complex path to publication with the interests of ethnographers, linguists and colonial officials overshadowing any sense of agency for the Swahili storytellers" (Hodapp 92). The subjective perspectives of the storytellers Tip and Chande as Native informants remain buried under the information essential for the colonial enterprise.

This is evident in the introductory note to the English translation of Chande's "My Journey Up-Country in Africa" in a collection edited by Lyndon Harris published in 1965. It begins with the remark that "the special interest of this account by an African of a journey up-country to get ivory is that it provides detailed information about the route" (Chande 233). The rest of the text describes the route giving the names of the places that Chande traveled through. Nowhere does the text mention his name, let alone his biography. The perspective of the storyteller is actively suppressed while highlighting the transactions and interactions that help Chande navigate the route. Similarly, Michelle Decker notes the "undifferentiated narratorial attention" to utilitarian interactions with villages in Tippu Tip's autobiography. Questioning the classification of the text as an autobiography, Decker argues that Tip "withholds his interiority" as he "fashions himself as a collection of silences" (754).

One of the ways these texts silence the subjectivity of the authors in service of the colonial enterprise is through the leveling of the linguistic difference. Both Tip's and Chande's accounts are largely monolingual and barely mention the presence of other languages across the vast geography they traverse even when describing encounters with different non-Swahili-speaking communities in the interior. Both accounts are rife with descriptions of conflicts, often violent, costing lives, whether because of the villagers' hostility toward the traders or due to the failure to reach a deal. Except in rare instances, the conversations with different village chiefs are given in Swahili without any indication of a different language being spoken.[8] Just as in the colonial dictionaries where the trajectories and the sources of the words in Indigenous languages were often erased or rewritten to assert control over local knowledge, the translator is made invisible in the Swahili texts written primarily to consolidate colonial knowledge about the ivory trade. Since the only translations that mattered were the translations from Swahili to European languages, the linguistic difference among different communities within Africa remains concealed.

In contrast, Gurnah's rewriting of these accounts in *Paradise* accentuates the problem posed by language. Gurnah models the character Aziz after Tip and borrows several plot elements from Chande's account of his travel, making some notable modifications. For instance, he changes the name of the chief of an inland village from Chata to Chatu. Noting the Swahili meaning of *chatu*, which is "python," Fawzia Mustafa observes that the disguised meaning "allows for both the Biblical

---

[8] There is one exception, in Tippu Tip's autobiography, where Tip admits the limits of his linguistic abilities (65). For more discussion on this, see Decker.

allusion to Eden as well as the locally mythical one" (18). This wordplay in Swahili remains inaccessible to non-Swahili speakers, including Chatu himself, placing him at once inside and outside the Swahili linguistic sphere. However, the most significant addition Gurnah makes is the insertion of the translator Nyundo, who becomes indispensable once the crew passes the limits of the Swahili-speaking territory.

Gurnah devotes significant blocks of texts describing Nyundo's attempts to translate between the traders and the villagers. These passages draw attention to the language difference and highlight the impossibility of a transparent communication and the anxieties generated by it. Consider the following exchange between Aziz ("the merchant") and a village sultan who offers him some beer, as Nyundo, the translator, translates between them:

"I am grateful, but I must decline," the merchant said.

"He asks why?" Nyundo said, grinning. "It's good beer. Is it because you think there's poison in it? He's already tasted it for you. Don't you trust him?" The sultan then said something else and the elders laughed among themselves, cackling with long-toothed merriment. The merchant looked at Nyundo, who shook his head. His gesture was ambiguous, perhaps he had not understood or thought it best not to translate.

"I'm a trader," Uncle Aziz said, looking at the sultan. "And I am a stranger in your town. If I drink beer I'll begin to shout and get into fights, and this is not how a stranger on business should behave."

"He says it's because your god won't let you. He knows about that," Nyundo said, as the sultan and his people laughed again among themselves. Nyundo took a long time before translating the sultan's next remark. The grin had disappeared from his face and he spoke carefully to give the impression that he was striving for a faithful delivery. "He says what kind of cruel god is it which doesn't allow men to drink beer?" (139–40)

The sultan's words are made available to both the reader and Uncle Aziz through Nyundo's translations. However, far from giving a faithful, unaltered translation, Nyundo takes on interpretive and evaluative functions as well. His "grinning" gesture recognizes the sarcasm in the sultan's question and insistence that they accept the drink, anticipating the laughter from the sultan. In paraphrasing the sultan when he asks, "Don't you trust him?" he removes the attribution and appears to speak for himself, adopting a derisive attitude toward Aziz, aligning with the sultan and the elders. However, if the translator disappears in the first part of the dialogue, right after this, Nyundo does not translate what the sultan says next, leaving both Aziz and the reader in the dark. Instead, Nyundo just shakes his head, a gesture that is lost to Aziz in the uncertainty of the "perhaps." So not only the translations, but the translator himself becomes opaque at this point. In attempting to translate a single exchange, Nyundo oscillates from extreme transparency in which he coincides with the source to total opacity where he himself becomes untranslatable. The difficulty of linguistic translation is further compounded by the perils of cultural translation when Aziz refuses the drink. Although the sultan knows that Aziz's religion forbids him from drinking, this knowledge does not translate into a cultural understanding, leading the sultan to mock Aziz's religion.

Later in a different village, its chief Chatu confiscates all of their trading goods as restitution for the harm caused by a different group of coastal traders who had kidnapped members from his village to sell them at the coast as slaves. Aziz protests, insisting that he has "only come to trade," but Chatu ignores him and alerts him to the fact that coastal traders like Aziz have enslaved and robbed Chatu's people and treated them as animals, invoking the history of slave raids by coastal groups in the region (160). Nyundo's struggle to translate this heated exchange reflects the fragility of the relation structured by the economy of the caravan trade. His translations are unable to mediate the irreconcilable understandings of the history of exchange between the two groups. While Chatu conflates Aziz with other slave raiders and demands material restitution for human loss, Aziz's insistence on the transactional nature of his relationship to Chatu blinds him to the irremediable damage done to communities by such trading expeditions. When the Germans arrive at the scene of this exchange with guns, imposing their own hierarchies, the number of translators and interpreters multiplies, creating further divisions, misunderstandings, and erasures. Claiming to enforce "the law of the government" over the village, the Europeans purport to resolve the conflict by forcing Chatu to return the goods to the traders, and dismissing Chatu's demand for restitution for harm done by coastal traders in the past (170). The imposition of the colonial order erases the history of exchange between the groups and their conflicting understandings of the past compounded by linguistic differences.

Conclusion

The multiplying chain of translators in *Paradise* serves a self-reflexive metafictional function projecting Gurnah himself as another node in the chain linking the Indian Ocean past with the present. Like the translators in his novel, Gurnah is what Neel from *Sea of Poppies* would call a "linkister," which Neel glosses as an "extension of the word 'link'—one that came to be applied to translators because it so perfectly fitted their function" (533). Gaurav Desai has similarly posited Amitav Ghosh as a "linkister" since his works are concerned with making links across histories, geographies, and languages, previously thought as separate ("Novelist" 1532). While Desai's emphasis is on the term *link*, I stress the translative component in Neel's definition as I apply it to both Ghosh and Gurnah. The precarity of translation depicted in *Sea of Poppies* and *Paradise* extends to the novelists who too become errant and unassimilable excesses in their fictional reconstructions of the past. The figures of Neel and Nyundo draw attention to the text as mediated narratives, written in English but existing in between several languages, which flow into each other but also, to a certain extent, always remain opaque to each other and to the novel's contemporary readers. As Ghosh insists in the epigraph of this article, the movement of languages "is more like that of liquids; they mingle and flow not just between groups but often within individuals," but he also reminds us that there are "dimensions of opaqueness inherent within linguistic fluidity" ("Speaking" 286, 293). Subject to asymmetrical relations of power in the Indian Ocean world, the fluidity and opacity of languages undermine the "realist" aesthetic of the novels and disrupt their mimetic relationship with the past. In the intertext between fiction and history, Nyundo and Neel restore the undetermined and indeterminable "zones d'ombre" (shadowy zones) of uncertainty to the archival past as well as the narrative present (Lionnet, *Le su* 13).

To conclude, my reading of *Sea of Poppies* and *Paradise* has shown two ways in which contemporary novelists from the Indian Ocean region appropriate and transform archival elements. Both texts retrieve the figure of the translator from the archives in different ways. By appropriating the form of the dictionary, Ghosh disavows the binary structure imposed by colonial claims over local languages, revealing the multidirectional movements of words, mirroring the trajectories of migrants across the Indian Ocean. Similarly, the processes of translation in *Paradise* point to the fragile yet complex web of economic relations that exist outside and alongside colonial incursions. Through the figures of Neel and Nyundo, *Sea of Poppies* and *Paradise* reconfigure the opposition between the global and the local, or the colonial and the postcolonial, in terms of multiple yet asymmetrical overlapping relations among languages. The past becomes less settled as the archive turns fugitive, errant, drifting between languages in the interspace between land and sea. The oceanic framework reveals an aesthetic that retrieves the archive from the regime of facts and frees languages from insular borders into the domain of the narrative imagination responsive to the shifting power relations of the Indian Ocean world.

Reed College

Works Cited

Anand, Ari Singh. "Cosmopolitanism in Hobson-Jobson: Remaking Imperial Subjects." *Comparative Studies of South Asia, Africa, and the Middle East* 31, no. 2 (2011): 521–37.

Baderoon, Gabeba. *Regarding Muslims: From Slavery to Post-apartheid.* Johannesburg: Wits University Press, 2014.

Baucom, Ian. *Specters of the Atlantic: Finance Capital, Slavery, and the Philosophy of History.* Durham, NC: Duke University Press, 2005.

Berman, Nina. "Yusuf's Choice: East African Agency during the German Colonial Period in Abdulrazak Gurnah's Novel *Paradise*." *English Studies in Africa* 56, no. 1 (2013): 51–64.

Blum, Hester. "The Prospect of Oceanic Studies." *PMLA* 125, no. 3 (2010): 670–77.

Brozgal, Lia. *Absent the Archive: Cultural Traces of a Massacre in Paris: 17 October 1961.* Liverpool, UK: Liverpool University Press, 2020.

Brozgal, Lia. "In the Absence of the Archive (Paris, October 17, 1961)." *South Central Review* 31, no. 1 (2014): 34–54.

Burton, Antoinette. "Introduction: Archive Fever, Archive Stories." In *Archive Stories: Facts, Fictions, and the Writing of History*, edited by Antoinette Burton, 1–23. Durham, NC: Duke University Press, 2006.

Chande, Selemani bin Mwenye. "My Journey Up-Country in Africa." In *Swahili Prose Texts: A Selection from the Material Collected by Carl Velten from 1893 to 1896*, translated by Lyndon Harries, 233–59. Oxford: Oxford University Press, 1965.

Decker, Michelle. "The 'Autobiography' of Tippu Tip: Geography, Genre, and the African Indian Ocean." *Interventions: International Journal of Postcolonial Studies* 17, no. 5 (2015): 744–58.

DeLoughrey, Elizabeth. "Submarine Futures of the Anthropocene." *Comparative Literature* 69, no. 1 (2017): 32–44.

Derrida, Jacques. "Archive Fever: A Freudian Impression," translated by Eric Prenowitz. *Diacritics* 25, no. 2 (1995): 9–63.

Desai, Gaurav. *Commerce with the Universe: Africa, India, and the Afrasian Imagination.* New York: Columbia University Press, 2013.

Desai, Gaurav. "The Novelist as Linkister." *American Historical Review* 121, no. 5 (2016): 1531–36.

Desai, Gaurav. "Oceans Connect: The Indian Ocean and African Identities." *PMLA* 125, no. 3 (2010): 713–20.

Forter, Greg. *Critique and Utopia in Postcolonial Historical Fiction: Atlantic and Other Worlds.* Oxford: Oxford University Press, 2019.

Ghosh, Amitav. "Of Fanás and Forecastles: The Indian Ocean and Some Lost Languages of the Age of Sail." In *Eyes across the Water: Navigating the Indian Ocean*, edited by Pamila Gupta, Isabel Hofmeyr, and Michael Pearson, 56–62. Pretoria: Unisa Press, 2010.

Ghosh, Amitav. *Sea of Poppies*. New York: John Murray, 2008.

Ghosh, Amitav. "Speaking of Babel: The Risks and Rewards of Writing about Polyglot Societies." *Comparative Literature* 72, no. 3 (2020): 283–98.

Guilhamon, Lise. "Global Languages in the Time of the Opium Wars: The Lost Idioms of Amitav Ghosh's *Sea of Poppies*." *Commonwealth Essays and Studies* 34, no. 1 (2011): 67–76.

Gurnah, Abdulrazak. "An Idea of the Past." *African Studies Bulletin*, no. 65 (2003): 26–36.

Gurnah, Abdulrazak. *Paradise*. New York: Penguin, 1995.

Han, Stephanie. "Amitav Ghosh's *Sea of Poppies*: Speaking Weird English." *The Explicator* 71, no. 4 (2013): 298–301.

Hartman, Saidiya. "Venus in Two Acts." *Small Axe*, no. 26 (2008): 1–14.

Hodapp, James. "Imagining Unmediated Early Swahili Narratives in Abdulrazak Gurnah's *Paradise*." *English in Africa* 42, no. 2 (2015): 89–108.

Hutcheon, Linda. "'The Pastime of Past Time': Fiction, History, Historiographical Metafiction." In *Essentials of the Theory of Fiction*, edited by Michael J. Hoffman and Patrick D. Murphy, 275–95. Durham, NC: Duke University Press, 2005.

Kent, Eddy. "'Ship-Siblings': Globalisation, Neoliberal Aesthetics, and Neo-Victorian Form in Amitav Ghosh's *Sea of Poppies*." *Neo-Victorian Studies* 8, no. 1 (2015): 107–30.

Kertzer, Jon. "Amitav Ghosh's Zubben: Confluence of Languages in the *Ibis* Trilogy." *Journal of Postcolonial Writing* 54, no. 2 (2018): 187–99.

Lavery, Charné. "White-Washed Minarets and Slimy Gutters: Abdulrazak Gurnah, Narrative Form, and Indian Ocean Space." *English Studies in Africa* 56, no. 1 (2013): 117–27.

Lionnet, Françoise. *Le su et l'incertain: Cosmopolitiques créoles de l'océan Indien*. Trou d'Eau Douce, Ile Maurice: La Librairie Mauricienne Numérique, 2014.

Lionnet, Françoise. "World Literature, Postcolonial Studies, and Coolie Odysseys: J.-M. G. Le Clézio's and Amitav Ghosh's Indian Ocean Novels." *Comparative Literature* 67, no. 3 (2015): 287–311.

Luo, Shao-Pin. "The Way of Words: Vernacular Cosmopolitanism in Amitav Ghosh's *Sea of Poppies*." *Journal of Commonwealth Literature* 48, no. 3 (2013): 377–92.

Martin, Theodore. "The Currency of the Contemporary." In *Postmodern, Postwar, and After*, edited by Jason Gladstone and Andrew Hoberek, 227–39. Iowa City: University of Iowa Press, 2016.

Mbembe, Achille. "The Power of the Archive." In *Refiguring the Archive*, edited by Carolyn Hamilton, 19–27. Dordrecht: Springer, 2002.

Mohan, Anupama. "Maritime Transmodernities and The Ibis Trilogy." *Postcolonial Text* 14, no. 3–4 (2019). www.postcolonial.org/index.php/pct/article/view/2488.

Moorthy, Shanti. "Abdulrazak Gurnah and Littoral Cosmopolitanism." In Moorthy and Jamal, 73–102.

Moorthy, Shanti, and Ashraf Jamal, eds. *Indian Ocean Studies: Cultural, Social, and Political Perspectives*. New York: Routledge, 2010.

Mustafa, Fawzia. "Swahili Histories and Texts in Abdulrazak Gurnah's Paradise." *English Studies in Africa* 58, no. 1 (2015): 14–29.

Mwangi, Evan. *Africa Writes Back to Self: Metafiction, Gender, Sexuality*. Albany: State University of New York Press, 2009.

Nasta, Susheila. "Abdulrazak Gurnah, *Paradise*." In *The Popular and the Canonical: Debating Twentieth-Century Literature, 1940–2000*, edited by David Johnson, 294–343. New York: Routledge, 2005.

Niranjana, Tejaswini. *Siting Translation: History, Post-structuralism, and the Colonial Context*. Berkeley: University of California Press, 1992.

Olaussen, Maria. "The Submerged History of the Indian Ocean in *Admiring Silence*." *English Studies in Africa* 56, no. 1 (2013): 65–77.

Orsini, Francesca. "The Multilingual Local in World Literature." *Comparative Literature* 67, no. 4 (2015): 345–74.

Prestholdt, Jeremy. "Locating the Indian Ocean: Notes on the Postcolonial Reconstitution of Space." *Journal of Eastern African Studies* 9, no. 3 (2015): 440–67.

Roebuck, Thomas. *A Laskari Dictionary; or, Anglo-Indian Vocabulary of Nautical Terms and Phrases in English and Hindustani, Chiefly in the Corrupt Jargon in Use among Laskars or Indian Sailors.* London: Crosby Lockwood, 1881.

Rollason, Christopher. "'Apparently Unbridgeable Gaps of Language': Amitav Ghosh's *River of Smoke* and an Emerging Global English?" *International Journal on Multicultural Literature* 2, no. 1 (2012): 8–14.

Said, Edward W. *Orientalism.* New York: Vintage Books, 1979.

Samuelson, Meg. "Coastal Form: Amphibian Positions, Wider Worlds, and Planetary Horizons on the African Indian Ocean Littoral." *Comparative Literature* 69, no. 1 (2017): 16–24.

Sheriff, Abdul. *Dhow Cultures of the Indian Ocean: Cosmopolitanism, Commerce, and Islam.* New York: Columbia University Press, 2010.

Spivak, Gayatri Chakravorty. *A Critique of Postcolonial Reason: Toward a History of the Vanishing Present.* Cambridge, MA: Harvard University Press, 1999.

Spivak, Gayatri Chakravorty. *Death of a Discipline.* New York: Columbia University Press, 2003.

Steinberg, Philip E. "Of Other Seas: Metaphors and Materialities in Maritime Regions." *Atlantic Studies* 10, no. 2 (2013): 156–69.

Steiner, Tina. "Writing 'Wider Worlds': The Role of Relation in Abdulrazak Gurnah's Fiction." *Research in African Literatures* 41, no. 3 (2010): 124–35.

Tip, Tippu. *Maisha ya Hamed bin Muhammed el Murjebi, yaani Tippu Tip, kwa maneno yake mwenyewe.* Kampala: East African Literature Bureau, 1974.

Trouillot, Michel-Rolph. *Silencing the Past: Power and the Production of History.* Boston, MA: Beacon, 1995.

Yule, Henry, and A. C. Burnell. *Hobson-Jobson: Being a Glossary of Anglo-Indian Colloquial Words and Phrases, and of Kindred Terms; Etymological, Historical, Geographical, and Discursive.* London: J. Murray, 1886.

ANANYA JAHANARA KABIR

Creole Indias, Creolizing Pondicherry: Ari Gautier's *Le thinnai* as the Archipelago of Fragments

Sur ce thinnai, l'Histoire et les histoires se mêlent: des marins Breton font naufrage aux Maldives, des coolies partent vers les Antilles vivre des destins brisés, des enfants malheureux sont jetés dans les rues sordides de Bombay, et Gilbert Tata erre, muni d'une pierre précieuse funeste et mystérieuse.

On this thinnai, History and stories mingle: Breton sailors are shipwrecked in the Maldives, coolies leave for the West Indies to live broken destinies, unhappy children are thrown into the sordid streets of Bombay, and Gilbert Tata wanders, armed with a fatal and mysterious precious stone.[1]

— Ari Gautier, *Le thinnai*

A Creole identity is an accident of birth: a mode of belonging that connects one to a history of coerced contact that produced unpredictable cultural formations and linguistic variations.

— Françoise Lionnet, "Cosmopolitans or Creole Lives?"

The goal is not to map out (new) territory, but to conceive of a vectoral space.

— Ottmar Ette, *Writing-between-Worlds*

"Creolization" is not a concept customarily applied to the material or literary culture of the geographical space known as the Indian subcontinent. If invoked at all, it is to suggest a gap, a lack, or the closing of certain historical possibilities (Markovits; Rai). The most commonly accepted connections of Indic culture with creolization are in linguistics (Cardoso), and through displacement: of

---

I thank Ari Gautier for the conversations and collaboration that have helped me develop the arguments for this essay and for my larger project of Creole Indias.

[1] All translations from French to English are mine, including those of the chapter and section epigraphs. Blake Smith's English translation of *Le thinnai*, published as *The Thinnai* (Hachette India, 2021) omits large sections of the original text. Hence, I do not use it in this essay.

Comparative Literature 74:2
DOI 10.1215/00104124-9594839 © 2022 by University of Oregon

indentured laborers from Indian heartlands to the Indian Ocean and Carib-bean islands where the plantation system had pressed out "Creole" as a recog-nized descriptor (for language, people, food), and that in turn generated a political praxis (e.g., of *créolité*), and an academic discourse (around creolization). Even here, however, there is controversy as to whether people of Indian heritage can be, should be, or want to be called "Creole" or described as "creolized," stemming from an aspirational Brahminism that interprets creolization as a loss of purity detrimental to the Indic world's privileging of caste and religion-based boundaries (Kabir, "Beyond"). Swimming against these tides, my essay demonstrates that "Creole Indias" is an analytical and historical category to take seriously. Moreover, I do so by applying it to peninsular India rather than the insular contexts of Indian labor diasporas. Creole Indias are not just good to think with, I argue, but best when thought with in conjunction with the Indian coastline.

The regnant vision of Indian nationalism mobilizes the Deccan Peninsula's west-ern and eastern coastlines as defining the anthropomorphized, sari-clad, lower body of *Bharat Mata* (Mother India), whose territorial integrity has to be defended fervently against fissures and fragmentation of all kinds (Ramaswamy). The coast-line is thus hermetically sealed in by a persistent "land-centric" imagination (Byl and Sykes 398) that centers "Indian culture" within the Gangetic plains as Indic heartland. The contingency of this construct becomes apparent, however, if we shift our gaze to the numerous settlements, forts, and lodges that different Euro-pean powers founded and fought over up and down these very coastlines since the advent of the Portuguese after Vasco da Gama's disembarkation near Calicut in 1498. They were followed by the Dutch, the Danes, the French, and, of course, the British. Britain's emergence as the strongest imperial power in India has eclipsed the early and continuing "polycoloniality" (Bhaduri) of multiple European pres-ences here, that became concentrated in the littoral enclaves to which British ascen-dancy increasingly confined them. However, precisely the denseness and longevity of "inter-imperial" cultural exchange (Doyle; Boatcă and Parvulescu) within these enclaves made them hotspots for creolization over the *longue durée*—as this essay will demonstrate through fiction's ability to retrieve and valorize the hidden, lost, or marginalized histories that crystallize in them.

The coastal enclave instigates both a particular history of encounter and literary reactivation of memories around that encounter and its consequences. This twofold approach to the enclave that I propose converges with Meg Samuelson's argument for a "littoral literature" predicated by the "coast as a heuristic device and unit of analysis" (16), in response to Michael Pearson's call ("Littoral Society: Case"; "Lit-toral Society: Concept") for increased historiographic focus on "littoral society." But I move beyond their shared view of the littoral as a frontier zone, to present, instead, the enclave on the littoral as a *contact zone* (Pratt). If creolization, a concept both "descriptive and analytical" (Shih and Lionnet 2), signals certain historical processes that generate new, adaptive, often unexpected cultural forms, the contact zone is its locus classicus. Creolization involves physical intimacy between peoples, but creolized cultures are disseminated through proximate cohabitation, often vio-lent and coerced, sometimes negotiated and adjusted. The contact zone is where this cohabitation and its unpredictable consequences take place. It thus brings to creolization theory a spatial specificity. Here unfold "the lived realities of subaltern subjects," from which creolization emerges as an "epistemology that remains connected to those realities" so as to bring forth a "a theoretical framework" imbued with the "experiential" (Shih and Lionnet 2).

As a specific kind of contact zone for creolization, the coastal enclave confers an analytical granularity to historiographic and literary studies of the littoral. But it also involves a shift from island to the *island-like*. Creolization has come to imply the encounter of Africans and Europeans in the Atlantic world through enslavement (Kabir, "Beyond"), with the privileged site for the concept's theoretical elaborations being the Caribbean sugar plantation islands, though it is varyingly applied to Indian Ocean insular contexts (Chaudenson; Vergès and Marimoutou; Lionnet) and to Cape Verde (Cohen and Toninato). Extending these uses, I deploy "creolization" to analyze island-like enclaves as sites for exchanges between Africans, Europeans, and Asians on the one hand, and merchants, artisans, go-betweens, the enslaved, and colonizers, on the other. These multidirectional encounters result from and illuminate the material circularities linking the Indian, Atlantic, and Pacific Ocean worlds and the hinterland. Through this *transoceanic* heuristic (Kabir, "Elmina"; Kabir, "Creolization"; Kabir, "*Rapsodia*"), I reinterpret enclaves carved out of continental littorals such as peninsular India as "sites where a plurality of possible agents can produce the unpredictable linguistic and social formations characteristic of creolization" through "rhizomatic multidirectionality" (Lionnet 25). One such enclave is Pondicherry. In this essay, I conduct a literary critical reading of Ari Gautier's novel *Le thinnai*, to conceive Pondicherry as a creolized "vectoral space"—in the words of Ottmar Ette cited in my third epigraph—constituted through *archipelagic* connections between continents and islands.

A Franco-Tamil author based in Oslo, Gautier writes historical fiction about Pondicherry that recalls its centuries-long function as a vital node within the intersecting circularities of commerce and colonialism that developed the modern world. *Le thinnai*, his second novel, confirms Gautier's affiliation to what Françoise Lionnet in my second epigraph identifies as a "Creole identity" through his investment in the "unpredictable cultural formations and linguistic variations" that connect him to a "history of coerced contact." How can this history be spatialized through Pondicherry, and how can Pondicherry, as threshold between the peninsular Indian hinterland and the Indian Ocean, help reconfigure our theories of creolization to suit the Indian context? In answer, I examine how the "thinnai," an integral element within Tamil domestic architecture, is creolized by Gautier linguistically, narratologically, and conceptually. Linking the thinnai as contact zone to the community in Pondicherry historically known as the "Bas Créoles," Gautier mobilizes the embodied culture of this community, particularly as deposited in language and cuisine. He thereby emplaces Pondicherry in an archipelagic map defined by two circuits: the transoceanic, which connects the Indian and Atlantic oceans, and the littoral, which connects enclaves up and down the peninsular coastline. An affective cartography of the hoped-for, the denied, the lost, and the retrieved emerges, which I explicate epistemically as "the archipelago of fragments": a transversal crisscrossing of transoceanic and littoral vectors via the coastal enclave that is culturally and historically shaped through their intersections.[2]

---

[2] The "archipelago of fragments" is a term jointly conceived of by me in conjunction with Ari Gautier, in the course of our collaborative work on the cultural platform "Le thinnai kreyol" that we cofounded in

Renouncing Hierarchies, Creolizing the Thinnai

Vu sa proximité du boulodrome du quai du Gingy, les amis de mon père se réunissaient souvent sur le thinnai après leurs parties de pétanque pour l'apéritif. Le soir arrivé, nous nous asseyions sur le thinnai pour bavarder et regarder la vie défiler devant nous en écoutant le silence tomber sur la ville entrecoupé du son de la cloche du marchand de Sonepapadi et le cri d'autres marchands ambulants qui se dirigeaient vers le temple du Perumal.

—Ari Gautier, *Le thinnai*

Given its proximity to the boulodrome on the Quay of Gingy, my father's friends often met up on the thinnai for an aperitif after their games of pétanque. As evening fell, we would sit on the thinnai to chat and watch life parade past us as we listened to silence descend on the town, interspersing the resounding clock of the Sonepadi vendor's cries with those of other perambulating hawkers heading toward the temple of Perumal.

What is *le thinnai* of this novel's title, that Gautier uses not merely as a key site for the narrative action but as an organizing principle? Structurally a combination of a porch and a veranda, a "thinnai" is a raised platform supported by pillars and shaded by an extension of the same roof that covers the house proper (Padmavathi). It is a well-recognized feature of domestic vernacular architecture within the Tamil-speaking world, including its Indian Ocean diasporas (Pillai; Shangeetha and Pillai), though space restrictions in modern urban India have impacted its incorporation into contemporary architecture or indeed retention within renovations of older homes (Sadanand and Nagarajan). Nevertheless, its historical longevity ensures that, as a word, *thinnai* is instantly recognized and understood by speakers of Tamil as well as cognate South Indian languages. At the same time, Gautier defamiliarizes this Tamil lexeme by inscribing it textually as *le thinnai*, as in the quote above. In conjunction with the French masculine definite article, it takes on a dual valence: sounding Tamil while behaving French. "Most of the novel's characters are Tamil speakers, and both their words and the language of the narrator are regularly interspersed with untranslated Tamil words and phrases," notes Blake Smith within his argument for Gautier's "translingualism" (Smith 77). I would go a step further. Gautier's profuse incorporation of Tamil words and syntactical formations creates new linguistic forms that operate simultaneously within and outside both languages. Its privileged position, announced by the book's title and its cover photograph, makes the construct "le thinnai" only the most prominent example of a stylistic strategy that surpasses the implications of "translingual" as a phenomenon that merely reconciles difference by skating over them. This is a literary language that surmounts difference by generating newness: it is *creolized*.

Gautier's two-way creolization of Tamil lexis and French syntax alerts us to other ways in which he deviates from the Tamil *thinnai* and the highly regulated sociocultural universe in which it is embedded. The traditional thinnai's position between the domestic interior and the street as exterior certainly gives it the architectural property of a threshold. However, "India has a caste system and hierarchy in caste was spatially manifested in settlement plans and houses" (Sadanand and Nagarajan

May 2020. See Le thinnai kreyol, Facebook page, www.facebook.com/lethinnaikreyol; Le Thinnai Kreyol, YouTube channel, www.youtube.com/c/LeThinnaiKreyol (both sites last accessed January 4, 2022).

COMPARATIVE LITERATURE / 206

2). The transformative potential that anthropological theory confers on the threshold as *limen* is in this case subordinated to the protocols of caste and gender that dictate everyday life: as "transition spaces" in upper-caste houses, thinnais certainly "permit dualities" (Sadanand and Nagarajan 2), but to maintain rather than disrupt the status quo. The complementary phenomenology of horizontal level changes and the verticality of pillars creates a "front and male zone" that is by default masculine and public (Sadanand and Nagarajan 8). Hence, while a thinnai provides space for social interaction with neighbors and family, it also performs a semipublic gatekeeper's role. Elaborate codes govern what activities can take place on it, who can enter or access the private interior or indeed, who from that interior can emerge to sit on the thinnai. In keeping with fears of pollution, eating can be discouraged on it (Sadanand and Nagarajan). This regulatory function of the thinnai as threshold is confirmed by its multiplication inside the home to provide spaces for the segregation of menstruating women and demarcated routes for low-caste sweepers and domestics to enter, clean the home, and exit without disrupting upper-caste purity.

The Tamil thinnai, then, is a threshold space, but one that perpetuates caste-based hierarchies rather than dissolve them. This paradox is most spectacularly manifested in the celebrated vernacular institution of the *pallikutam vikatam* (veranda school), a pedagogic institution located on the domestic thinnai (Babu 20). The formidable computational and mnemonic skills cultivated therein were restricted to upper-caste scholars; the Tamil social order denied children from the manual laboring caste groups access to these institutions (Babu 20). Even in rare instances of schools with "a multicaste clientele, sectarian and caste distinctions were carefully maintained," with "lower caste children . . . made to sit separately and taught different things" (Raman 111). Cultural capital was amassed and retained through spatialized ejection of unwelcome elements (Mines), rather than their absorption: hence even the newly arrived colonizer was neutralized, as it were, by being configured within satirical tracts on *pallikutam* learning as "the sinister presence of an outsider" who stands "looming" on the thinnai (Raman 117–19). Historically, the thinnai school could not implement such an ejection of European presence in India. Instead, its elitist practices were mobilized into the continuation of Brahmin monopoly over education during colonial rule. Hence the indigenous pedagogic institution supported by the thinnai eventually became part of an "Anglo-vernacular" arsenal, through which the upper castes could collaborate with British colonial structures of the mission school on the one hand, and the Company officers on the other (Raman 132–33).

These co-opted fortunes of the thinnai in British India, which scholarship has shed light on via the *pallikutam vikatam*, vividly contrast with its metamorphosis in Gautier's novel. His is a *Pondicherry* thinnai, an architectural element within a Franco-Tamil home, part of a Franco-Tamil world of post-pétanque aperitifs and hawkers' cries announcing Indic sweets.[3] The novel's cover photograph is of a

---

[3] The Franco-Tamils are the specific group in Pondicherry descended from the "renonçants," or those who renounced Indian personal laws in favor of becoming French citizens; see Guesquin; Pairaudeau 40–53. They very often came from the lowest caste or pariah groups. In the twentieth century, this group also entered the French army to create a distinct "soldat" subculture within Pondicherry, and many of these

Figure 1. The thinnai on the cover of Ari Gautier's *Le thinnai*. Cantine Street, Pondicherry; demolished in December 2020. Photograph courtesy of Mouhamed Moustapha.

house that stood on Cantine Street, the boundary between the historic White Town or the French Quarter, and the Black Town, where Indians lived (fig. 1). However, these demarcations were already blurred during French rule. Indistinctly racialized communities with access to cultural capital lived in the White Town, while lower-caste and "outcaste" groups refashioned themselves via access to the same cultural capital of religion and language after "renouncing" formally Hindu customary laws in favor of French citizenship, Catholicism, and education: Gautier himself belongs to such a "renonçant" family. Finally, mercantile communities such as the Chettiar both amassed economic capital through their participation within the "ocean of trade" (Machado), and converted it to cultural capital through building extravagant homes in between the Black and White Towns, with thinnais among the elements drawn from numerous architectural and ornamental traditions. Divergences between the British colonial system, which reified caste-based exclusions, and the French colonial system, with its alternative genealogy for subject formation through possibilities of co-opted citizenship (Pairaudeau), thus predicate a distinctly Pondicherrian material genealogy for Gautier's thinnai. It is shaped in contradistinction to thinnais elsewhere in the Tamil-speaking world, which he is nevertheless aware of thanks to the proximity and porousness of "discrepant empires" (Arondekar 151) and their postcolonial afterlives.

families opted for French citizenship after 1947, thus creating a straight line between the "renonçants" and "optants"; see Rai 120–21.

Figure 2. Pondicherry thinnai as equalizing social space. Photograph courtesy of Mouhamed Moustapha.

No schoolmaster's disciplining ground structured by the persistence of caste, this thinnai is a Rabelaisian site of transformation through eating, drinking, lazing, transacting, and storytelling (fig. 2). The lexical form *le thinnai* graphically signals how creolization restores liminality to this limen by instigating these transformations.

From Refuge to Centrifuge: The Creolizing Contact Zone

Du fait de sa position idéale placée à l'entrée du hameau, nos thinnais ne désemplissaient jamais. Il était fréquent de voir nos voisins ou des gens de passage l'occuper à leur guise sans que cela nous importune. À ses débuts, Lourdes ne pouvait supporter la présence des étrangers et des habitants du quartier qui envahissaient les thinnais de façon importune. Mais elle comprit rapidement que nos thinnais avaient la particularité d'être un refuge à toutes personnes indigentes qui sillonnaient les routes nébuleuses de l'existence.

—Ari Gautier, *Le thinnai*

Because of its ideal position at the entrance of the village, our thinnais were never emptied of people. One could often see our neighbors or passersby taking their place on it at their convenience without it bothering us. In the beginning, Lourdes couldn't tolerate the presence of strangers or neighbors who invaded the thinnais in this intrusive manner. But she soon understood that our thinnais had the particular feature of being a refuge for all manner of destitute people who crisscrossed life's nebulous pathways.

The socioeconomic history of Tamil Nadu's thinnais, and their changing function within the postcolonial context, were shaped by a combination of nativist and colonialist pressures that derived from British administrative policies in the Deccan. The Pondicherry thinnais that inspire Gautier are products of a different trajectory: of cross-cultural transfusion, negotiation, compromise, and unpredictable innovation within the compacted space of a French enclave in India. This trajectory answers to the specific conditions under which creolization as a cultural process operates to generate new cultural products. Gautier's mobilization of the Pondicherry thinnai allows us to refine our understanding of how such processes unfolded in India's littoral enclaves, even while that understanding in turn sheds light on why an author writing about such an enclave would choose to transform an architectural element into the governing trope for his work of fiction. In Gautier's novel, this architectural element, "le thinnai," is a space which enables travelers and locals to meet and merge. The novel's blurb, cited as the first epigraph, makes sure we get this point. Actors circulating in the transoceanic frame linking the Atlantic and Indian Ocean worlds—Breton sailors on the one hand, coolies on the other—are some of the vectors for those stories. Gautier's intention in bringing together on his thinnai these subaltern characters, the flotsam and jetsam of History, goes beyond the urge to memorialize "les hommes d'orage aux pieds nus" (Torabully 16; the men of storms with bare feet). The divergences this quirky cast of characters embodies—including complexions, religious beliefs, relationship to French and Frenchness, and reasons for traversing the oceans—give rise to the diverse narrative threads through which he weaves a richly variegated Pondicherry.

As a historical novelist, Gautier's interest lies not in character development or intricacies of plot: rather, he mines archival sources to tell us why such people, and the stories they carry, would pass through Pondicherry. In the process, he builds the scaffolding for a hitherto untold history of this inter-imperial space, shaped by rivalries between European trading powers, the empires that they devolved into, and the postcolonial arrangements that emerged in their wake. This history goes beyond the Anglo-French rivalry among the Deccan privileged by those writing imaginatively and historically about Pondicherry. The reduction of French imperial ambitions in India to five tiny *comptoirs* after Pondicherry fell to the British in 1793 generated a certain obsession with *l'Inde perdue* (lost India) focalized through Pondicherry, as exemplified by the French colonial author George Delamare's novel, *Désordres à Pondichéry*. Srilata Ravi reads Delamare's Pondicherry as a "a border zone" of disorder and chaos, which cannot however realize the potential of liminality. Mired in "the dual dimension of desire and regret [that] continues to reduce the trading post to an imagined space . . . connect[ed] nostalgically with a 'museified' past," this "border zone" fails to emerge as a space of resistance (Ravi 387). But Pondichéry's subsequent status as an outpost outside British jurisdiction also encouraged another view: its function as a "strategic sanctuary" (Edwards), a place of "liberty, equality and fraternity" where political refugees from the British Empire could take asylum while remaining geographically on Indian soil. One such refugee was the renegade guru Sri Aurobindo, whose relocation to Pondicherry led to the establishment there, in 1926, of the Aurobindo Ashram for his growing band of followers, and, in 1968, the international, utopian settler community called Auroville on Pondicherry's outskirts.

Gautier's first novel, *Carnet secret de Lakshmi* (2015), mercilessly satirizes Sri Aurobindo, the Ashram, and Auroville as representing the messy (post)colonial inheritances and incomplete decolonization of French India (Namakkal). In writing *Le thinnai*, however, he is able to respond to these stereotypes of Pondicherry in a more complex manner. On the one hand, the thinnai is indeed a sanctuary that offers refuge to a number of maverick characters. On the other, as threshold of a house located in an impoverished fisherman's village on the outskirts of town, it replicates fractally Pondicherry's position as inter-imperial border zone. But Gautier reinvests these associations of Pondicherry to evoke the thinnai as a space where "peoples geographically and historically separated come into contact with each other and establish ongoing relations, usually involving conditions of coercion, radical inequality, and intractable conflict" (Pratt 8). While these relations are established through storytelling, Gautier urges us to take seriously the transformative power of the space rather than the act of storytelling.[4] His thinnai is the privileged site in the novel from which all stories radiate; along with the young boy who is the novel's protagonist, we remain captive to those stories, almost never allowed to enter the home. The thinnai instead draws out onto it the denizens of the home, imposing on all characters a spatialized equality that avoids the hierarchies of an elaborated domestic interior. Troped thus, the thinnai can function as the ideal contact zone: it "treats the relations among colonizers and colonized, or travellers and travellees, not in terms of separateness, but in terms of co-presence, interaction, interlocking understandings and practices, and often within radically asymmetrical relations of power" (Pratt 8). The thinnai is not just a refuge but a *centrifuge* for cultural dynamism, powered by the mélange of those who converge on it, their pasts, and their presents.

The thinnai thus becomes a *mise en abyme* of Pondicherry. More than a threshold whose liminality is a prelude to transformation, the liminality of the thinnai-as-Pondicherry is perpetually productive; it is contact zone as motor of creolization, where transformation is unpredictable, chaotic, but ongoing. Just as remapping Europe to include its creolized island territories "helps creolize our collective geographic imaginary" (Boatcă 15–16), so too does this creolizing presentation of Pondicherry reverberate on the metanarrative level. Through its ability to absorb characters and their stories, Gautier's thinnai creolizes the picaresque mode: the novel doesn't actually go anywhere, even while taking us everywhere. Because this peculiar spatiality imprisons everyone (reader and author included), on the limen between the house and the world for the entire duration of its diegesis, the thinnai is not just a trope, but equally a *chronotope*. "Au mépris du temps," the narrator announces at the very start of the novel, "le thinnai avait réussi à garder le mystère de la temporalité" (Gautier 14; In defiance of time, the thinnai had managed to keep the mystery of temporality). This mystery recalls Michel-Rolph Trouillot's pronouncement on the "miracle of creolization" or the genesis of new culture from, and as resistance to, the most inhospitable circumstances (15). Like the dialogic dynamics of creolization itself, this antagonistic relationship between "temps" and the thinnai's "temporalité" gives rise to new narratological possibilities: "Des souvenirs poussiéreux emprisonnés dans les crevasses du mur du vieux thinnai s'echappèrent comme des sylphes soulagés d'une liberté longtemps rêvée" (Gautier

---

[4] In this spatial and transformative emphasis, Gautier's thinnai and my theorization of it diverge from the discussion of the Bengali "adda" as practice offered by Dipesh Chakrabarty (1999).

14; Dusty memories trapped in the crevices of the wall of the old thinnai escaped like sylphs relieved of a long dreamed-of freedom).

Indianized French? Creoles, Creolized, Creolizing

Déjà que nous jonglions entre le français que nous parlions avec mon père et le tamoul que nous uti-lisions avec mon oncle, ma tante et les voisins ; à cela était venu s'ajouter le créole de Lourdes. D'une façon, cela aurait été la langue idéale. Ce mélange de français et de tamoul aurait pu être notre lingua franca de la famille. Mais mon père s'était véhémentement opposé à ce que Lourdes nous parlât en créole.

—Ari Gautier, *Le thinnai*

We already juggled the French we spoke with our father and the Tamil we spoke with our uncle, aunt, and neighbors. Now we had to add Lourdes's Creole. In a sense, it should have been an ideal language. This mix of French and Tamil could have been our family's lingua franca. But my father violently resisted the idea of Lourdes speaking to us in it.

The thinnai as chronotope enables dynamism through apparent stasis: to arrest the linear flow of time on the thinnai is to release the exchange of stories as the cre-olizing impulse. Yet, like the stories themselves and their bearers, the creolization that occurs in this contact zone is highly contingent; it is neither uniformly distrib-uted nor apparent in every aspect comprising its habitus. Creolization processes in general are deeply implicated with issues of power, prestige, shame, and self-censorship. This novel shows us how these affective burdens drive the Indic creol-ized habitus under the radar of the everyday, making it difficult to detect. In keep-ing with the intellectual genealogy connecting the contact zone as concept and "the contact languages of linguistics … which develop among speakers of different tongues who need to communicate with each other consistently" (Pratt 8), the foun-dational elusiveness of Indic creolization is located in language itself. The multiple nodes of linguistic variegation running through Gautier's prose include the par-ticular language spoken by Lourdes, the domestic help and de facto nurse of the protagonist. Several clues give away the emotional importance Gautier invests in her. Not only is she the only female character, stepping into the vacuum left by the early death of the protagonist's mother, but she is also the only one who crosses back and forth between the exterior and the domestic interior, bringing nourish-ment in the form of food and drink to those who sit on the thinnai telling or listen-ing to stories. This narratological function as go-between and symbolic function as maternal substitute are contoured historically and linguistically by the way Gautier makes Lourdes speak.

The direct speech Gautier fashions for Lourdes is French characterized by "a set of typical phrases and structures" (Smith 78) attributed by the narrator to the Pondicherry community known as the Bas Créoles, to which she belongs. The nar-rator carefully distinguishes them from the Hauts Créoles, who descend from early French settlers in Pondicherry. The Hauts Créoles are the bastions of cul-tural, economic, and social capital in Pondicherry, living in the mansions of the White Town and the custodians of impeccable French. In contrast, the Bas Cré-oles are a racially métis group that crystallized in the first centuries of European encounters with locals and with each other in peninsular India's coastal enclaves.

This "subaltern and creolized" (Carton 585) community that a nineteenth-century British observer characterized with some horror as "tawny-faced Frenchmen and their families" (Hervey 284) descended from "early alliances between Portuguese traders and Indian or Christian free women of colour... testifying to a racial landscape... already complex and hybridized before the first French traders arrived in India to stake their claim in the lucrative East India trade" (Carton 586). Lourdes, the sole representative of this community in *Le thinnai*, is also "the only character in the novel presented as speaking Pondicherrian Creole, a language that has received almost no scholarly attention or literary documentation outside of Gautier's novel" (Smith 77). While the way Lourdes speaks is not perceived by her as anything out of the ordinary, it "appears to some characters (and sometimes to the narrator) as an independent language marking its speaker's social exclusion, [and] at other times as a degenerate and corrupted French" (Smith 77).

The single monograph-length study to date of the language of Pondicherry Bas Créoles provisionally calls it PCF (Pondicherian Creole French), assesses the evidence for Tamil and French syntactical interactions therein, and concludes that "one cannot seriously claim that PCF is a Creole.... This variety can be termed as *Indianized French*" (Kelkar-Stephen 104). What is at stake in simultaneously calling this language *Creole* and disavowing its creoleness? The apparent inability for this "Indianized French" to attain status of a Creole language adheres to a pattern discernible in peninsular Indian enclaves: the Indic languages local to these enclaves absorb lexis from a number of European languages but fail to fit textbook definitions of "Creoles" or even "Pidgins." The absence of linguistic creolization in the present does not imply, of course, that there were no Creole languages that had developed in the past (Cardoso): these could well have disappeared without entering the archive, leaving behind lexical and syntactic remnants recoverable from the oral domain of marginalized groups that can, as in this case, also bear the label of "Creole." One can hypothesize that a feature of cultural creolization in peninsular India is the absence of circumstances that lead to linguistic creolization as a stable feature over time (Cardoso). Whether we call Lourdes's mode of speaking (and being), "Creole," "créole," or "Indianized French" (distinct, of course, from the "Indianized French" that is the language of the novel as a whole), it is not something that Gautier has invented: growing up in Pondicherry, he had heard it spoken by Bas Créoles and absorbed its idiosyncrasies. Like his protagonist, he too was banned from speaking it by his father.

This paternal interdiction, which blurs the boundary between the fictive and the personal, only intensifies the complex symbolic value that Lourdes and her language is made to bear in the novel. On the one hand, the narrator declares that "le créole pondichérien est un français corrompu" (Gautier 69; Pondicherrian Creole is a corrupted French); on the other, he wishes that it could have been their family's lingua franca. Gautier uses Lourdes's Bas Créole identity to not only interject in his prose their particular variety of French, but to acknowledge these tensions and fissures around the historical presence of such a community in Pondicherry through their linguistic trace that should have but did not become Pondicherry's lingua franca. Lourdes's language may not be a recognizable textbook "Creole," but it is creolized and creolizing; what Gautier shows, inter alia, is the response to this creolizing impulse by other micro-communities in Pondicherry, in particular Franco-Tamils such as the protagonist of *Le thinnai* (and himself). Between that resistance and his authorial preference for succumbing to that impulse, his novel is fiction's testimony to the unpredictable yet inevitable ways in which creolization as cultural process linked different groups in this densely layered space. The thinnai is where a Bas Créole woman converses freely in her "créole pondicherien," and where its rhythms and interjections are learned by the protagonist and ventriloquized by the author. It is a fictive space of wish fulfillment created by an author whose childhood mirrors that of his protagonist. It is therefore also a creolizing chronotope, activated by a Bas Créole broker between interior and exterior, which acknowledges *and* disobeys the father's order.

Transoceanic Sensorium: Singing, Dancing, Tasting Creole

Malgré ce handicap, cette communauté avait une façon désinvolte d'affronter la vie et cette société raciste. Il y avait en eux cette mystérieuse insouciance et une légèreté mélangée à une certaine fierté. Ils noyaient leur chagrin et leur mal de vivre dans un pas de Chega en entonnant une Rosa Poudina ou même un Marie le pêcheur qui étaient des chansons créoles.

—Ari Gautier, *Le thinnai*

Despite these disadvantages, this community had a way to confront life in this racist society. They had in them this mysterious insouciance and a lightness mixed with a certain pride. They drowned their grief and their happiness in a step of the Sega while singing a "Rosa Poudina" or even a "Marie the fisherman," which were Creole songs.

After all, the father's order comes ambivalently packaged. He "violently" resists the language that Lourdes speaks but displays no disdain whatsoever toward the food she cooks, which the men in the novel compulsively and repeatedly ask for. A superficial reading might dismiss this alignment of feminine presence with the culinary arts as a predictable, even politically retrogressive, portrayal of womanhood. However, a very different interpretation is urged on us by the conjunction of Lourdes's Bas Créole identity and the thinnai as threshold and contact zone. The Franco-Tamil world that the father represents would reject some aspects of Lourdes's Bas Créole habitus, but it cannot do without others. This is precisely the ambivalence that the novel codes: even while noting that her language cannot become its lingua franca, it grants extraordinary metanarrative power to the food she makes. Without her food there can be no stories. The dishes Lourdes prepares deep inside the home literally and emotionally fuels the novel's raison d'être: the storytelling on the liminal thinnai. In the kitchen's fecund interiority, the cultural potential encoded in Lourdes's creolized and creolizing speech finds full expression. It is also metonymically connected to a specific exteriority: Bas Créole expressive culture, that in turn links Pondicherry to a transoceanic frame. The quote above reveals the narrator's care in emphasizing the names of their songs ("Rosa Poudina," "Marie le pêcheur") and the genre of their dance ("Chega"). Minor deviations of orthography notwithstanding, these very songs and the same dance circulate within the Creole repertoire of the Mascarene islands, while the masquerades are part of creolized Christian revels that flourish across the Atlantic and Indian Ocean worlds (Kabir, "Creolization"; Kabir, "*Rapsodia*").

The Rabelaisian streak running through the novel owes to this embodied culture that flows between kitchen, street, and ocean, to suspend the thinnai—and Pondicherry—in an ephemeral yet palpable creole sensorium, as breathtakingly transoceanic as it is intensely localized on the littoral. Precisely this valence radiates from the food Lourdes cooks, on which the author lavishes much attention. Not only are specific dishes named; long passages are devoted to their ingredients and the culinary techniques involved. These narratorial deviations are of extreme strategic value. They offer reminders of the highly mobile lives of Franco-Tamils interpellated as citizens within the French empire (Pairaudeau), and the "vectoral space" (Ette) that Pondicherry becomes as a consequence. If the father and his friends developed their taste for Vietnamese snacks because of the transcolonial connections between Indochine and Pondicherry, a material consequence of this preference is the entry of these dishes into Lourdes's repertoire. But the most spectacular showcasing of Lourdes's talent is through the Pondicherrian specialties that the narrator groups under "cuisine créole." From his descriptions, I extract four categories of ingredients used therein: local/coastal (coconut milk, greens, vegetables); generic Indic (ginger and garlic, onions, coriander, spices, poppy seeds, ghee, cashew nuts); New World imports (green chilies, tomatoes); and animal protein (chicken, prawns, beef). These ingredients are combined with the same mysterious lightness the narrator bestows on the Bas Créoles: a nonchalant disregard for Brahminical taboos around "non-vegetarian" food in general and beef in particular. The names the dishes bear—*baffade*, *fougade*, *kousid*, and *moily*—lexically tie their insouciant rejection of Indic "purity" to a history of transoceanic creolization that sediments in the Deccan.

These names attach themselves to dishes not just in Pondicherry but also on the Konkan and Malabar coasts. Appearing in a variety of orthographic forms depending on whether they are transliterated into the Roman alphabet in Konkani-, Malayalam-, or Tulu-speaking regions, they are all creolized Portuguese words. *Fougade*, also spelled *foogat(h)*, is from Portuguese *refogado* (fried in hot oil); *Kousid*, also spelled *k(o)ucid(e)*, is from Portuguese *cozido* (boiled); *bafad*, also spelled *baf(f)at/d(e)*, is from Portuguese *abafado* (choked, stifled); and *moily*, variously seen as *moilee*, *molly*, and *molee*, is from Portuguese *molho* (sauce). In keeping with the polysemy and lack of standardization typical of creolized cultural products (Kabir, "Creolization"), the dishes corresponding to these names can vary across the Deccan. While *fougade* is always a dry vegetable dish incorporating grated coconut, usually made with cabbage or green beans, *kousid*, which across the Portuguese-speaking world is a creolized rendering of the Portuguese boiled meat dish *cozido*, in Pondicherry names a dish made of coconut milk, greens, and prawns. The *baffade* that Lourdes cooks is chicken marinated in coconut milk and stewed with various whole spices; but in Goa and Mangalore it is a spicy stew made with pork and a special spice powder, *bafat masala*. Up and down the Deccan coastlines, *moily* and its variations signals a coconut milk–based stew, usually cooked with fish but also on occasion incorporating duck and other meats. This Portuguese-derived lexicon of the creolized *kucini* (Tamil *kitchen*, from Portuguese *cozinha*) thus locates Pondicherry on two, intersecting vectors: one linking the Atlantic and Indian Ocean worlds, and the other linking coastal enclaves elsewhere in peninsular India.

This lexicon's talismanic charge is not diluted even by the occasional folk etymology the narrator reaches for—as when he connects *moily* to Mexican *mole*. "Savait-elle que cette sauce importée par les Portugais était d'origine aztèque?" he asks of Lourdes (Gautier 75; Did she know that this sauce imported by the Portuguese had an Aztec origin?). Lexis works in conjunction with the sensorium to retrieve transoceanic pasts that are embodied in Lourdes under the sign of *Créole.* Just as "the fragrance of her Moily had the power to cross seas and oceans" (Gautier 75), so too does Lourdes's genealogy. The narrator tells us that her mother Bébé was descended from an aristocratic Portuguese line; one of the intervening ancestors had landed in a Goan convent via an ill-fated convoy of "king's daughters" destined for Portuguese men overseas. Through various twists and turns, including widow-hood, she traveled from Goa to the Danish settlement of Tranquebar near Pondicherry (Gautier 74). To make the mother of Bébé then land up in Pondicherry as a nurse in an Haut Créole household is a veritable cakewalk for the author of historical fiction: the archive is replete with such individuals through whose peregrinations and liaisons the Bas Créole community eventually emerged as a distinct group (Carton; Arondekar). Bébé is the result of her mother's transformation from nurse to mistress in Pondicherry's White Town. That this was but a precarious elevation is borne out by the ever-descending fortunes of Bébé and Lourdes. Lourdes's genealogy thus brings on the thinnai the agentive yet marginalized women who literally moved culture between coastal enclaves established by different European powers. It enables Gautier to evoke the Bas Créoles as custodians of Pondicherry's creolized history, even while making visible the lineaments of the "vectoral space" (Ette) that it spatializes.

Archipelago of Fragments

"Literature goes back, in its encounter between history and place, to the inventory of its phantoms and fantasies" (Vergès and Marimoutou 28). The creole sensorium associated with Lourdes is precisely such an inventory, through which Gautier retrieves disappeared and disappearing pasts of Pondicherry for his thinnai. The sensorium is described as irradiating the existence of the Bas Créoles in spite of the double racism they suffer, reviled by the Hauts Créoles and caste-conscious Hindus alike. The self-confessed inability to make "creole pondichérien" the novel's lingua franca acknowledges this "racial, cultural economic and linguistic deficit" indexed by the creole subject (Lionnet 29). Yet Gautier valorizes other aspects of their embodied culture as a source of "alegropolitics" (Kabir, "Fleeting"), or resistance through the expression of collective joy, generated through creolization that draws its ingredients from both transoceanic and littoral sites. By "pars[ing] out" (Lionnet 30) these ingredients, Gautier avoids reembedding the creolized culture of Pondicherry into a territorial episteme. Instead, he uses its liminal position to rework an "understanding of land [that] includes the ocean" (Vergès and Marimoutou 13). Through this understanding he configures Pondicherry as "le thinnai," a vital node in the circulation of objects, peoples, ships, tastes, and stories not only through the Indian Ocean and the Atlantic world, but also between European-established enclaves on the Indic coast. It is at the intersection of these two vectors, that I am calling the littoral and the transoceanic, within genealogies such as Lourdes's, that Pondicherry emerges as not just a creolized but a creolizing site. It creolizes not merely through *métissage* as biological (f)act, but, more importantly, through affiliative bonds enabled by proximate cohabitation.

The alegropolitical dimension that activates the resistive potential of creolizing Pondicherry is not only manifested in the creole sensorium; it is also articulated to an archipelagic structure. Édouard Glissant (vii) once observed in passing that the remnants of French India, "these exiguous territories, distant from one another, were always grouped together as Pondichéry, Chandernagore, Yanam, Karikal and Mahé, giving the impression of a single body of land or rather, of a fairly integrated archipelago." This perspective certainly redeems the supremely scattered and dispersed spatial nature of Pondicherry, whether we consider it the French quarter, the town, or the present-day Union Territory, which includes all the former French settlements and lodges in the Deccan. Once incorporated within the fractal logic of creolization, the fragments of Pondicherry reveal themselves as part of a web of connections, a pattern of repeating islands (Benítez-Rojo). Gautier extends this archipelagic impression to comprehend coastal enclaves founded and controlled by European powers other than the French—most obviously the Portuguese, but also, as Lourdes's ancestral connection to Tranquebar confirms, the Danes; elsewhere in the novel, he brings in details from the peninsular copresence of the Dutch. At the same time, hidden histories of indentured laborers transported to the French Antilles from Pondicherry also return to the thinnai, as the central raconteur-traveler Gilbert Tata progressively reveals his life story in response to the hospitality of the protagonist's family and the ministrations of Lourdes. The creole sensorium levers the thinnai as connector of multiscalar worlds, across the Indian and Atlantic oceans and along the Deccan Peninsula's coastlines and enclaves, to generate an episteme I call the archipelago of fragments.

The archipelago of fragments allows us to interpret the creolizing chronotope of the thinnai as the modus operandi for Pondicherry's cartographic reorientation. Its geopolitical subsumption within postcolonial India since 1962 has led to a reinscription of its geographical position within the Deccan Peninsula. But if Pondicherry's back is to the peninsular hinterland, it also faces the Indian Ocean. As "hinge" and "mediator" between hinterland and sea (Pearson, "Littoral Society: Case" 4), Gautier's Pondicherry responds to Pearson's presentation of "littoral society" as a "tin-opener" ("Littoral Society: Case" 7) for newer concepts by offering us the enclave, the thinnai, and creolization itself as examples. By keeping us on the thinnai for the duration of his novel, Gautier obliges us to participate in storytelling as a memorializing act through which the Creole sensorium is activated. Through this activation reemerges the transoceanic and littoral circularities supporting an archipelagic episteme that not only challenges Indian postcoloniality as Anglophone, but also renders the coastline porous (Pearson, "Littoral Society: Case" 4; Pearson, "Littoral Society: Concept" 356; Samuelson 17), through an ocean-facing, multilingual cosmopolitanism of "creole lives" (Lionnet) that move back and forth across the hinterland and coastline. The dusty memories trapped in the crevices of Gautier's thinnai can finally escape in pursuit of their long dreamed-of archipelagic freedom.

King's College London

Works Cited

Arondekar, Anjali. "What More Remains: Slavery, Sexuality, South Asia." *History of the Present* 6, no. 2 (2016): 146–54.

Babu, Senthil. "Memory and Mathematics in the Tamil Tinnai Schools of South India in the Eighteenth and Nineteenth Centuries." *International Journal for the History of Mathematics Education* 2, no. 1 (2007): 15–32.

Benítez-Rojo, Antonio. *The Repeating Island: The Caribbean and the Postmodern Perspective.* Durham, NC: Duke University Press, 1996.

Bhaduri, Saugata. *Polycoloniality: European Transactions with Bengal from the Thirteenth to the Nineteenth Century.* London: Bloomsbury Publishing, 2020.

Boatcă, Manuela. "Thinking Europe Otherwise: Lessons from the Caribbean." *Current Sociology* 69, no. 3 (2021): 389–414.

Boatcă, Manuela, and Anca Parvulescu. "Creolizing Transylvania: Notes on Coloniality and Inter-imperiality." *History of the Present* 10, no. 1 (2020): 9–27.

Byl, Julia, and Jim Sykes. "Ethnomusicology and the Indian Ocean: On the Politics of Area Studies." *Ethnomusicology* 64, no. 3 (2020): 394–421.

Cardoso, Hugo C. "The Indo-Portuguese Creoles of the Malabar: Historical Cues and Questions." In *India, the Portuguese, and Maritime Interactions,* edited by Pius Malekandathil, Lotika Varadarajan, and Amar Farooqui, vol. 1, 345–73. Delhi: Primus Books, 2019.

Carton, Adrian. "Shades of Fraternity: Creolization and the Making of Citizenship in French India, 1790–1792." *French Historical Studies* 31, no. 4 (2008): 581–607.

Chakrabarty, Dipesh. "Adda, Calcutta: Dwelling in Modernity." *Public Culture* 11, no 1 (1999): 109–45.

Chaudenson, Robert. *Creolization of Language and Culture.* London: Routledge, 2002.

Cohen, Robin, and Paola Toninato. *The Creolization Reader.* London: Routledge, 2010.

Doyle, Laura. "Inter-imperiality: An Introduction." *Modern Fiction Studies* 64, no. 3 (2018): 395–402.

Edwards, Penny. "A Strategic Sanctuary: Reading *l'Inde française* through the Colonial Archive." *Interventions* 12, no. 3 (2010): 356–67.

Ette, Ottmar. *Writing-between-Worlds.* Berlin: De Gruyter, 2016.

Gautier, Ari. *Le thinnai.* Paris: Le lys bleu, 2017.

Glissant, Édouard. Preface to Rai, iv–vii.

Gueusquin Marie-France. "Les Pondichériens de citoyenneté française: Entre va-et-vient et retours accomplis." *Diasporas: Histoire et sociétés,* no. 10 (2007): 187–205.

Hervey, Albert. *Ten Years in India; or, The Life of a Young Officer.* London: William Schoberl, 1850.

Kabir, Ananya Jahanara. "Beyond Créolité and Coolitude, the Indian on the Plantation: Re-creolization in the Transoceanic Frame." *Middle Atlantic Review of Latin American Studies* 4, no. 2 (2020): 174–93.

Kabir, Ananya Jahanara. "Creolization as Balancing Act in the Transoceanic Quadrille: Choreogenesis, Incorporation, Memory, Market." *Atlantic Studies* 17, no. 1 (2020): 135–57.

Kabir, Ananya Jahanara. "Elmina as Postcolonial Space: Transoceanic Creolization and the Fabric of Memory." *Interventions* 22, no. 8 (2020): 994–1012.

Kabir, Ananya Jahanara. "The Fleeting Taste of Mazaa: From Embodied Philology to an Alegropolitics for South Asia." *South Asia: Journal of South Asian Studies* 43, no. 2 (2020): 243–254.

Kabir, Ananya Jahanara. "*Rapsodia Ibero-Indiana*: Transoceanic Creolization and the Mando of Goa." *Modern Asian Studies.* Published online 11th January 2021. doi.org/10.1017/S0026749X20000311.

Kelkar-Stephan, Leena. *Bonjour Maa: The French-Tamil Language Contact Situation in India.* PhD diss, Martin Luther University of Halle-Wittenberg, 2005.

Lionnet, Françoise. "Cosmopolitan or Creole Lives? Globalized Oceans and Insular Identities." *Profession,* 2011, 23–43.

Machado, Pedro. *Ocean of Trade.* Cambridge: Cambridge University Press, 2014.

Markovits, Claude. "On the Political History of Britishness in India: Lord Cornwallis and the Early Demise of Creole India." In *Memory, Identity, and the Colonial Encounter in India: Essays in Honour of*

Peter Robb, edited by Ezra Rashkow, Sanjukta Ghosh, and Upal Chakrabarti, 55–70. London: Taylor and Francis, 2017.

Mines, Diane P. "Making the Past Past: Objects and the Spatialization of Time in Tamilnadu." *Anthropological Quarterly* 70, no. 4 (1997): 173–86.

Namakkal, Jessica. *Unsettling Utopia: The Making and Unmaking of French India*. New York: Columbia University Press, 2021.

Padmavathi, V. "Climatic Architectural Tradition of India." Paper presented at the International Conference "Passive and Low Energy Cooling for the Built Environment," 1103–8. Santorini, Greece, May 2005.

Pairaudeau, Natasha. *Mobile Citizens: French Indians in Indochina, 1858–1954*. Copenhagen: NIAS, 2016.

Pearson, Michael N. "Littoral Society: The Case for the Coast." *Great Circle* 7, no. 1 (1985): 1–8.

Pearson, Michael N. "Littoral Society: The Concept and the Problems." *Journal of World History* 17, no. 4 (2006): 353–73.

Pillai, Shanthini. *Colonial Visions, Postcolonial Revisions: Images of the Indian Diaspora in Malaysia*. Cambridge: Scholars Publishing, 2007.

Pratt, Mary Louise. *Imperial Eyes: Travel Writing and Transculturation*. New York: Routledge, 2007.

Rai, Animesh. *The Legacy of French Rule in India (1674–1954): An Investigation of a Process of Creolization*. Puducherry, India: Institut français de Pondichéry, 2008.

Raman, Bhavani. *Document Raj: Writing and Scribes in Early Colonial South India*. Chicago: University of Chicago Press, 2012.

Ramaswamy, Sumathi. *The Goddess and the Nation: Mapping Mother India*. Durham, NC: Duke University Press, 2010.

Ravi, Srilata. "Border Zones in Colonial Spaces: Imagining Pondicherry, Mauritius, and Lucknow." *Interventions* 12, vol. 3 (2010): 383–95.

Sadanand, Anjali, and R. V. Nagarajan. "Transition Spaces in an Indian Context." *Athens Journal of Architecture* 6, no. 3 (2020): 193–224.

Samuelson, Meg. "Coastal Form: Amphibian Positions, Wider Worlds, and Planetary Horizons on the African Indian Ocean Littoral." *Comparative Literature* 69, no. 1 (2017): 16–24.

Shangeetha, R. K., and S. Pillai. "Diasporic Dwellings: The Family House and its Role in the Creative Imaginary of Selected Malaysian Indian Writers." *Pertanika* 22, no. 3 (2014): 903–16.

Shih, Shu-Mei, and Françoise Lionnet. Introduction to *The Creolization of Theory*, edited by Françoise Lionnet and Shu-Mei Shih, 1–34. Durham, NC: Duke University Press, 2011.

Smith, Blake. "Translingualism in Francophone Writing from South Asia." *L'esprit créateur* 59, no. 4 (2019): 68–80.

Torabully, Khaleel. *Cale d'étoiles: Coolitude*. Paris: FeniXX, 1991.

Trouillot, Michel-Rolph. "Culture on the Edges: Caribbean Creolization in Historical Context." In *The African Diaspora and Creolization Literary Forum*, edited by ACTION Foundation, 9–22. Fort Lauderdale, FL: A.C.T.I.O.N. Foundation, 2006. http://internationalcreolefest.org/images/CahierICF06-Booklet.pdf.

Vergès, Françoise, and Carpanin Marimoutou. "Moorings: Indian Ocean Creolizations." *PORTAL: Journal of Multidisciplinary International Studies* 9, no. 1 (2012): 1–39.

NIKHITA OBEEGADOO

An Archipelagic Node in Global Migration? The Stakes of Comparison and Irony in Nathacha Appanah's *Tropique de la violence*

> When that Syrian boy was found washed up on a Turkish beach, it gave me hope. I told myself that someone somewhere would remember this French island and would point out that here, too, children are dying on beaches.... But nothing ever changes and sometimes I feel as though I'm living in a parallel dimension in which what happens here never crosses the ocean and doesn't have any effect on people.... Lives on this land matter just as much as all those lives on other lands, don't they?[1]
>
> —Nathacha Appanah, *Tropic of Violence*

THE QUESTION THAT ends this epigraph is troubling. It unsettles and provokes. Enunciated by Olivier, a policeman from the French island of Mayotte in the Indian Ocean, the epigraph points out that in September 2015, at the very same time as lifeless migrant corpses—including that of a three-year-old Syrian toddler, Alan Kurdi—washed up on European shores at the height of the continent's migration "crisis," another migratory tragedy was claiming countless lives, albeit away from the global media spotlight. In the Indian Ocean, off the eastern coast of Africa, thousands of people have lost their lives to the seventy-kilometer clandestine sea crossing from the Comoros, one of the poorest nations in the world, to the French island-territory of Mayotte. Mauritian author Nathacha Appanah's 2016 novel *Tropique de la violence* (*Tropic of Violence*) grapples with this ongoing human catastrophe, as well as its precarious positionality within global imaginaries of mobility and (non)belonging.

---

[1] In this article, I cite the published English translation of *Tropique de la violence*. In general, all translations are mine, unless the source cited is a published translation. When I have modified a quotation from a published translation to highlight an original meaning, this has been noted following the quotation.

Comparative Literature 74:2
DOI 10.1215/00104124-9594852   © 2022 by University of Oregon

But why, exactly, do Olivier's words make us uncomfortable? Are we ill at ease because his interrogation reveals the hollowness of our theoretical understanding of all human lives as equally valuable? Are we put off by the explicit attempt to compare tragedies, that is, to judge suffering in one part of the world according to images emerging from another? Might our unease be due to voice rather than content—would we have preferred to hear this message from the migrants themselves, rather than the policeman charged with greeting their corpses on the Mahoran shore? Is the policeman, then, taking up space that is not his, even as he resets a narrative asymmetry that privileges continental Europe? Interestingly, this line of inquiry can be extended to *Tropique de la violence* itself: should the novel be lauded for drawing attention to an invisibilized part of the world, or criticized for turning human suffering into literary raw material? As I demonstrate in this essay, these questions not only tether together disparate geographies, but also reach the very heart of the practice of comparison in an unequally globalized world.

Tropique de la violence depicts clandestine migration in the Indian Ocean as intimately linked to its counterpart in the Mediterranean, as well as to other migratory movements across time and space. Appanah's approach, I argue, exists on a precarious ledge between the creative and ethical potential of new approaches to global migration, and the violence of the foreign gaze. This precarious equilibrium is crystallized in what I term the novel's incomplete polyphony: *Tropique de la violence* explores the crisis through metropolitan French and Mahoran subjectivities while paradoxically not engaging with those of the Comoran migrants themselves, the people *around* and *about* whom the entire text is woven. Particularly compelling, I demonstrate, is the narrative silencing of Mo's mother, which forces us to engage with two different kinds of literary violence: voicelessness and appropriation. Can silence, in making itself felt, be more impactful than the story it conceals?

Going beyond migration, the novel ironically highlights the cleavage between metropolitan France and the most destitute French overseas department. As the following section explains, Mayotte formed part of the Comoran archipelago until excised from it by the French in 1975. Its status as "French," therefore, is fraught with tension. Appanah's careful linguistic leitmotif underlines how Mayotte's poverty undermines its French status: Mayotte is perceived as *too poor* to be properly French. Simultaneously, it emphasizes how Mayotte's French status undermines the perception of its poverty: a French territory cannot be understood as *veritably poor*. Mayotte's political status as French, which can be twisted in contradictory ways, is thus ultimately rendered meaningless.

Weaving these strands together, I argue that *Tropique de la violence* takes a nuanced and often ironical approach to the facile equivalences between the Indian Ocean and the Mediterranean (in terms of migratory tragedy), as well as between Mayotte and France (in terms of political status). Finally, having addressed its entanglements of irony, global comparison, and silence, I examine the work's own complex positionality in the "global creative economy" (Lionnet and Jean-François). As a French-language novel written by a Mauritian author about Mayotte, does *Tropique de la violence* join the island itself in being too foreign, and yet not foreign enough?

The Lagoon-Cemetery

Grande Comore, Anjouan, Moheli, and Mayotte are the four islands comprising the volcanic archipelago of the Comoros, nestled in the Mozambique Channel between Mozambique and Madagascar. In addition to being culturally and historically linked to East Africa, including Madagascar, the Comoros have also been a French colony. The first three islands obtained independence in 1975, while Mayotte remained under French control. Although the United Nations has recognized the Comoros' sovereignty over Mayotte and urged France to leave the territory, Mayotte has officially been a French overseas department since 2011.

The political boundary erected between Mayotte and the rest of the Comoros disrupts an archipelagic ecosystem that has historically functioned through movement and exchange, and thus creates the inevitability of clandestine migration. Historically, geographically, culturally, and religiously, the four islands continue to form a cohesive unit, with numerous Anjouanese families dispersed across the two islands of Anjouan and Mayotte (Wicker). However, the two territories are now separated by significant economic disparity: the Comoros are among the poorest nations in the world, while Mayotte is a French territory and therefore part of the European Union. Since 1995, movement between Mayotte and the rest of the Comoran islands is restricted by the Balladur visa, the obtention of which is an important logistic and financial hurdle. It is therefore impossible for many Comorans to legally set foot on their ancestral land. The heartbreaking irony of the situation is best expressed in Comoran poet Soeuf Elbadawi's words: "Can one be a stranger or clandestine in the land of one's ancestors" (25). While Elbadawi's poetry in *Un dhikri pour nos morts: La rage entre les dents* (2013; *A Dhikr for Our Dead: Teeth Clenched in Rage*) generally subverts grammatical conventions by eliminating the use of punctuation marks, the absence of a question mark is here especially powerful. Even though the interrogative phrasing seeks to open up the possibility of non-belonging, its absurdity is its own answer.

As a result of the restrictions on movement between islands, Comoran migrants regularly lose their lives as they attempt to illegally cross the waters between Anjouan and Mayotte in little fishing boats known as kwasa kwasa. Official statistics are scarce, and vary across the border: As of February 2016, the minimum number of fatalities ranged from the French suggestion of seven thousand to its Comoran counterpart of fifty thousand ("Island of Death"). The waters of the Lagoon Island thus function as an "ultramarine cemetery" (Elbadawi 52). The irony of this fact is not lost on Appanah's character Stéphane, a young volunteer from metropolitan France: "Yes, now you're sure of it, it's the most beautiful lagoon in the whole world, since you've seen this emerald and opaline domain with your own eyes and, even if you know that hundreds of people drown there, you still say *It's the most beautiful lagoon in the world*" (118–19; italics in original). The circular emphases of Stéphane's assertion (beautiful-tragic-beautiful) highlight the island's illusory tropical beauty at the expense of its invisible tragedy.[2]

---

[2] As it challenges this misplaced emphasis, *Tropique de la violence* can be considered as part of a wider Indian Ocean literary trend of exploring "the underside of the postcard" when it comes to exotic insular locations, with notable examples including Ananda Devi's *Ève de ses décombres* (2006; *Eve out of Her Ruins*) and Shenaz Patel's *Paradis blues* (2014; *Paradise Blues*).

Tragedy, indeed, constitutes the driving impulse of the novel. *Tropique de la violence* follows the life trajectory of a young boy, Moïse, nicknamed Mo. He reaches Mayotte as a swaddled newborn in the arms of his mother, a clandestine migrant from the Comoros. Abandoned that very night, Mo is adopted by a white nurse, Marie, and spends a comfortable childhood with her. But when Marie abruptly passes away, a teenage Mo is drawn into the orbit of Bruce, the young gang leader of Mayotte's shantytown Kaweni, also known as Gaza. Under Bruce's influence, Mo gets caught up in a downward spiral of violence and poverty that characterizes the lives of many clandestine teenagers on the island. Despite the best intentions of Stéphane, the NGO volunteer from metropolitan France, and Olivier, the Mahoran police officer who is sensitive to the complex reasons for youth delinquency, Mo meets a heartbreaking end.

A Novel Cartography of Migration

In the early days of September 2015, a three-year-old Syrian child, Alan Kurdi, drowned in the Mediterranean Sea as his family tried to reach Europe. The picture of the toddler's corpse immediately became a symbol of the Mediterranean refugee crisis. It prompted strong reactions from heads of state around the world, who committed to taking a more proactive stance to stanch the human costs of migration. However, even at this juncture of heightened global awareness and media sensationalism with respect to clandestine migration, Mayotte's crisis remained utterly ignored by France.

For Emmanuel Bruno Jean-François, the effectiveness of the quote from Olivier's chapter that I cite as this essay's epigraph, as well as Appanah's broader project of linking migratory histories, lies in its ability to generate "transoceanic empathy." By showing how the tragic loss of lives transcends geopolitical boundaries but is paradoxically regulated by the "selective ordering of human lives" (126), it places much-needed focus on our common humanity. *Tropique de la violence* thus successfully "mediates a form of recognition" of the migrants from the Comoros, and strategically generates empathy for their plight (127).

However, unlike Jean-François, I argue that the above assimilation between the (presumably familiar) Mediterranean tragedy and the (presumably unknown) Indian Ocean situation, as well as the empathy it generates, may be problematic. The text represents the humanity of the Comoran migrants as a logical progression to that of their Mediterranean counterparts, rather than a self-evident truth. This mediation itself reads like a form of violence. What are the effects of going "there" and then saying "here, too," as though the "here" did not mean as much without the "there"? What are the dangers of using the continental European reference point to understand the tragedy in the Indian Ocean, and of making the Mediterranean the de facto center for conversations on contemporary migration—similar, perhaps, to the way in which the Holocaust was long used as the benchmark for academic discussions of trauma? As R. Radhakrishnan reminds us, "comparisons are never neutral: they are inevitably tendentious, didactic, competitive, and prescriptive. . . . Comparisons are never disinterested" (454). And even less so when the two areas under comparison are Africa and Europe, continents already entangled in a long history of power asymmetries, with the former constantly being judged by the standards of the latter.

As reviewer Fouad Ahamada Tadjiri points out, by representing Comoran clandestine migrants as moving principally for economic reasons, like their Mediterranean counterparts, *Tropique de la violence* negates the specificity of Comoran migrants on Mahoran land—land which is *ancestrally theirs*. The Comoros/Mayotte situation is reduced to the illegal movement of people over the border; there is no consideration of the prior—and equally illegal—*movement of a border* over a single people. Additionally, the presumption of familiarity with the Mediterranean context also makes clear that the intended audience of the work is metropolitan French. It means that the Mauritian, Haitian, or New Caledonian francophone reader learning about Comoran clandestine crossings through Appanah's work must necessarily pass through the references to Lampedusa and Alan Kurdi, when other migration crises might be as close, if not closer, to their lived experiences, and thus just as relatable. Empathy, then, is unidirectional. It flows from the "default humans" who have the luxury of feeling it to the "empathy vehicles" who have the misfortune of evoking it (Serpell).

I argue that the power of Appanah's project lies less in its (problematic) evocation of empathy across oceans, and more in its direct confrontation of the unequal terrain across which connections are made. As Shu-mei Shih argues in her definition of relational comparison, to compare ethically is to actively engage with this unequal surface:

Comparison as relation means setting into motion historical relationalities between entities brought together for comparison, and bringing into relation terms that have traditionally been pushed apart from each other due to certain interests, such as the European exceptionalism that undergirds Eurocentrism. The excavation of these relationalities is what I consider to be the ethical practice of comparison, where the workings of power are not concealed but necessarily revealed. Power, after all, is a form of relation. (79)

Adopting precisely this commitment to address rather than ignore power relations, Appanah underscores that despite the similarities between the two cases, Mayotte remains stuck in a "parallel dimension" (*Tropic* 42). As the following section demonstrates, if this separate realm is itself a product of global asymmetry, disequilibrium also exists even *within* it: while Olivier has the narrative space to decry injustice, Comoran migrants, such as Mo's mother, do not enjoy the same privilege.

An Incomplete Polyphony

In *Tropique de la violence*'s polyphonic structure, two of the five foregrounded voices are from metropolitan France (Marie and Stéphane), and the remaining three are Mahoran (Bruce, Mo, and Olivier), with Olivier also the law enforcement function of the French state.[3] The clandestine migrants themselves, those around and about whom this entire story is woven, are silenced: "Do they even have a story?" (Tadjiri) This fact is best evidenced through Appanah's narrative treatment of Mo's mother. Despite the author's avowed commitment to "the life of the nonpowerful, the outsiders, those forgotten by history" (Appanah, *Une année* 59), Mo's mother is only ever heard uttering a couple of fearful sentences in a language that

---

[3] Appanah brilliantly crafts Mahoran identity to mean something unique to each of these characters. Mo, for example, is "the illegal *with papers*" (Ravi 77), given his situation as the child of an undocumented migrant, who was subsequently duplicitously legally recognized by Marie's husband.

is clearly not her own—"Him baby of the djinn," "Him bring bad luck with his eye," "You love him, you take him" (*Tropic* 14)—before disappearing into the night. We see her committing the unadmirable act of abandoning her child on account of his heterochromia, but never learn about the harsh circumstances—such as extreme poverty and lack of education—that led her to this course of action. The closest we come is Mo's reconstruction of the past:

> My mother handed me over, like an old parcel, to the first person who came along but I know now that it wasn't her fault, I know now you need money to go on a kwassa-kwassa, you need courage to go on board these fragile boats. I know now what it looks like, that beach at Bandrakouni, with its baobab trees that resemble ramparts, I know you need to feel something else in your bowels apart from just pity and fear. I know you need a little love. (*Tropic* 124–25)

Despite Mo's attempt to place himself in his biological mother's shoes, neither he nor the reader ever gains access to the latter's subjectivity. In this respect, she is like other poor women of color evoked in the novel, such as the second wife of Marie's ex-husband Cham, who is herself an undocumented immigrant (*Tropic* 9–11), Bruce's mother (69), and the Malagasy prostitute that Bruce sleeps with (117). In *Tropique de la violence,* the only woman to be heard is Marie, the white nurse from France. In the novel's first chapter, we gain access to her early adulthood (*Tropic* 3–4), her love story with Cham (4–5), and the female infertility that drives a wedge in their marriage and leads Marie to act with bitter virulence toward other women: she fantasizes about denouncing the clandestine status of Cham's second wife to the authorities (*Tropic* 11), harshly judges the pregnant women who come to give birth on Mayotte's shores (8), and chases away, with a stick, the little clandestine girl who is only looking for food (9). Marie's questionable attitudes make it somewhat uncomfortable for us, as readers, to inhabit her thoughts. However, precisely because we are privy to her deep, unfathomable sadness at being without child, we are able to understand, if not excuse, her actions. *Tropique de la violence* does not give us any such possibility of intimacy with the subaltern women figures. At the end of the day, we are ultimately left holding an asymmetrical narrative between our hands, where those from metropolitan France once again dominate the narratives.

However, Appanah's choice to leave the Comoran migrant's story shrouded in mystery merits deeper reflection. After all, when one is unable to engage in accurate or ethical representation, there might be more value and respect in drawing attention to silence without trying to fill it in. If *Tropique de la violence* does not offer us the migrant's subjectivity, it nonetheless points to its *past existence* and *present irrecoverability.* During the first chapter, Appanah's choice to render the Comoran migrant's words in grammatically incorrect French hints at an insurmountable linguistic barrier: no matter how much the migrant might wish to speak with complexity and abundance, she is constrained by the (colonial) language she will be understood in, both within the novel (by Marie) and beyond it (by the reader). The linguistic violence committed unto the migrant trickles down to the reader in the form of an incomplete narrative *that makes itself felt.* The absence of the migrant's narrative from the novel is a self-aware reflection of the world's inhospitability to such stories—the self-awareness being evidenced by the shift from Marie's fluid prose to the migrant's short, hacked fragments of speech. For Srilata Ravi, Appanah's rejection of straightforward representation, to instead make us aware of our own "intrusive gaze" on the clandestine migrant, is precisely what distinguishes *Tropique de la violence* from common discourse on clandestine migration (83).

Additionally, rather than removing Mo's mother from the novel after her narrative function is completed, Appanah later leads us all the way to the Bandrakouni beach and forces us, together with Mo, to confront the questions that the text leaves unanswered: "The tides had washed away their footprints on the black sand, the wind had blown back their shouts across the open sea.... Had she been afraid then? In the dark during the crossing? Had I cried?" (*Tropic* 111). These questions have no answers, but it is nonetheless crucial to pose them. As Saidiya Hartman tells us, it is important to acknowledge the impossibility of knowing the female subaltern experience that is lost to history and to "respect the limits of what cannot be known" (4) rather than "committing further violence in [one's] own act of narration" (2).[4] For Ravi, this conundrum productively challenges the novelistic project itself, by making us, readers and writers, aware of our own invasiveness and inadequateness when it comes to accessing the clandestine migrant's experience. The violence of silence, here, might be less brutal than that of narrative appropriation. Sometimes, a story must refuse to be told.

Beyond the Mediterranean

Ultimately, *Tropique de la violence* tethers the clandestine migration in Mayotte to not only illegal movements in the Mediterranean but also to migration across distinct historical and geographical contexts, that both encompass and exceed Indian Ocean circularities:

> But in the end maybe it's just the same old story, one heard a hundred times before, one told a hundred times before. The story of a country that shines brightly, where everyone wants to be. There are names for it: El Dorado, mirage, paradise, chimera, utopia, Lampedusa. It's the story of those boats that people here call kwassa-kwassas, elsewhere they're known as barques, dugout canoes, ships, vessels. They have existed since the dawn of time, carrying people from place to place, willingly or against their will. It's the story of the human beings aboard these vessels and since the dawn of time these are the names they've been given: slaves, volunteers, lepers, convicts, repatriated settlers, Jews, boat people, refugees, stowaways, illegal immigrants. (*Tropique de la violence* 42–43)

In the above quote, which inspires Jean-François's conception of "kinships of the sea," Appanah's intention is to foster identification for the Mahoran tragedy by assimilating it to other migratory movements, including, but this time also *transcending*, the Mediterranean context. Her insistence on linguistic constructions of alterity—"that people here call," "elsewhere they're known as," "these are the names they've been given"—suggests that the differences between migrations might be more the product of human compartmentalization rather than inherent. Let us note that Appanah has previously written about two of these crossings: the *kala pani* crossing of indentured laborers (the "engagés" mistranslated as "volunteers") in her first novel *Les rochers de Poudre d'Or* (2003; *The Rocks of Gold Dust*), and the doomed odyssey of Jewish refugees in her fourth novel *Le dernier frère* (2007; *The Last Brother*). Both novels productively engage in what Michael Rothberg calls "multidirectional memory": they show how memories of different historical traumas—enslavement and indentured labor in *The Rocks of Gold Dust*; the postcolonial

---

[4] Drawing from Glissant, Jean-François argues that such opacity co-constitutes rather than opposes the project of empathy—one should not have to completely penetrate the other's mind in order to empathize with them (125).

condition and the Holocaust in *The Last Brother*—co-constitute rather than oppose each other.[5] In the same vein, the aforementioned quote engages in a multidirectional approach to migration: To weave the following migratory movements in an enumerative sequence is to compare relationally—that is, to examine how such movements form part of a dynamic, global ecosystem that is constantly, and intentionally, portrayed as fragmented. If Shih is clear that comparison as relation aims to "[bring] into relation terms that have traditionally been pushed apart from each other due to *certain interests*" (79; emphasis mine), Ravi is even more forceful and specific with regards to the political necessity of a more holistic approach toward migration: "Indeed, the 'migrant crisis,' a sociopolitical construction created by rich countries, deserves a transnational treatment in order to demystify the 'threat' that it is supposed to present, and expose the human rights violation perpetrated everywhere in the world in the name of national security" (75). Thus, in a world where sensational rhetoric surrounding migration "crises" has led to a rise in xenophobia and fulfills specific political agendas, Appanah's attempt to portray migration as a multifaceted yet coherent human history (rather than the separate histories of separate peoples) might allow us to see beyond politically expedient mirages and pave the way for a deeper understanding of this timeless phenomenon. It is the same commitment to nuance that leads Appanah to dismantle the facile equation between the island-territory of Mayotte and the French nation, which I explore in the next section.

"Mayotte, c'est la France"

Examining the leitmotif of "Mayotte, c'est la France" ("Mayotte is France"; translation modified) throughout *Tropique de la violence* sheds important light on the complexities of Mayotte's political status as a French territory. The first assertion of "Mayotte, c'est la France" underlines the cleavage between a "developed" nation and its most impoverished region. Landing in Mayotte for the first time, Stéphane is stupefied at the diseased bodies and abject poverty that he encounters: "I then made the stupidest remark of my life, *But, for heaven's sake, we're in France here!*" (*Tropic* 96; italics in original). His statement betrays deep cognitive dissonance: how to reconcile the idea of a "developed" nation with the dehumanizing conditions that he witnesses? The linguistic equivalence that Stéphane draws between France and Mayotte rings more powerfully in French rather than English: "Mayotte, c'est la France" (*Tropique* 112) translates literally to "Mayotte is France," (translation modified) rather than translator Strachan's more elegant but less literal "Mayotte is still part of France" (95), which unfortunately does away with the ambiguities of Appanah's ironic phrasing.

Tadjiri argues that Appanah simply reproduces the French *mappa mundi*: "For Nathacha Appanah, Mayotte is France. No ambiguity on the subject." Tadjiri interprets the statement as the author's own perspective, rather than that of a flawed character who is himself *ironically* put into question. Françoise Lionnet and

---

Jean-François argue that irony is one of the multiple "survival tactics" deployed by minor francophone authors in order to covertly critique, rather than flagrantly contradict, the demands of a global capitalist market anchored in the French metropole (1234). However, critics holding stereotyped expectations of minor texts may completely overlook such literary complexity (1229). Tadjiri thus fails to notice that Stéphane's technically correct factual statement is preceded by the qualification "the stupidest remark of my life," and met with laughter from the local fireman who shows him around: "Chebani laughed until tears came into his eyes" (*Tropic* 96). Chebani's laughter indicates the ridiculousness of a legal identity that does not translate into lived experience.

Throughout the novel, Appanah brilliantly conditions her characters' statements (which essentially convey the same thing: Mayotte is very different from France) to reflect their different class belongings: while Stéphane, with the privilege of money and distance, is indignant to realize the cleavage that exists between Mayotte and France, Bruce is equally incredulous of any possible equivalence. Recalling Mo's idyllic descriptions of his childhood, the teenage gang leader explodes into a furious, sometimes even vulgar, crescendo of rhetorical questions: "This is Mayotte here and you say it's France. Fuck off! Is France like this? . . . In France are there scores of kwassa-kwassas arriving with people landing on beaches, some of them already half dead? . . . In France do people shit and sling their trash into gullies like they do here?" (*Tropic* 80–81). The deep misery that Bruce evokes is thus veiled by a misleading political status, as the following section explores more deeply.

Searching for "Authentic" Poverty

Although Mayotte remains one of the most destitute parts of France, its designation as part of the European Union—"Mayotte, c'est la France"—is irreconcilable with popular conceptions of poverty. Thus, because of its affiliation with France, Mayotte's suffering remains illegible to institutions designed to identify and remedy need, such as the NGO that employs Stéphane. After all, despite its seemingly altruistic aims, the NGO itself is inscribed within a neoliberal framework, and its attractiveness to volunteers depends on a problematic commodification of poverty and legitimization of suffering:

> Just two of us had volunteered to come here. Mayotte is still part of France and no one was interested in that. The others wanted to go to Haiti, Sri Lanka, Bangladesh, Indonesia, Madagascar, Ethiopia. They wanted the "authentic" poverty. . . . The favorite destination that looks great on your CV was still Gaza, and I mean the real Gaza, in Palestine, but that was reserved for the most experienced volunteers. (*Tropic* 95)

Appanah mockingly draws up a list of regions that are fetishized as more exciting volunteer locations than Mayotte, and then dismantles it by multiplying the signified locations that can be attributable to the signifier "Gaza." Thus "the real Gaza, in Palestine" is contrasted with Mayotte's Gaza, the nickname given to the shantytown of Kaweni. Deprived of its own name, just like Mayotte is deprived of its own political status, Kaweni finds itself excluded from this global imaginary of violence. Positioning herself in Mayotte, Appanah thus creates a world that functions as multiple nodes in a network of violence, but in which Kaweni can only exist via linguistic and geographical proxy: "Gaza is a shantytown, a ghetto, a trash pile, a bottomless pit, a favela, a vast encampment of illegal immigrants, open to the skies. . . . Gaza is Capetown, it's Calcutta, it's Rio. Gaza is Mayotte, Gaza is France" (*Tropic* 41). The last line extends the parallel between Mayotte and France to enfold Gaza, the multiply signified space of violence. In the world of *Tropique de la violence*, it is linguistically— and therefore, ethically?—impossible to reflect upon poverty in a single spot: to feel for the poor people of Kaweni is also to feel for the poor in the constellation of other Gazas.

Appanah's commitment to centering Mayotte's invisibilized plight sometimes overflows into stereotypes. Let us examine, for example, Stéphane's inner struggle to comprehend the violence he feels is fermenting in Mayotte: "So you have a vision of hundreds of blacks coming down into the street with machetes and you no longer know whether it's an image from Rwanda or Zimbabwe or the Congo and you say *That'll never happen in a* département *of the French state*" (*Tropic* 119). The irony of Stéphane's last assertion is made clear at the end of the novel, when violence erupts on the streets of the island. However, no such nuance seems to underlie the textual depiction of Rwanda, Zimbabwe, and Congo as regions of violence par excellence. Thus, Appanah's effort to highlight the difference between Mayotte and the stereotype of a French department has the undesirable effect of erasing the differences between these individual African nations: all that remains are their common representation as interchangeable spaces of (imagined) violence, and their opposition to the French department (despite geographical and racial links that cannot be ignored).

Similarly, in the Mahoran context, Appanah's descriptions of Gaza's youth as invariably imbricated in theft and drugs correspond to prevalent clichés. Her attempts to go beyond this initial image—such as her exploration of the events leading up to Bruce's departure from the family home (*Tropic* 66–72)—evoke feelings of pity and indignation. Tadjiri points out all that she misses by relaying the words of Mahoran philosopher Touam Bona: "There are not only kids intoxicated by synthetic drugs. . . . There are especially lots of stigmatized young people and inhabitants, who struggle to stay afloat, who create solidarities, who experiment, who found micro-enterprises, who recycle, who do slam, who continue to go to school, despite everything." For critical race theorist Eve Tuck, attempts to portray and study communities that have undergone trauma may be described in two ways. A "damage-centered" approach is one that views trauma as a community's defining feature (412). On the other hand, a "desire-based" lens acknowledges trauma as part of the diversity and ambiguity of human experience (416). Drawing from Tuck's framework, Appanah is unable to move beyond a "damage-centered" view to one that is "desire-based": she traps the youth of Gaza in an oversimplified narrative of trauma that does not make space for their complex and ever-shifting experiences, including those of agency and resilience.

A Toothbrush of One's Own

The crowning irony of "Mayotte, c'est la France" is that those capable of improving the situation, such as French decision-makers, cannot comprehend it; simultaneously, those with on-the-ground experience, such as Olivier, are divested of the agency to effect change. Olivier, the Mahoran policeman, can be surprisingly tender toward those who are on the opposite side of the law. He is careful as he gathers up little Comoran corpses that wash up on the beach (*Tropic* 42), and he recognizes Bruce and Mo as children, instead of locking them in a narrative of criminality (*Tropic* 40,141). Olivier's reflections—including the one enshrined in the essay's epigraph—are nuanced and perceptive, much more so than the media rhetoric that reaches decision-makers in Paris. However, he divests himself of all agency— "I'm only a cop" (*Tropic* 42)—instead placing it in faraway figures of authority. Olivier keeps hoping "that someone, somewhere in the teams of top civil servants who follow in the wave of ministerial visits, among the historians and intellectuals who read newspapers, that someone would truly understand what's going on here and find a solution" (*Tropic* 42). It may seem here that *Tropique de la violence* is advocating for urgent awareness and action by metropolitan France in order to avert tragedy. However, the novel itself warns against the fallacy of imported knowledge, that can ultimately be irrelevant to the local context. Although Stéphane and Mo slowly become friends over the course of the novel, Mo hesitates to truly open up:

Stéphane could never understand things like that.... I've seen guys like him spending a few months in Gaza.... They know a lot of things, those guys, they know the figures on poverty, they know the statistics on petty crime, they study graphs of violence, words like culture and leisure spring readily to their lips, but they never truly understand anything.... There's no film screening or soccer match that can equal the fact of owning something, some object that belongs to you and you alone, even if it's only an old toothbrush. (106–7)

At the end of the quotation, Mo's assertion that no philanthropic activity could ever come close to true ownership suggests that no amount of seemingly benevolent foreign intervention can rival with the fact of having a country to call one's own. While *Tropique de la violence* constantly underlines the discrepancies between Mayotte's lived reality and its status as a French department, this may be the closest that the novel comes to truly questioning France's authority (rather than simply advocating for a better administration of this authority) over Mayotte.[6]

Literary Circulations: Mauritius to Mayotte, via France

Having explored how *Tropique de la violence* imagines the globe as a network of migration, as well as the complexity of Mayotte as a node that is both too-French and yet not-French-enough, it is now fitting to consider the novel's own migration and identity as a literary and commercial object. *Tropique de la violence* was first published in 2016 by the prestigious French publishing house Gallimard. It received a plethora of awards and was staged as a play in Paris in January 2021. The novel placed Mayotte's migratory tragedy on contemporary francophone literature's radar, and remains the most well-known work on the issue today.[7] Its author, Nathacha Appanah, was born and grew up in Mauritius, in a family whose ancestry can be traced to India. Appanah moved to metropolitan France in her mid-twenties, where she has since been living and writing. Like her compatriot Ananda Devi,

---

[6] This may be a case of the text speaking for itself, rather than reflecting the author's own political views: when speaking to the press, Appanah underscores the "immense attachment" that Mahoran people feel for France (Appanah, "Sur l'île Maurice").

[7] Appanah's commitment to centering Mayotte also modulated her weekly columns for *La croix*. See, for example, "Si vous vous étiez arrêté, Monsieur Macron, devant le cimetière des kwassas-kwassas...," published on June 8, 2017, and later reproduced under the title "Merci, Monsieur le Président" in *Une année lumière* (65–68).

Appanah is "a writer now considered major but linked to a minor location" (Lionnet and Jean-François 1229).

Just like the phrase "Mayotte is France" has been contorted to fit opposing arguments, the author's Mauritian origins have been weaponized to contradictory ends: they have been used to suggest that she is too foreign to write about Mayotte, but also that she cannot legitimately write about another context than the Indian Ocean. The author frontally addresses the debate in an interview in *Le monde*, a popular French daily:

But when I said in Mauritius that I was writing on Mayotte, I was sometimes told a very simple sentence: "Ah, you are returning to the Indian Ocean," as though it was good to return to the drawer to which I had been consigned. It's as though I was not legitimate to speak about anything else, but that I am with respect to the Indian Ocean. And, in Mayotte, I was made to understand that I was not Mahoran, but Mauritian.

Appanah thus joins Mayotte in being too foreign and yet not foreign enough. As evidenced by the quote above, Appanah is not seen as eligible to write about contexts other than the Indian Ocean by virtue of her birthplace. On the other hand, she also suffers from the suggestion that she is not Mahoran enough to be writing about Mahoran issues. This latter sentiment is echoed by Tadjiri, who seems to consider Appanah as a sellout who writes about her region for the European market, hence her choice of "a selling theme for an occidental reader, permanently solicited with respect to migrant questions." For Tadjiri, "[the novel] participates in a symbology [original: un *imaginaire*] of contempt towards the Comoran. . . . The same that has been pitting the Mahoran against his brothers from other islands for years, *except that here the re-writing of history emanates from a neighboring island, Mauritius*" (emphasis mine). While Tadjiri notes that Appanah creates from a space that is neither Mayotte nor Europe, he opines that the well-worn narrative and audience both ultimately fall into the latter's camp.

Both positions, however, raise important objections. To demand that a writer only write about what they know, or where they hail from, is to severely reduce the imaginative possibilities afforded by literature. For Appanah, it puts into question the very "objective" of the craft: "I always thought that the objective of my work was to write stories but especially to incarnate *others* than I" (*Une année* 58). Such criticisms also fall into the trap of "peg[ging] authorial identity as fixed and rooted rather than dynamic and linked to multiple and simultaneous spaces of belonging" (Lionnet and Jean-François 1229). By overlooking the fact that "the division between the local and the global has never been intellectually viable for multitudes of border-crossing cultural agents" (Lionnet and Jean-François 1228), they fail to take into account the fact that not only is it possible and legitimate for Appanah to write about migrations both in the Indian Ocean and in the rest of the world, but it is also quite natural, given her simultaneous and multiple belongings, that she should think and write them *with* and *through* each other. However, like other minor francophone authors making their voices heard in France and beyond, she must do this in a way that both exists within and yet subverts the non-trivial expectations linked to her origins (Lionnet and Jean-François 1229). Both the author and the island that she describes, thus, survive in a space of tension, imbricated within a global system of circulation that however resists fully embracing them.

Conclusion

Ultimately, not "French" enough to fulfill the golden dreams of migrants who risk their lives to reach its shores, and yet too "French" to fit into the fantasies of the metropolitan's volunteers who want an immediately recognizable charity-destination, Mayotte is caught in a painful limbo of clandestine migration, poverty, and violence. This situation can be productively linked, but not neatly reduced, to other migratory movements across time and space. And therefrom arises the question at the heart of *Tropique de la violence*: as she strives to explore the complexity of the Mahoran situation in a way that is accessible to a French audience, does Appanah compromise the very literary quality and ethical premises of her work?

The answer to this question is not straightforward. *Tropique de la violence* is clearly not without weaknesses. Its attempt to link clandestine migration in the Indian Ocean to the Mediterranean does not take crucial differences into account and represents the humanity of the Comoran migrants as a logical progression to that of their Mediterranean counterparts, rather than a self-evident truth. It channels voices from metropolitan France while silencing at best, and stereotyping at worst, those from the Comoros.

Nevertheless, the silence of the Comoran migrant does not simply fade into the background, but rather foregrounds the unrepresentability of certain stories. *Tropique de la violence*'s comparative approach carves a new landscape of global migration and violence that pushes against politically expedient discourses of difference. It makes skillful use of irony to shed light on the discrepancy between Mayotte's legal status and lived experience. And ultimately, looking at the broader picture, the widely acclaimed novel undeniably performs the important work of combating the very apathy that Appanah decries and that continues to shroud the island today. As the Mahoran situation itself swells in complexity, with rising numbers of clandestine migrants arriving from Madagascar and the African Great Lakes area, the value of such work cannot be underestimated.

If Appanah does reproduce the foreign gaze, then, it is not without a degree of ironical self-awareness, or demonstrated commitment to drawing attention to the plight of Mayotte's clandestine migrants. Both conversation and irony, however, must be actively engaged with. Such engagement is not easy, but it is necessary. Migratory movements around the world are increasingly intertwined, in reality as well as in the news and art that we consume. Whether we are aware of it or not, as citizens of an (unequally) globalized world, we are, just like Appanah, inevitably thinking of these migrations in relation to each other. But connection does not imply equality. The politically correct answer to Olivier's question—"Lives on this land matter just as much as all those lives on other lands, don't they?"—may be obvious, but it remains untrue. By forcing us to examine the connections and disjunctions created by our own (sub)consciousness, as well as the treacherous terrain across which they stretch, *Tropique de la violence* refuses to let us turn away from this discrepancy.

Harvard University

Works Cited

Appanah, Nathacha. *The Last Brother,* translated by Geoffrey Strachan. Minneapolis, MN: Graywolf Press, 2011.

Appanah, Nathacha. *Le dernier frère*. Paris: Olivier, 2007.

Appanah, Nathacha. *Les rochers de Poudre d'Or*. Paris: Gallimard, 2003.

Appanah, Nathacha. "Sur l'île Maurice, il y a une vraie dynamique littéraire." Interview by Gladys Marivat and Pierre Lepidi. *Le monde*, September 14, 2016. www.lemonde.fr/afrique/article/2016/09/14 /nathacha-appanah-a-l-ile-maurice-il-y-a-une-vraie-dynamique-des-auteurs_4997365_3212.html.

Appanah, Nathacha. *Tropic of Violence*, translated by Geoffrey Strachan. Minneapolis, MN: Greywolf, 2020.

Appanah, Nathacha. *Tropique de la violence*. Paris: Gallimard, 2016.

Appanah, Nathacha. *Une année lumière: Chroniques*. Paris: Gallimard, 2018.

Devi, Ananda. *Ève de ses décombres*. Paris: Gallimard, 2006.

Devi, Ananda. *Eve out of Her Ruins*, translated by Jeffrey Zuckerman. Dallas, TX: Deep Vellum, 2016.

Elbadawi, Soeuf. *Un dhikri pour nos morts: La rage entre les dents*. Paris: Vents d'Ailleurs, 2013.

Hartman, Saidiya V. "Venus in Two Acts." *Small Axe*, no. 26 (2008): 1–14.

"Island of Death." *Al Jazeera World,* February 3, 2016. https://www.aljazeera.com/program/al-jazeera -world/2016/2/3/island-of-death.

Jean-François, Emmanuel Bruno. "Kinships of the Sea: Comparative History, Minor Solidarity, and Transoceanic Empathy." In *Reframing Postcolonial Studies*, edited by David Kim, 113–34. London: Palgrave Macmillan, 2021.

Lionnet, Françoise, and Emmanuel Bruno Jean-François. "Literary Routes: Migration, Islands, and the Creative Economy." *PMLA* 131, no. 5 (2016): 1222–38.

Patel, Shenaz. *Paradis Blues*. Paris: Vents d'ailleurs, 2014.

Radhakrishnan, R. "Why Compare?" *New Literary History* 40, no. 3 (2009): 453–71.

Ravi, Srilata. "Eaux troubles: Migrations clandestines dans *The Illegal* de Lawrence Hill et *Tropique de la Violence* de Nathacha Appanah." *Canadian Review of Comparative Literature* 47, no. 1 (2020): 74–87.

Rothberg, Michael. *Multidirectional Memory: Remembering the Holocaust in the Age of Decolonization*. Redwood City, CA: Stanford University Press, 2009.

Serpell, Namwali. "The Banality of Empathy." *New York Review,* March 2, 2019. www.nybooks.com/daily /2019/03/02/the-banality-of-empathy.

Shih, Shu-mei. "Comparison as Relation." In *Comparison: Theories, Approaches, Uses*, edited by Rita Felski and Susan Stanford, 79–98. Baltimore, MD: Johns Hopkins University Press, 2013.

Tadjiri, Ahamada. "Critique: *Tropique de la violence* de Natacha Appanah." *Africultures*, December 15, 2016. africultures.com/tropique/de/la/violence/13894.

Tuck, Eve. "Suspending Damage: A Letter to Communities." *Harvard Educational Review* 79, no. 3 (2009): 409–28.

Wicker, Elise. "France's Migrant 'Cemetery' in Africa." *BBC News*, October 19, 2015. www.bbc.com/news /magazine-34548270.

WEIHSIN GUI

Indian Ocean Narratives, Tidalectics, and Perth's Centre for Stories

INTRODUCING *WAVE AFTER Wave: Writers from the Indian Ocean*, editor Robert Wood states that this anthology, besides being informed by the contributors' "places and identities," is also about "how we frame, narrate, and write about our worlds" to show "other forms of belonging" that include and go beyond "the national" (10). Wood's statement recognizes the multiple histories of the anthology's contributors, who hail from different countries surrounding the Indian Ocean. It also suggests the anthology's form shapes and frames how Indian Ocean experiences are narrated, and furthermore creates a sense of transnational sociality and belonging that critiques national imaginaries without canceling them out. These transnational social bonds are alluded to by Wood when he describes how the contributors to *Wave after Wave* were "encouraged by mentors within a community" at the Centre for Stories in Perth, Western Australia, "that cares about where we come from, and that has rhizomes and roots and branches in a great many spaces elsewhere" (introduction 10–11) both in Australia and along the Indian Ocean's rim. Using Wood's meditations as a starting point, I argue in this essay that scholars working on the literatures of the Indian Ocean should pay attention to literary anthologies such as *Wave after Wave* in addition to single-author texts by acclaimed authors such as Amitav Ghosh. Through their form and arrangement, anthologies collecting the works of new and emerging writers can generate fresh ways of understanding the overlapping, polyphonic histories and socialities of those who traverse and look back across the Indian Ocean. Examining two literary anthologies resulting from writing mentorships organized by the Centre for Stories, I propose that reading the Indian Ocean anthologically requires attention to what Kamau Brathwaite calls tidalectics, an aesthetics informed by cyclical movements that overlay and interleave the meanings expressed by disparate, individual pieces in an anthology. On a larger level, I suggest that literary scholars might think about anthologies beyond their utility as instruments for teaching or canon formation. Instead of selectively reading pieces from an anthology (as is often the case with classroom-facing anthologies), it may be productive to peruse a thematic anthology cover to cover and treat it as a circulatory and fluid form, representing

Comparative Literature 74:2
DOI 10.1215/00104124-9594865   © 2022 by University of Oregon

what Engseng Ho calls the circulation and disaggregation-reaggregation of socio-cultural elements within its pages (919).

Reading Anthologically

It is worth distinguishing between two main types of literary anthologies. First, there are anthologies specifically designed for pedagogical use, the most famous being those published by W. W. Norton. As Jeffrey Di Leo observes in the collection *On Anthologies*, "anthologies are shaped by pedagogies, and pedagogies shape anthologies" ("Analyzing" 1–2); anthologies "have a key role in canon-formation" and are often contested sites when national literary traditions are taught in schools (5). Several critics in that volume discuss the cultural capital and politics of such canon-forming, classroom-facing anthologies (see Damrosch; Lawall; Kilcup). However, I am interested in another type of anthology that has a specific thematic focus, because the two published by the Centre for Stories are not ostensibly intended for pedagogical use. In contrast to Norton's anthologies that are assertively marketed by the publisher to schools and educators, *Ways of Being Here* and *Wave after Wave* are publications of small, independent presses and lack mass-market circulation and distribution. Instead, they aim to give (mainly Australian) readers a sense of writing from and about the Indian Ocean. A thematic anthology, suggests Alan Schrift in "Confessions of an Anthology Editor," aims at something "much smaller than tradition-creation; it can introduce a new field to an audience" that "doesn't yet know enough about the particular field to be interested" (193). This introduction can offer a critical lens instead of a panoramic survey, as Tsitsi Jaji argues in "Zimbabwe in Verse: Anthologizing an Alternative Historiography." Examining poetry anthologies instead of novels (which are more commonly associated with national imaginaries), Jaji argues "that anchoring a literary reading of national history in the poetry anthology reveals how such collections chant an ever-evolving polyphonic vision, a crucial counterpoint to the political rallies that chant their presbyopic slogans in strict unison" (611). These Zimbabwean anthologies "establish the trope of a collection as an act of constitution, gathering individuals into a cooperative" instead of a monolithic national subject (612). Adopting a regional approach in "'Towards a New Oceania': On Contemporary Pacific Islander Poetry Networks," Craig Santos Perez describes how reading Pacific Islander poetry anthologies was an introduction not only to a body of verse but also the region's multifaceted history and aesthetic practices. Perez coins the phrase "reading *anthologically*" to describe how these anthologies "encouraged [him] to address the major themes that past generations have addressed but from [his] own perspective and experience" and reading in this fashion "also gave [him] permission to explore diverse aesthetics knowing that there is no single style that defines Pacific literature" (245). Furthermore, "these anthologies can be imagined as maps of the New Oceania, as vessels upon which readers can imaginatively journey across and learn about the region" (245).

Perez's metaphors of anthologies as maps and vessels or ships mark a turn away from earlier tropes of literary anthologies as culinary feasts or floral garlands (discussed by Barbara Benedict in *Making the Modern Reader: Cultural Mediation in Early Modern Literary Anthologies*). Maps and vessels instead gesture toward imaginative acts of relational wayfinding and knowledge production. Even though Perez is working in the context of the Pacific Islands, his account of how anthologies enable a thematic conversation with earlier poets and make him aware of multiple aesthetic practices from which he can draw and to which he can contribute echoes what Engseng Ho, in a discussion of inter-Asian socioeconomic spaces, describes as circulation and disaggregation-reaggregation. Adapted for my analysis, circulation can be understood as movements of literary-cultural actors and elements creating spatiotemporal "stability" and "substance" without the monolithic "fixity" and "perdurance of relations" associated with "notions of structure" (Ho 921). A literary-cultural approach to disaggregation and reaggregation would "unpack" and recognize individual authors and texts within a larger body of work, then trace how their "mobilities" allow them to be "transplanted" within a different literary-cultural space as part of another collective corpus (919). Perez's process of reading anthologically tracks the circulation and different iterations of major themes across literary space-time in the Pacific Islands anthologies; he is able to disaggregate aesthetic practices employed by poets past while reaggregating and transplanting them into verse of his own, providing maps and vessels for readers to imagine the Pacific Islands through anthologies that look to the past while voyaging toward a new present.

While it may seem unusual to employ Perez's idea of reading anthologically, mooted in a Pacific context, to analyses of literature about the Indian Ocean, several studies of the latter have assayed an inter- or transregional approach. Gaurav Desai's *Commerce with the Universe* brings African and South Asian literatures into conversation with each other, highlighting an "Afrasian imagination" that can "shed light on the circulation of people, ideas, and goods over the longue durée in conditions of relative conviviality and also those of gross injustices and inequalities" (18). Shifting from continents to islands, in their essay "Literary Routes: Migration, Islands, and the Creative Economy" Françoise Lionnet and Emmanuel Bruno Jean-François focus on francophone writers from the western arc of the Indian Ocean who "exemplify forms of translocality capable of undermining notions of static belonging" (1228) and convey an "alternate geography of transnational connections and minor relations" (1234). In *The Global Indies*, Ashley L. Cohen looks at how the East Indies and the West Indies were imagined in eighteenth-century British literature through a "discursive practice of linking Britain's colonies in India and the Americas" (9), staging an inter-regional comparison between Indian Ocean and Atlantic worlds. The Atlantic is also a comparative body in Isabel Hofmeyr's essay "The Black Atlantic Meets the Indian Ocean," which argues that a three-way comparison of "the black Atlantic, the Indian Ocean, and Africa" can bring about new approaches in Global South scholarship (4). In another essay on "Styling Multilateralism: Indian Ocean Cultural Futures," Hofmeyr situates Indian Ocean literary-cultural texts within overlapping global frameworks of colonialism and Cold War geopolitics, coupled with anti-imperial resistance and nonalignment, suggesting that Indian Ocean writing evinces a "depth of temporalities forged through a longue durée of connection and disconnection, mobility and dislocation" (99).

This is not to say that contemporary novels cannot represent such (dis)connections and movements. Françoise Lionnet's "Shipwrecks, Slavery, and the Challenge of Global Comparison: From Fiction to Archive" looks at Amitav Ghosh's novels to show how "one can read between the lines in order to begin to imagine another world than the one presented in archival materials that mainly reflect a colonialist mentality," and "how historic proximities" across the Indian Ocean "created new hybrid cultures, structured mentalities, and transformed languages" (452, 453). However, bearing in mind the polyphonic and collective importance of poetry anthologies highlighted by Jaji and Perez, is it not possible that anthologies containing pieces by multiple authors may be just as, if not more, representative of the Indian Ocean's proximities and hybridities in comparison to a single-author novel? If, according to Hofmeyr, the Indian Ocean world is constituted by connection-disconnection and mobility-dislocation across time, then Indian Ocean literary anthologies may be apt vehicles to represent a circulation of ideas, cultures, and people as they are disaggregated and reaggregated within an anthology's pages. Thematic anthologies invite readers to actively trace obvious and oblique connections and resonances between separate but adjacent authors and texts, to reaggregate meaning in specific clusters of constitutive pieces that may be guided by but also depart from the editorial vision. Thinking of the anthology as a circulatory and fluid form rather than a strictly structured container of various pieces allows us to consider how Caribbean poet and critic Kamau Brathwaite's idea of tidalectics might be a useful way to read anthologically.

Thinking Tidalectically

For Kamau Brathwaite, tidalectics departs from Western philosophy's "Hegelian" dialectic, with its "the notion of one-two-three" (thesis, antithesis, synthesis), and is inspired by "the movement of water backwards and forwards as a kind of cyclic . . . motion, rather than linear" ("Interview" 14). Brathwaite speaks of "discovering" his own experiences and fashioning them into poetry; he tries "to overlay [them], one on top of the other, and interleave them wherever possible. But it is an effort there to try to perceive some coherence out of the various shafts of intuition" (18). Brathwaite further emphasizes the overlapping and intercalated aspects of tidalectics when he remarks on "an increasing interleaving of experience rather than a linear movement" in his recent poetry (19). Tidalectics is also informed by "the history of the sense of migration" (23) in which "people have by their very contiguity influenced each other" in an "interlapping of experiences" (23–24). This stress on interleaving, interlapping, and contiguity suggests a formal and structural arrangement very similar to that of an anthology with its arrangement of distinct yet contiguous and sometimes interlapping pieces.

Here it is worth noting that, regarding Indian Ocean literary form, Meg Samuelson offers the idea of an amphibian aesthetic related to coastal form developed through astute analyses of Indian Ocean novels. In "Abdulrazak Gurnah's Fictions of the Swahili Coast: Littoral Locations and Amphibian Aesthetics," Samuelson focuses on Gurnah's novels, in which the "most consistent structure of feeling that the coast elicits" is a prevalent "melancholia that attends ambivalent loss" (502, 500). The beach as a distinctive coastal feature generates Gurnah's "complex vantage point" that is "poised between land and sea, ambivalently constituted and abjected by colonial and nationalist orders" (506); on its sandy shore "fragments of stories" are "washing up" and from these "flotsam and jetsam" larger narratives are constructed (511). In "Coastal Form: Amphibian Positions, Wider Worlds, and Planetary Horizons on the African Indian Ocean Littoral," Samuelson explains that in an amphibian aesthetic "sensory reception is oriented simultaneously towards land and sea, interior and exterior, here and there," and it "present[s] different voices jostling alongside one another and stories-within-stories that complicate distinctions between inside and outside" (20). Without taking anything away from Samuelson's insights, I argue that amphibian aesthetics might not be best suited for understanding Indian Ocean anthologies. First, Samuelson's analysis focuses on single-author novels by Abdulrazah Gurnah and Mia Cuoto, whereas anthologies are, obviously, the product of multiple authors and editorial choices. The reaggregated visions of *Ways of Being Here* and *Wave after Wave* set them qualitatively and quantitatively apart from novels that are authored by an individual, even if that single author may juxtapose multiple voices and perspectives. Second, amphibian aesthetics seems to rely on the liminal geographical and metaphorical site of the beach or coast for its constitution, but in many of the anthologies' pieces there are no mentions of littoral locations. In fact, sometimes it is hard to pin down a specific place described or evoked in a particular piece of writing. Third, melancholy is arguably not the prevailing feeling or mood in both anthologies. While some contributors do look wistfully to their countries of origin, many more express a determination to make themselves heard and at home in Australia, their country of residence, with humor and conviviality. Therefore, Brathwaite's formulation of tidalectics may offer a better framing of the aesthetics in the Centre for Stories' Indian Ocean anthologies.

One might even argue that, when Brathwaite brings up tidalectics in his long prose poem "New Gods of the Middle Passages," he elaborates the idea by crafting a miniature anthology consisting of disparate pieces by separate authors. Near the poem's end, Brathwaite alerts readers about "what happenin to this talk: the repetition the overlapping of xperiences the concept at last of what I call tidalectics" (45). Over the next six pages, as he explains the meaning and importance of tidalectics, Brathwaite offers long quotations from texts by four writers to flesh out his thinking: Angela Cole's collection of essays *In the Spirit of Diana* (46), another of Brathwaite's long poems *Soweto* (47), James Baldwin's novel *Tell Me How Long the Train's Been Gone* (47–48), and Philip Sherlock's poem "Long Mountain Rise" (48–49). Together, this combination of poetry and prose by different Caribbean and African American writers enables Brathwaite to explain how tidalectics is a Sisyphean idea that refuses to give in to lamentation or despair when "something is slowly—sometimes almost immediately—once again being eroded," and bears a "responsibility . . . to start again. To pick up that burden of Sisyphus & try again and again" (47). In addition to Sisyphus, at the end of the tidalectics section Brathwaite offers "a second icon": a personification of the country of Rwanda, "her heart almost now hopeless but still hopefull—that's the point—still movingly tidalectic even as she reaches the eye of the desert of yr camera" (51). Brathwaite's idea of tidalectics as a persistent, cyclical effort performed in the face of repeated failure might be useful for thinking about the anthology as form. Even if anthologies contain clear thematic sections defined by an editorial preface, they do not always move toward a telos that resoundingly knits together all their component pieces. Instead, there may be clusters or accretions of meaning in each section. Brathwaite's movingly tidalectic turn toward the almost hopeless but still hopeful personification of Rwanda is also pertinent for the Centre for Stories' Indian Ocean anthologies. Despite overtones of sadness and anger in several pieces, there is nonetheless a persisting sense of determination and hope for the future.

Founded in 2015, the Centre for Stories promotes both oral and written "storytelling to inspire social cohesion and improve understanding of diverse communities" in Western Australia.[1] Several of the center's projects mentor and train individuals in Western Australia who have connections to Indian Ocean countries and cultures. In 2017, the center's mentorship for writers of African heritage resulted in a short fiction anthology, *Ways of Being Here*. Its Indian Ocean mentoring project involved participants from Mauritius to Malaysia and produced the 2019 anthology *Wave after Wave*. In 2021 the center started *Portside Review*, a journal dedicated to Indian Ocean writing with editorial board members from Australia, Singapore, and India. These Indian Ocean–centered projects can be seen as interrogating Australia's history of racism toward immigrants and People of Color, which persists to this day despite the official termination of discriminatory immigration laws (often called the White Australia policy) in the 1970s. While this essay is not the venue for a comprehensive critique of Australian race relations, it is worth remembering Ghassan Hage's argument that Australia as a nation is "structured around a White culture, where Aboriginal people and non-White 'ethnics' are merely national objects to be moved or removed according to a White national will" (18). The emergence, demise, and subsequent resurgence of the politician Pauline Hanson and her One Nation party with its populist anti-immigrant rhetoric "has enabled White Australians to unleash a new phase" of "White national exclusionism" that co-opts liberal multiculturalism to politely portray immigrants as "debatable problematised objects" who are "safely positioned in the liminal spaces of inclusion/exclusion" rather than as human subjects deserving care (Hage 246). In this sociopolitical context, it is not a stretch to think of the center's Indian Ocean projects, especially the anthology *Wave after Wave*, as a response and rejoinder to noxious statements such as those by conservative columnist Andrew Bolt, who fears Australia is threatened by "a tidal wave of immigrants sweep[ing] away what's left of our national identity."

Interleaving Africa and Australia

Introducing *Ways of Being Here*, Maxine Beneba Clarke employs a tidal metaphor to describe the twists and turns of its four stories: they are "flooded with the rhythms, poetry and patterns of the mother continent" (8). These African Australian stories offer a rich palette of emotional experiences exceeding melancholia that contribute to "an expansive understanding of African territories and identities" if one looks eastward to the Indian Ocean instead of only westward to the Atlantic (Desai 6). "Light at the End," by Rafeif Ismail, sets the movingly tidalectic tone and structure for the anthology. The unnamed narrator, who came to the country as a child, tries to cope with her friend Nadia's sudden suicide while they are on a holiday trip in a large Australian city attending a party hosted by relatives

---

[1] "Our Purpose," Centre for Stories, June 21, 2021, centreforstories.com/artistic-statement-of-intent.

and friends from their African diasporic community. While the narrator's country of origin is never specified, the fact that she and Nadia speak in a mixture of Arabic and English suggests that she is likely of Sudanese background like the author. The story's structure is tidalectic, told in four sections that move backward and forward in time centering on Nadia's suicide. It tidalectically and temporally interleaves the narrator's different recollections of Nadia's suicide as she struggles to cope with the emotional aftermath, and also juxtaposes her memories of Nadia with a family history centered around the narrator's mother. Although the narrator sees Nadia on a telephone call with her family in Sudan, receiving news that possibly triggered her suicide, she lacks "the vocabulary" to "navigate" and talk about such painful situations with her devastated friend (32). The narrator acknowledges this reticence to talk about pain comes from her mother: the latter "has buried friends and family and carried on" quietly with a new life in Australia, while such "loss is unfamiliar" to the narrator who came as a child (29, 30). In contrast to women of her mother's generation, who were "forced to be more than human in their capacity to feel love and endure pain," the narrator starts a posthumous conversation with Nadia through their social media chat that still exists on her smartphone. Typing "*I was tired once too. I miss you*," the narrator echoes the last words Nadia spoke to her at the party (33). The Sisyphean task of restarting a conversation with Nadia even after death has literally eroded their friendship leads to a tentative sense of hopefulness and healing: "It feels like acceptance. It feels like an apology and forgiveness" (33). The tidalectic structure of Ismail's story, where knowledge is gained or produced through the back and forth motion or shifting between two states of mind or experiential frames, carries over to the anthology's other stories.

"When the Sky Looks Like the Belly of a Donkey," by Yirga Gelaw Woldeyes, juxtaposes exteriors with interiors and the protagonist Ermi's impressions of Australia with memories of Ethiopia. Ermi's encounters with Australian racism are framed in terms of ignorance rather than violent altercations. Extremely conscious of being a new immigrant in Australia, Ermi constantly introduces himself with his name and his country of origin when he starts working as a night-shift university security guard (43). His white Australian colleagues, however, snub his enthusiastic attempts at friendship; Ermi internalizes this rejection because he thinks "it was his fault, his stilted English putting people off" (37). Yet the story does not dwell on this cold shoulder; instead, the physical exteriors of the university buildings Ermi patrols begin interlapping with fond memories of his homeland and parents. Ethiopia and Australia are represented as contiguous impressions, filling Ermi not only with homesickness but also comfort and hope. Perhaps prompted by how the CCTV screens in the central guardroom "cycled through hundreds of locations around the university" (39), Ermi adopts a less panoptic and more reflective mindset as he "cycle[s] through memories" of Ethiopia upon seeing some eucalyptus trees (47). These are "the same sort of trees his father had used to build their home in the village" where Ermi remembers "his mother's sweet quiet singing" (47). These memories keyed to his Ethiopian family home provide Ermi emotional succor and support, in contrast to the cold faceless buildings of the Australian university Ermi repetitively secures on his patrols. Another powerful moment of sense memory occurs when Ermi watches daybreak from the roof of the economics building and recalls how in Ethiopia this "moment when the sun glowed within the womb of the horizon" is called "the belly of the donkey" (55). The phrase pulls Ermi from the Australian rooftop to a memory of watching the sunrise from an Ethiopian mountaintop as "a little boy" as his father "raised his stick and pointed out" important features in and stories about their landscape and community. The rooftop of the economics building where Ermi presently stands, with its connotations of a world-system of calculated inequalities, is overlaid with Ermi's memories of the luminous donkey's belly and his father's oral history of their Ethiopian lifeworld.

The anthology's tidalectic structure reaches its high point in Tinashe Jakwa's story "No Child of One's Own," where there are two streams of consciousness: an italicized second-person stream and a first-person stream presented in roman type. Both narratives belong to the same protagonist, but they offer distinct accounts and commentaries complementing each other because of the inconsistent and eroding nature of diasporic memory—in the words of the first-person narrator, "ruins as memory and memory as ruins" (79). The two narrators trace the protagonist's multistage journey from Zimbabwe (Jakwa's country of origin) to Australia through Botswana and South Africa: "*Botswana had been no diaspora but a mere neighbouring country*" (65); "*you felt ill-conceived as a Zimbabwean in a sister country . . . these fatherlands recognised no daughters*" (66). The alienation faced by the protagonist in other African countries turns into outright discrimination when she arrives in Australia, as her "*eleven-year-old self*" is asked by a teacher to write about the racist politician Pauline Hanson for an assignment about "*a woman leader who has done many a great thing*" (67). The ebb and flow of the two narratives gradually uncovers the diasporic protagonist's estrangement from her family and lack of kinship with fellow Zimbabweans, as seen in the first-person narrator's statement that "*what's in a name is non-recognition as lineages are cast away to be built anew*" (66). As tides of memory rise and ebb throughout the story, the protagonist begins recovering ties to her family by recalling anecdotes and episodes. The men resurface as an amalgam, "brother, uncle and grandfather altogether in an intricate bond" (75), who "remain with us in the flesh of their offspring and soft-spoken with care" and as one gestalt figure "his voice carries clarity and understanding often denied young men of eighteen" (76). The protagonist's mother, speaking in Shona, is more distinct: "a common thread weaves through the years, kudza amai, mazuva awedzerwe; you must cherish and respect your mothers so your days on earth may increase. These are my mother's words as I let her voice ring in my ears, a cherished song" (82). As the story concludes, we discover that the two narratives are not only an exercise in familial reconciliation but also a process of learning how to know and listen: "*You ask after a body's health and are your ears open to its bruises, the subtle ways it makes its pain known, its joys?*" (84). This recalls Brathwaite's comment that tidalectics conveys the contiguity and interlapping of experiences, of pains and joys, in this case not between groups of people but within a single diasporic subject.

The concluding piece by Yuot A. Alaak, "The Lost Girl of Pajomba," juxtaposes two conventional tropes regarding Africa and Australia to destabilize them both. In a story that likely draws on Alaak's own background as a former child refugee from South Sudan, the first two-thirds of the story recount the suffering of Akeyooi, a young girl who is captured as a child bride by a warlord in a nameless African country. Akeyooi is "hungry and exhausted" but forced to march "even faster" and "whipped even harder" by her captor (92). The last third of the story jumps forward in time and space, where the adult Akeyooi, now an accomplished lawyer, watches "as the glorious summer sun slides down over the Sydney Opera House" during a celebratory event with colleagues (93). While this story may risk reproducing a stereotype of immiserated Africans rescued and uplifted by first-world beneficence, the ambivalent ending qualifies any sense of a completely redemptive or assimilative journey. The adult Akeyooi reflects that "beneath the bright celebratory smile lies a dark past. Vivid recollections instantaneously transform a prominent lawyer into a terrified lost little girl. The lost girl of Pajomba. But I suppose it is a way. My way. My way of being here" (94). By acknowledging her troubled past and how it makes her vulnerable despite her present success, Akeyooi's assertion that this is her "way of being here" suggests that being African Australian requires an understanding and affirmation of the pains and joys of the other continent on the other side of the Indian Ocean as much as it depends on fitting into Australia despite facing discrimination.

Akeyooi's phrase also provides the title for the anthology, *Ways of Being Here*, a tidalectic cycling back to the book's beginning that underscores the volume's arrangement. The dialogue that the narrator in "Light at the End" reopens with her dead friend is thematically echoed and extended in the split narratives within "No Child of One's Own"; interleaved between them are two other stories—"When the Sky Looks Like the Belly of a Donkey" and "The Lost Girl of Pajoomba"—in which African places are overlaid onto Australian spaces. These emotionally resonant stories certainly speak of the struggles faced by Black Africans in Australia. According to Hyacinth Udah, mainstream media in Australian reinforces stereotypes of them as "unwanted migrants, victims, refugees, fraudsters" (394), resulting in many Black Africans being perceived as ethno-racial others who cannot integrate into Australia (393). But these stories do not dwell on melancholia. Instead, reading anthologically and using Brathwaite's phrasing, we might see how they express "the xperience" and "movemant of . . . the tide w/in myself," a tide bringing Africa and Australia into proximity through prose, attending not only to "the savage" stereotypes and their resulting racism but also what is "the special & the sacred" in the experiences of an oft-overlooked segment of the African diaspora ("New" 50).

Ebb and Flow of Stories

While *Ways of Being Here* spotlights African Australian stories, *Wave after Wave* represents a wider arc of the Indian Ocean. The anthology's tidalectical structure and thematics are alluded to by editor Robert Wood when he highlights how the "ebb and flow" of the Indian Ocean's "waters" provide a trope for the anthology's "ethical and aesthetic attention to being in the region, which engages with the fact and fiction of what happens here" ("Introduction" 11). *Wave*'s title refers not to white ethno-racial fears of an immigrant tidal wave threatening Australia but rather a sine wave oscillating between ethics and aesthetics, between fact and fiction. Oscillation does not mean opposition. The anthology's sinuous unfolding draws on each term to enrich another; it enables ethico-aesthetic responses to displacement and diaspora that combine fact with fiction, and also articulates voices laying claim to a society where "the discourse of White decline" can "express itself in the pathological political language of a home-grown Australian neo-fascism" (Hage 22).

Wave after Wave comprises three thematically distinct but unmarked sections, each concluding with a set of poems, and a final story that reprises some of the topics raised in earlier pieces. The first two stories and set of poems represent the struggles of migrating and fitting into a new place on emotionally and physical intimate registers. In Raphael Farmer's story "Island Boy," Solan, a Mauritian teenager who has just migrated to Perth, is disappointed by the "lifeless" Australian city (17). His culture shock is compounded by a cutting rejection from a classmate he is attracted to — *"Leave me alone. I'm not like you"* (24) — and his family's explicit homophobia, with Solan's father stating that a gay son would "bring such shame to our family" (20). The story ends with a sliver of hopefulness when Max, another classmate, extends a sincere offer of friendship to share "some chips" with Solan and take a trip "into the city after school" together (26). A similar struggle is experienced by Tina in Belinda Hermawan's "Fly In Fly Out," who realizes she is "a trophy wife" in Perth's suburbs while her husband works in Sydney "on the other side of the country" (35). Although Tina's ethnic background or identity is never specified, her ambivalence about learning "the rules, the social codes" necessary to assimilate into her wealthy new neighborhood as the "only option" to fit in is a sentiment shared by many immigrants (30, 34). The figurative presence of the Indian Ocean underscores Tina's emotional discomfort: her "anxiety" regarding assimilation is "like sand after a beach visit — every time she's shaken it off, she finds grains in her hair, under her nails, in her navel" (34). Her husband's occasional conjugal visits cannot help Tina shake off her feelings of being "forever on the sidelines" of a world that may never fully accept her (34), a common predicament of many diasporic subjects. The feeling of being sidelined and overlooked is expressed in one of Patrick Gunasekara's poems, "Both/And." Gunasekara's speaker is keenly aware of how his Sri Lankan identity and skin color mark his difference in Australia: "I've never seen a body like mine: brown // nipples and olive skin" (40–41). But simultaneously, the speaker is aware, like Solan in Farmer's story, that he is "one of the invisible // Asian queers" because being gay is one of many "dangerous Sri Lankan / taboos" (41). The speaker's predicament of being doubly sidelined, like Tina in Hermawan's story, is not uncommon for many queer People of Color, who still wish to participate in their diasporic communities where they are "still learning how to exist . . . as all of ourselves" (41). Yet Gunasekara's poem "Thinking of a Man Who Is Better Than an Apartment on Bulwer St" rounds out this first section with hopefulness. The speaker projects the loving, physical intimacy they share onto their apartment: "There are so many curves in the front room / they outdo each other without touching / I am flowing with roundness and reality" (46). The emotions expressed here are not clashing but companionate and contiguous, flowing alongside each other into the second section of the anthology.

The second section delves thematically into sociocultural aggregation-disaggregation. Prakash, the narrator in Rushil D'Cruz's "Vulture," attends a South Asian cultural festival but finds that, because he is from "Malaysia," he does not know any of the South Asian languages spoken by the other participants who are "in the centre of the room" (49). Prakash cannot fully identify with South Asia as a central, originary culture, symbolized (when the story takes a fantastical turn) by the festival host, who morphs into a Hindu goddess with "four fully-formed arms" bestowing her "blessing" upon the crowd (53). Prakash's refusal of the goddess's imperative—"My Child. Come Home. I Will Watch Over You" (54)—marks his dis-aggregation from an essentialist form of diasporic identity and asserts linguistic and cultural differences among members of the South Asian diaspora in Australia. Sarah Marchant's "Nyoka," which is the "Swahili word for serpent" (58), is a series of vignettes tracing her personal and professional life back and forth across Tanga-nyika (now Tanzania), Kenya, Uganda, and finally alighting in Australia. March-ant's piece, positioned in the middle of the anthology, links the western and eastern arcs of the Indian Ocean: while her own journey takes place in African countries, she brings each of her "grandchildren" to visit "a country with a different culture from Australia's," such as Indonesia, Vietnam, and Sri Lanka (67). Like the sine wave alluded to in the anthology's title, snakes "continued to wind their way, river-like, through" Marchant's personal and family lives (66), and through these symbolic serpents various countries along the Indian Oceans are placed in contiguous relation without conflation. Continuing the sine wave analogy, Priya Kahlon's poems oscillate between a daughter and memories of her mother. In "Wildflowers," a girl with "skin the colour of driftwood and eyes like emeralds / in a pool of black" is subject, like many immigrants of color, to curious and intru-sive questioning (68). Often asked "Where are you from," she defiantly replies "*Here and everywhere*" (68). The speaker suspects she inherits this defiant attitude from her mother, who would also be accosted by "strangers in whose eyes / she could not belong" (68). This connection between mother and daughter is repeated in "Dear Mama" where it is hinted that they might be of South Asian background, as the daughter asks if her mother was away "at masiji's place" when she called (71) and if Mama "could show me how to make roti again" (72). These attempts at connection are severed, however, when the speaker finally reveals that her mother has died: she asks if Mama "could give me your number for up there / So I can call to tell you I miss you" (72). Although ending with a poignant and personal loss, thematically the poems echo D'Cruz's story about the difficulty of seeking South Asian roots in Australia and Marchant's life writing about family connections across the Indian Ocean.

The third section extends the pain expressed in Kahlon's poems to the pressures placed on diasporic subjects of color by members of their own community. In Sim-eon Neo's "A Bowl of Soft-Boiled Eggs" unemployed creative-writing graduate Nick is reprimanded by his ethnic Chinese mother for not being as successful as John, the son of her close friend June, now working as a magazine editor (76). Desperate to please his mother but suffering from agoraphobia, Nick agrees to be a travel writer for John's magazine without having to physically travel because he will only use "research on the internet" (82). While Nick realizes he could "get caught" for such "fraud," his desire to "make his mother proud" pushes him to this ethically dubious act (82). The youtiao (fried dough sticks) and eggs "soft-boiled to perfec-tion" (75) that Nick's mother makes for breakfast every morning represent her over-whelming love for Nick and desire for him to turn out as perfect as John. Sunitha, a single mother, faces another kind of pressure in "Cosmic Dance," by Priyardarshini Chidambaranathan: she is denied a promotion by her manager, who is also South Asian, unless she gives him sexual favors. Sunitha angrily resigns and, at home, starts painting to vent emotions she had "bottled up over the past fifteen years" (88). Sunitha's painting is also an act of rebellion against her abusive ex-husband who had "paroxysms of fury" when Sunitha painted, until she "finally stopped" (89). The cathartic painting Suntha produces is symbolic, depicting the goddess "Shakti in cosmic dance" with Shiva, her male counterpart, only "a shadow in the distance" (91). Unlike Nick's utterly fabricated travel pieces in the previous story, Sunitha's painting, emerging from a diasporic "life in all its tragedy," empowers her to "finally [be] in control of her own story" (91) against misogynistic men from the South Asian community. The two stories trace a sinuous curve and tidalectic ebb and flow between ethics and aesthetics. Similarly, Michael Joboy's poems rounding out the third section turn diasporic subjects' pain and despair into purpose and determination, even though none of them have any specific geographical or ethno-cultural references. "End of the Line" has second-person and first-person speakers who talk at or over, rather than to, each other. The last two lines— "You are the conductor / And the passenger. // 'I thought it would be different'" (93)—encapsulate the experiences of many in diaspora who have to conduct themselves or their communities into a new country they thought would be different in terms of welcome and affirmation. The emotional toll of surviving in diaspora, conveyed in Neo's and Chidambaranathan's stories, takes a poetic and psychological turn in Joboy's "Somnambulism" where the speaker suddenly "disintegrate[s] and paint[s] the ground with my fibres" (99). This figurative rupture is accompanied by an aphasia familiar to immigrants who are not fluent in their host land's local language: "I'm wishing for the words. / I forget how to say 'hello,' / My tongue has evaporated" (99). Despite these difficulties, like the personification of Rwanda in Kamau Brathwaite's poem-lecture on tidalectics, Joboy's speaker still seems hopeful in an apparently hopeless situation, ending the poem by declaring "I have become resolute" (99). Here is a Sisyphean challenge of resolving to live again despite the odds, which might seem foolish in reality but is resounding in poetry.

Raihanaty A. Jalil's life-writing piece "Gaming the Skin" concludes the anthology by drawing together the preceding sections' thematic threads about the struggles against discrimination and assimilation, the difficulties of maintaining ties to one's culture and homeland, and the pressures placed on individuals by their diasporic community in an unwelcoming country. It also recirculates the Indian Ocean as a cultural space: Raihanaty's "parents are from Indonesia," but "she was born in Malaysia" and has been "living in Australia since [she] was three" (103). As a practicing Muslim she wears the hijab (headscarf) and is friends with other Muslim women in Perth, such as Diyana, from nearby Singapore (106), and Reema, who is of Palestinian descent (108). Her family and friends are reminders of the close historical connections between Australia and Malaysia and Indonesia as contiguous regions along the Indian Ocean's eastern arc, and also of the movement of Islam as both religion and culture across this ocean. Raihanaty's piece shifts between episodes from her past and present. In the former she recounts incidents of verbal discrimination and physical harassment due to her skin color and religion; these racist incidents inform her decision in the latter episodes, where Raihanaty and her cousin Tara (who both speak English fluently) pretend to be inarticulate Indonesians when questioned by Australian immigration officers at the airport. Raihanaty's choice to "ben[d] the rules in the game of skin" (102) is a humorous, if pyrrhic, act of resistance against institutionalized and casual racism in Australia. She and Tara know that although their passports are Australian, because of their appearance and religion they will always suffer additional questioning and luggage searches by the authorities. By "pretend[ing] we can't speak English" (112) they can at least poke silent fun at the Australian immigration officers; in Raihanaty's words, "in spite of being underdogs in the game of skin, we found an edge—using the assumptions we had to grin and bear to our advantage" (113). Faced by a predicament that cannot be dialectically resolved (no matter how good her English is, she is still considered un-Australian), Raihanaty chooses to move tidalectically backward into inarticulateness in order to put forward a socially minor but personally important act of resistance, at the same time maintaining the integrity of her religion and culture.

Conclusion

In *The Indian Ocean*, Michael Pearson's opening quotation from Joseph Conrad describes the sea as "a great circular solitude" surrounding the protagonist's ship, "ever changing and ever the same, always monotonous and always imposing" (29). Departing from Conradian solitude and imposing monotony, the anthologies produced by the Centre for Stories represent a range of narratives that are not limited to a single style. Reading anthologically, we see that the pieces within are informed by the Indian Ocean's histories of migration, circulation, and exchange. They disaggregate the Indian Ocean into particular collective and individual experiences that are contiguous with but not conflatable with each other; on the other hand, these experiences can be reaggregated to interrogate Australia's exclusionary and racially biased national imaginary. The urgency and variety of the anthologies' diasporic narratives bring to mind Kamau Brathwaite's sense of tidalectics as a Sisyphean task—a responsibility to pick up a burden and try again and again to bear it across the churning waters and turning pages.

University of California, Riverside

Works Cited

Alaak, Yuot A. "The Lost Girl of Pajomba." In Ismail et al. 87–94.

Benedict, Barbara. *Making the Modern Reader: Cultural Mediation in Early Modern Literary Anthologies.* Princeton, NJ: Princeton University Press, 1996.

Bolt, Andrew. "There Is No 'Us' as Migrants Form Colonies." *Herald Sun* (Melbourne), August 2, 2018. www.heraldsun.com.au/blogs/andrew-bolt/there-is-no-us-as-migrants-form-colonies/news-story/919f583813314a3a9ec8c4c74bc8c091.

Brathwaite, Kamau. "An Interview with Kamau Brathwaite," by Nathaniel Mackey. In *The Art of Kamau Brathwaite*, edited by Stuart Brown, 13–32. Bridgend, UK: Seren, 1995.

Brathwaite, Kamau. "New Gods of the Middle Passages." *Caribbean Quarterly* 46, no. 3–4 (2000): 12–58.

Chidambaranathan, Priyadarshini. "Cosmic Dance." In Wood, *Wave* 86–91.

Clarke, Maxine Beneba. Foreword to Ismail et al. 8–11.

Cohen, Ashley L. *The Global Indies: British Imperial Culture and the Reshaping of the World, 1756–1815.* New Haven, CT: Yale University Press, 2020.

Conrad, Joseph. *The Nigger of the* Narcissus. New York: Heritage Press, 1965.

Damrosch, David. "From the Old World to the Whole World." In Di Leo, *Anthologies* 31–46.

D'Cruz, Rushil. "Vulture." In Wood, *Wave* 47–57.

Desai, Gaurav. *Commerce with the Universe: Africa, India, and the Afrasian Imagination.* New York: Columbia University Press, 2013.

Di Leo, Jeffrey. "Analyzing Anthologies." In Di Leo, *Anthologies* 1–27.

Di Leo, Jeffrey, ed. *On Anthologies: Politics and Pedagogy.* Lincoln: University of Nebraska Press, 2004.

Farmer, Raphael. "Island Boy." In Wood, *Wave* 14–27.

Gunasekara, Patrick. "Both/And." In Wood, *Wave* 40–43.

Gunasekara, Patrick. "Thinking of a Man Who Is Better Than an Apartment on Bulwer St." In Wood, *Wave* 45–46.

Hage, Ghassan. *White Nation: Fantasies of White Supremacy in a Multicultural Society.* Annandale, Australia: Pluto, 1998.

Hermawan, Belinda. "Fly In, Fly Out." In Wood, *Wave* 28–39.

Ho, Engseng. "Inter-Asian Concepts for Mobile Societies." *Journal of Asian Studies* 76, no. 4 (2017): 907–28.

Hofmeyr, Isabel. "The Black Atlantic Meets the Indian Ocean: Forging New Paradigms of Transnationalism for the Global South—Literary and Cultural Perspectives." *Social Dynamics* 33, no. 2 (2007): 3–32.

Hofmeyr, Isabel. "Styling Multilateralism: Indian Ocean Cultural Futures." *Journal of the Indian Ocean Region* 11, no. 1 (2015): 98–109.

Ismail, Rafeif. "Light at the End." In Ismail et al. 13–33.

Ismail, Rafeif, Yirga Gelaw Woldeyes, Tinashe Jakwa, and Yuot A. Alaak. *Ways of Being Here: Short Stories.* Northbridge, Australia: Margaret River Press, 2017.

Jaji, Tsitsi. "Zimbabwe in Verse: Anthologizing an Alternative Historiography." *New Literary History* 50, no. 45 (2019): 609–39.

Jakwa, Tinashe. "No Child of One's Own." In Ismail et al. 61–85.

Joboy, Michael. "End of Line." In Wood, *Wave* 92–93.

Joboy, Michael. "Somnambulism." In Wood, *Wave* 96–99.

Kahlon, Priya. "Dear Mama." In Wood, *Wave* 71–72.

Kahlon, Priya. "Wildflowers." In Wood, *Wave* 68–69.

Kilcup, Karen L. "The Poetry and Prose of Recovery Work." In Di Leo, *Anthologies* 112–38.

Lawall, Sarah. "Anthologizing 'World Literature.'" In Di Leo, *Anthologies* 47–89.

Lionnet, Françoise. "Shipwrecks, Slavery, and the Challenge of Global Comparison: From Fiction to Archive in the Colonial Indian Ocean." *Comparative Literature* 64, no. 4 (2012): 446–61.

Lionnet, Françoise, and Emmanuel Bruno Jean-François. "Literary Routes: Migration, Islands, and the Creative Economy." *PMLA* 131, no. 5 (2016): 1222–38.

Marchant, Sarah. "Nyoka." In Wood, *Wave* 58–67.

Neo, Simeon. "A Bowl of Soft-Boiled Eggs." In Wood, *Wave* 73–85.

Pearson, Michael. *The Indian Ocean.* New York: Routledge, 2003.

Perez, Craig Santos. "'Towards a New Oceania': On Contemporary Pacific Islander Poetry Networks." *College Literature* 47, no. 1 (2020): 240–47.

Raihanaty, Jalil. "Gaming the Skin." In Wood, *Wave* 100–13.

Samuelson, Meg. "Abdulrazak Gurnah's Fictions of the Swahili Coast: Littoral Locations and Amphibian Aesthetics." *Social Dynamics* 38, no. 3 (2012): 499–515.

Samuelson, Meg. "Coastal Form: Amphibian Positions, Wider Worlds, and Planetary Horizons on the African Indian Ocean Littoral." *Comparative Literature* 69, no. 1 (2017): 16–24.

Schrift, Alan D. "Confessions of an Anthology Editor." In Di Leo, *Anthologies* 186–204.

Udah, Hyacinth. "'Not by Default Accepted': The African Experience of Othering and Being Othered in Australia." *Journal of Asian and African Studies* 53, no. 3 (2018): 384–400.

Woldeyes, Yirga Gelaw. "When the Sky Looks Like the Belly of a Donkey." In Ismail et al. 35–59.

Wood, Robert. Introduction to Wood, *Wave* 9–13.

Wood, Robert, editor. *Wave after Wave: Writers From the Indian Ocean.* Perth: Centre for Stories, 2019.

NEELOFER QADIR

Asia Rising Is an Imperial Fiction: A View from the Indian Ocean

IN THE SUMMER of 2018, the notion of rich Asians, indeed "crazy rich Asians,"
hit a fever pitch with the premiere of John M. Chu's feature film *Crazy Rich Asians*,
adapted from Singaporean American Kevin Kwan's 2013 novel of the same name.
Much of the conversation surrounding the film celebrated it for the representation
of Asian and Asian American actors it brought to the big screen. Yet, both the 2018
film and the trilogy that it is based on are far more concerned with depicting the
meteoric wealth of overseas Chinese in Singapore and, to a lesser degree, the newly
rich Chinese from mainland China. Focusing on the subset of contemporary
wealthy Chinese and their interpersonal dramas of marriage and inheritance
allows the film, especially, to take up a classic romance plot that sidelines any
actors, actions, or histories that do not ultimately prop up the love story. In so
doing, the narratives of a billion other Chinese who are not filthy rich, many
more billions of Asians, and centuries of dynamic histories are flattened out of
the frame. While for minoritized audiences in the United States, the film *Crazy
Rich Asians* satiates a desire for a certain kind of on-screen representation,[1] for
the mainstream, it reveals a broader concern among Euro-American political
and cultural economies about the role of rich Asians, in particular China as the
"new" frontier of economic power.

The specter of "rich Asians" has enchanted not only a white Euro-American
imagination, but multiple Asian ones as well. Since 2008, there has been a notice-
able increase in Anglophone literary and filmic representations from South Asian,
East Asian, and Asian American authors narrating the stories of old and new money

---

[1] The film's more critical reception coheres around the misrepresentation of racial and ethnic politics and their hierarchies in Singapore (Thanapal; Bhutto; Kirk; Tsen-Putterman), even by critics
who are themselves from elite backgrounds, such as Fatima Bhutto. While these reviews offer compelling criticisms, they nevertheless lapse into an East-versus-West narrative that this essay seeks to
circumvent.

Comparative Literature 74:2
DOI 10.1215/00104124-9594878   © 2022 by University of Oregon

Asians *in* Asia.[2] While such proliferation may make the counterclaim—that interest in fiction about rich Asians is inextricably intertwined with Euro-American fears of a changing world order—the work that many of these texts are doing undermines the totality of that narrative. In the vast majority of instances, these narratives are driven primarily by desires to highlight or recuperate the stories of entrenched, multigenerational Asian wealth in lieu of focusing exclusively or even predominantly on the Asian nouveaux riches. Without overrepresenting the relationship between aesthetic production and markets (in this case, the literary fiction market), I want to draw our attention to the coincidence between this "rise" in the production/circulation of fiction about rich Asians and the crash of the US economy that reverberated across the globe, driven as it was by a subprime mortgage crisis. Rather than attribute this "coincidence" to an easy teleological narrative about the baton of global capitalism's polarity passing from the West to the East, I suggest that foregrounding Indian Ocean circularities in our analyses reveals that Asian wealth cannot and does not exist outside the networks of global racial capitalism, nor does global racial capitalism exist without an imbrication across Asia.

Within the contexts of new and old Asian money, this essay follows representations of nineteenth- and twentieth-century Indian Ocean transits between the South Asian subcontinent, the Malay Archipelago, and China to explore overlapping and incongruent representations of Asian wealth accumulation. I put into conversation two contemporary writers, who form perhaps an unlikely pairing: the Indian writer Amitav Ghosh is an established and prolific writer, considered by literary critic Gaurav Desai to be "one of the most dedicated chroniclers of the Indian Ocean" (1531) and his Ibis trilogy—a sprawling narrative that connects India, China, Mauritius, Britain, and the United States around opium cultivation, indenture, and the first Anglo-Opium War—a "paradigmatic example . . . of more southerly routes . . . [that] provincialize Europe and North America" (Bystrom and Hofmeyr 2). Singaporean American writer Kevin Kwan, on the other hand, published his Rich trilogy, including the debut novel *Crazy Rich Asians*, in quick succession; the three novels narrate the multigenerational lives of the "crazy rich" Young, T'Sien, and Shang families modeled after "old establishment famil[ies]" like Kwan's own. Kwan writes, "our family tree goes back to the year 946" and includes "three families [who] intermarried . . . the Kwans . . . the Ohs . . . and the Hus" (Kwan, "Meet"). While Kwan's books do not enjoy the same prestige in the literary press and among scholars from a number of academic disciplines that Ghosh's Ibis trilogy has garnered,[3] the Rich trilogy quickly topped US book sale charts as a bestseller even as its scholarly reception has been quite different, with scholars calling the series "middle-brow" and remaining largely critical of its neoliberal complicities (Hong; Ding).

---

[2] Several of these works deploy genre fiction techniques—such as historical fiction, romance, self-help, and epistolary exchanges—even as they circulate in the literary marketplace as high fiction. In addition to Kwan's Rich trilogy, they include texts such as Tash Aw's *Five Star Billionaire* (2013), Mohsin Hamid's *How to Get Filthy Rich in Rising Asia* (2013), and Aravind Aidga's *White Tiger* (2008; adapted for film in 2021).

[3] In addition to being the subject of a number of journal articles, book chapters, and dissertations in literary studies, the Ibis trilogy has been the subject of a roundtable in the *American Historical Review*, a feat rarely awarded to literary texts ("History Meets Fiction in the Indian Ocean"); Ghosh has been interviewed about these works in *Cultural Anthropology* (see Stankiewicz).

My investment in reading Amitav Ghosh's Ibis trilogy in relation with Kwan's Rich trilogy emerges from a commitment to better understand how differently positioned figures across Asia and the Indian Ocean world were in relation to one another as European colonialism expanded its reach across both these waters and lands. Much scholarly attention has produced a binary focus, dividing communities into either colonizers or colonized, or framed the relation as one between a single metropole and a particular colony. Building on Lisa Lowe's assertion that "the 'coloniality' of modern world history is not a brute binary division, but...one that operates through precisely spatialized and temporalized processes of both differentiation and connection" (*Intimacies* 8), this essay zooms in on representations of wealthy Asians during the European colonial period and the postcolonial contemporary to query their desire for wealth and their practices of ensuring its accumulation across generations of their families. To do so, I read contemporary Anglophone fiction by Asian authors not only in relation to British colonial history, but also, more importantly, within a deep archive of Indian Ocean histories that reveal a millennia-long history of travel and exchange without romanticizing these histories, in spite of such tendencies within the novels themselves.

This essay shows how hollow the proclamation of Asia Rising truly is, for there have always been powerful entities in Asia that both resisted and collaborated with Euro-American colonial and imperial desires. Toward developing this argument through a study of Ghosh and Kwan's novels, I borrow the tools of relational thinking and provincializing made possible through a vibrant historiography of Indian Ocean routes and roots that constitute what historian Sugata Bose has termed an "interregional arena" (6–7) that has "continuing relevance...in a time of intense global interconnections," allowing for a "radically new perspective on the history of globalization" (3). Indeed, my purpose in stitching together these complicated histories to our present tensions responds to Sinophone studies scholars' programmatic suggestions for the field, such as Kuan-Hsing Chen's call to "decoloniz[e], deimperializ[e], and de–cold war" (4) and our studies of globalization and Shu-mei Shih's invitation to work against a "deracialized area studies" (57). I think alongside multiple geohistories to maneuver out of the containers of area studies that partition South Asia, Southeast Asia, and China to consider permutations of racial capitalism that become legible when these spaces are considered together and when European colonial actors are deprioritized: my analysis travels the heavily trafficked routes of the eastern Indian Ocean and the South China Sea; dwelling in the heterogeneity of Global Asias[4] through an oceanic perspective, I am able to "remain alive to those contingencies of place" rather than "hermetically seal [off] the contemporary present" (Burton et al. 498, 500). I focalize on elite Asian figures such as the Parsi and Armenian merchants, Bahram Moddie and Zadig

---

[4] In their introduction to the first issue of *Verge: Studies in Global Asia*, editors Tina Chen and Eric Hayot critique the "epistemological limits of twentieth-century historiography," noting that "Asia has been present in the world-making project of history and human life from the very beginning." They call upon us to "restor[e] a long view to the history of Asia's place in and as the world" (vi–vii). While they are most invested in bringing together Asian studies with Asian American studies (ix) to "cross-pollinate categories of analysis" (x), I argue that an Indian Ocean orientation to the study of Global Asias is critically important to showing how "'Asia' has been 'global' since long before the diasporas of the nineteenth-century" (xi).

Karabedian (in Ghosh's *River of Smoke* and *Flood of Fire*), and the matriarch Su Yi of the Shang, T'sien, and Young families (in Kwan's *Crazy Rich Asians* and *Rich People Problems*). I examine their mobilities, with attention to routes across the Indian Ocean and between the ocean and South China Sea ports as well as the kinship practices that condition their social and material worlds. I am particularly interested in how these trilogies published contemporaneously[5] rely on historical fiction (in the Ibis trilogy) and flashbacks, diaries, and storytelling (in the Rich trilogy) to query the status of Asia(s) and Asians across multiple decisive historical events: the first Anglo-Opium War, World War II, and the so-called Asian century of the contemporary. I read these moments of heightened anxieties and how those anxieties are resolved within these texts by situating them within the Indian Ocean's *longue durée*, a practice that illuminates the Asian mobilities and wealth accumulation that precede the historical settings of these texts and persist into the twenty-first century.

Indian Ocean Asias: A Historical View

The first two decades of the twenty-first century have been witness to a flourishing in historical scholarship on Indian Ocean contestations and connectivities. Scholars from Engseng Ho to Nurfadzilah Yahaya have shown us circuits of trade enmeshed with notions of cosmopolitanism, religious practices, and legal cultures. In Yahaya's telling, Arab and Persian merchants transited from the western Indian Ocean to ports across the Malaya archipelago from the seventh century onward, with settlements beginning in the late ninth century "when foreign vessels in the port of Canton, including Arab vessels, were expelled following the massacre of foreign merchants in the port" (17). Quoting Ghosh on difference as a modality of belonging in a heterogeneous worldscape, Yahaya argues that "port cities of Southeast Asia were shaped to an unusual extent by mobility" and that, in these cases, "the sea connects rather than separates" (17, 19). Sunil Amrith's scholarship on the Bay of Bengal underscores this idea. He writes that the Bay of Bengal's shores "were no tabula rasa for European newcomers to reshape in their own image" (35); rather, these "port cities were as plural as any on earth, and *more so than most*" (3; emphasis mine). "The Indian Ocean," Amrith shows, "was 'global' long before the Atlantic" (26). He suggests that the relationship of Europeans to these "webs of commerce" was "parasitic" (36–37, 61), and the movements across the eastern waterways, even in the nineteenth century at the height of British colonialism, remained circular: "Of the nearly 30 million people who left India's shores between 1840 and 1940, all but two million of them traveled back and forth [from India] to ... Ceylon, Burma, and Malaya" (28). As critical as these merchant networks were—and I would argue remain today—Anand Yang's insistence on illuminating the histories of subjugated laborers that weave together points across these ocean worlds is equally important. As Yang describes in his critical study *Empire of Convicts*, convict workers, in Singapore especially, were vital to transforming the island into an

---

5 Ghosh's Ibis trilogy's publication dates are as follows: *Sea of Poppies* (2008); *River of Smoke* (2011); *Flood of Fire* (2015). Kwan's Rich trilogy publication dates are as follows: *Crazy Rich Asians* (2013); *China Rich Girlfriend* (2015); *Rich People Problems* (2017).

"entrepot" and "hub" for the British. He shows how "convicts work[ed] in tandem with other types of unfree labor, chattel slaves from East Africa…and bonded labor or debt slaves from the nearby island of Nias" (6), arguing that the "island's natural and built environment," including "communication infrastructure and major edifices," would not exist without their labor. Indeed, their labor was critical to putting pressure on the Chinese on the island, and the largest workforce was dedicated to building roadways into the interior that disrupted the agricultural ventures of the Chinese (Yang 154). Carl A. Trocki's studies on opium show how farms that accounted for "between 40 to 60 percent of local revenues…became the favored instruments of capital accumulation among the wealthier Chinese.… Opium revenue soon became the major prop of the colonial states in Southeast Asia" (88–92). Not only did "opium smoking coolies literally pa[y] for Singapore's free trade" (91–92), "opium capital financed the production of all of Southeast Asia's other major commodities" (101). Thinking through these histories together—as histories of competition and collaboration among European colonial and Asian finance networks—critically revises our understanding of both the past and the present we are in, in which flows of migrant labor and transnational capital continue to make sites like Singapore a major node of global racial capitalism.

Historian Kris Manjapra calls on us "to work parallactically to explore these interwoven histories, while also striving to avoid the imposition of false equivalences" (13).[6] In his essay "Asian Capital in the Age of European Domination," Rajat Kanta Ray shows how "richly variegated…the trading world of Asia [was].… What was true of the Eastern Archipelago was not necessarily true of the Caliphate and of the Western Indian Ocean" (456). In particular, Ray shows how, as far back as an "obscure antiquity," there was a robust inland trade and forms of monetization (454), and "Asian traders had for centuries transacted a sophisticated and voluminous trade that included bulk cargoes of essential commodities" (456). He cites, for example, seventeenth-century Malaccan traders and Surat merchants who had stitched together a "tightly-controlled shipping network that stretched at one end to Manila and at the other end to Mokha" (456). Nor does the financial prowess of such merchants and traders disappear as the might of European imperialism grew across Asian lands and Indian Ocean waters; rather, he suggests that "Chinese and Indian financial and mercantile interests were not passive spectators.… Whether in the trail of imperialism *or* in advance of its territorial limits, the businessmen of China and India penetrated more deeply than ever into the finances and inland economies of princes, pedlars and peasants" until the middle of the nineteenth century, when, per Ray, "the imperial communications revolution…alter[ed] the very conditions in which Asian business communities would henceforward function" (466, 471–78; emphasis mine). I wish to linger here on the idea that Asian business communities had to "alter" the ways they engaged in these places and practices

---

6 In a chapter on ports, Manjapra offers a longer discussion of the European relationship to the histories of Asian and Pacific ports (102–15). Of particular interest to this argument is his focus on liberalism's role in colonial violence not as an "episodic" practice, as nineteenth-century liberal theorists have maintained; rather, Manjapra shows how colonial violence is "symptomatic of imperial liberalism itself" (107). In the readings of Ghosh's Ibis trilogy and Kwan's Rich trilogy that follow, I am analyzing the characters' arcs of elite Asian figures in times of imperial wars (the first Anglo-Opium War, World War II).

because I am curious about how "alterations" have been overrepresented in historical, political, economic, and cultural imaginaries as a complete break, such as that no aspect of these complex and robust networks persisted from the mid-nineteenth century onward. I suggest that such overrepresentations perform a powerful erasure that makes it possible to (re)produce the notion of "Asia Rising" or the "Asian century" as a break from an imperial teleology that cast Asian (and African) communities in forms of underdevelopment and belatedness while positioning the Western subject as civilized.

Reading against the possibility of such erasures is a vital practice. As Adam McKeown shows, rather than the "assumption that Chinese labor migrated only under conditions of direct European control . . . the bulk of the over 20 million Chinese who departed from South China from the 1840s to 1930s traveled under their own resources and organizations" (66).[7] The communication innovations, particularly infrastructural ones that (re)shaped the Singaporean built environment, are also deeply embedded within the stories that we tell about the period (Yang 8, 14, 146). Rajat Kanta Ray's "Chinese Financiers and Chetti Bankers in Southern Waters" reveals that the European communications innovations did *not* destroy the long-standing practices of Asian merchants fully. He writes that "these modern Asian enterprises of the twentieth century"—of Hokkien, Teochew, and Cantonese communities—"grew continuously out of nineteenth-century trading and banking groups rooted in an . . . Asian maritime and monetary activity. . . which not only proved perfectly capable of yielding large returns in the new colonial context, but which the colonial interests found sufficiently sophisticated for utilizations in their own operations on terms profitable both to themselves and to their Asian associates" (229). In the two literary trilogies that comprise the focus of my argument in the remaining pages, we see two opposing practices of incorporating such histories. Whereas Ghosh dedicatedly revitalizes plural Indian Ocean worlds in his Ibis trilogy,[8] in Kwan's Rich trilogy it is quite easy to rush past these older networked relationships, for they are most often referenced in passing, as minor gossip, rather than the central story. I read these two texts in conversation not only because of what they might share with one another—anxieties about family legacies and inheritance—but also for how they elucidate aspects of one another and what the stakes are for selective incorporation of complex histories by writers querying the status of Asia(s) in the twenty-first century.

---

[7] McKeown notes that the data commonly cited on Chinese labor migration relies on only three Western language sources that account for only two to eight million people (66).

[8] Epistolary exchanges between the Anglo-Indian painter Robin Chinnery and the French-Indian botanist Paulette Lambert reveal the rich and long history of Canton to readers who are privy to these letters. The Armeninan merchant Zadig Karabedian—typically called Zadig Bey—is responsible for illuminating this history of Canton for Robin, both in terms of the tensions unfolding in the novel's present day between the foreign merchants and their Chinese counterparts as well as the history going back as far as the Tang period (AD 618–907). These exchanges (Ghosh, *River* 262–64, 352–55) refer to well-known European figures such as Marco Polo (also referred to in an epigraph in Kwan's *Crazy Rich Asians*) as well as the lesser-known stories of "hundreds of thousands of Achhas, Arabs, Persians and Africans [who] had lived in Canton" (Ghosh, *River* 353). Robin's painting of Canton's Fanqui-town not only captures these diverse populations but also the built environment produced through their historic presence in Canton (Ghosh, *River* 516–17).

Asia Is the Past, Asia Is the Future

Amid the opium trade–fueled rising tensions between the foreign merchants in Canton's Thirteen Factories, or Fanqui-town, and the Chinese state, we encounter the "doyen of the [Parsis]" Bahram[9] as the Achha Hong[10] readies to host celebrations for Navroze,[11] the Persian new year. The day's festivities—dedicated to "cleansing and cleanliness . . . when the dark shadow of Ahriman was driven from the farthest corners of the house" (Ghosh, *River* 419)—prompt Bahram to reflect fondly on what his mother would have made of him becoming the powerful community elder among Canton's Parsi merchant community, given that his childhood was marred by their family's fall from grace when his well-known textile-dealer grandfather, at the end of his life, reduced the family to penury following a "slew of rash investments, incurring an enormous burden of debt" (Ghosh, *River* 43). When his longtime confidant Zadig Bey provokes him to consider the source of his own riches—a circuit of dispossession borne and nurtured by the opium trade that knits together Bihar and Bombay to Singapore and Canton—Bahram protests. He claims that his mother "would have understood that *opium* is not important in *itself*: it is just mud—it is what grows out of it that is important," adding that what grows out of it is "the future . . . a new way ahead—for myself, and maybe for *all of us*," because, as he elaborates, "*we* are living in a world not of our own making" (Ghosh, *River* 422; emphasis mine). The way out—from the confines of a world made by the East India Company's forced cultivation of opium in India to export to China, not only through their economic manipulations but also the juridical infrastructure crafted alongside it—is to "move our businesses to places where the laws can't be changed to shut us out. . . . With enough money we might be able to buy a country, no? A small one" (Ghosh, *River* 423). The exchange of "country" in the desire to buy one paired with the critique of a "world" where Bahram belies the reality that Bahram and merchants like him, simultaneously colonial subjects but not the subaltern, have a heavy hand in the world the opium trade made. Though Bahram and his fellow Parsis do not have parity in representation in Canton's Chamber of Commerce, he does hold a seat to represent the views of his community, and his particular position as a colonial Indian figure is one to whom many parties—Euro-American and Chinese—appeal in order to resolve the crisis prompted by Imperial Commissioner Yum-Chae's "edict . . . to surrender *all* the opium currently

---

[9] Mark Ravinder Frost celebrates Ghosh's characterization of Bahram, calling him "Ghosh's finest creation [in the novel], if not his entire trilogy" for how this figure "conjures into life . . . a more complex examination of the collaboration and complicity on which the edifice of an opium-fueled British Empire rested" (1543), whereas Pedro Machado takes a more critical position of Bahram and departs from Frost in identifying Bahram within the vein of "intermediary capital," as Bose terms it (Bose 29): Machado finds the representation of Bahram obscures the robust "indigenous commercial structures, institutional arrangements, and exchangement mechanisms . . . that allowed South Asian merchant networks to maintain positions and modes of business (Machado 1549).

[10] The Achha Hong is one of the Thirteen Factories where Bahram and his staff live when they are in Canton. Following Bahram's lead, many Bombay merchants began using it as their residence, departing from a previous norm of living in the Dutch Factory. Achha refers to people from India who "come from Sindh and Goa, Bombay and Malabar, Madras and the Coringa hills, Calcutta and Sylhet" (Ghosh, *River* 174–77).

[11] I follow the spelling convention in Ghosh's *River*; alternate spellings of the new year celebration include Nowruz.

stored in their ships . . . and furnish bonds, pledging that they will never again smuggle opium into China" (Ghosh; *River* 425, emphasis original). That the opium trade passed through many hands—from forced cultivation to refinement in the factories to the cutters that unloaded it from ships and brought them into Canton port—is not to hold each of these figures responsible equally for most of these hands labored under duress across scales of forced labor and coercive participation. But focusing on the wealthy and elite Asians who participated in its traffic is to account both historically and in the contemporary for the inequities that structure the past and the present.

Represented as a conversation between friends, in which they might joke with another, the "sly smile" Bahram gives Zadig Bey hides the panic underwriting Bahram's desires (Ghosh, *River* 423). The echo of his grandfather's "rash investment" is surely in his mind as he alone is in charge of persuading the family he married into—the Mistries, famed shipbuilders of Bombay—to trade in opium. One wonders, though, who constitutes the "we" that would constitute Bahram's purchased country. Are Chinese figures such as Co-Hong member Punhyqua, with whom the Parsis in Canton have an enduring relationship, part of that "we"? Likely not, if Bahram's reprimand to Zadig Bey calling him seditious is any evidence. "'What bakwaas! I am the most loyal of the Queen's subjects,'" he responds, ". . . laugh[ing], but mostly in astonishment" (Ghosh, *River* 423). Thus, in the very conversation in which he seeks a solution to his predicament, we find Bahram deeply embedded, and desiring to remain, within the contours of the British Empire. Such tensions in what appear to be diametrically opposed desires and affiliations ultimately cohere around a desire for dominant position, not one that seeks to interrupt the machinations of an already robust global capitalism. Indeed, in a historical moment that anticipates the 1857 Sepoy Mutiny, Bahram's desire to buy his way toward greater power shares no sympathies with anticolonial sentiments in British colonial India.

Bahram's desire for a country in which juridical and economic structures work hand in glove to assure profit for the already incredibly rich finds a home in contemporary Singapore. While in the era of his journeys from Bombay to Canton, including his final one in 1838, the "fledgling township" of Singapore appeared to him as a "junglee joke" compared to "one of his favourite cities," Malacca, where he stopped in the "old days" (Ghosh, *River* 58), the Singapore in Kwan's Rich trilogy is "a dense metropolis of skyscrapers . . . pulsating energy" (Kwan, *Crazy* 110). Our first look at the city-state in the Rich trilogy is from the perspective of the novel's ostensible protagonist, Chinese American Rachel Chu, who is visiting her boyfriend Nick Young's family; upon arriving at Changi Airport, Rachel exclaims that the airport "makes JFK look like Mogadishu" and she "feel[s] like [she is] at some upscale tropical resort" (Kwan *Crazy* 112).[12] What happens in between these two historical moments—that leads to, not only

---

[12] While I do not have the space here to offer an extended analysis of the remarkably racist ways that Bahram describes an early nineteenth-century Singapore and Rachel describes twenty-first century John F. Kennedy International Airport, it is worth noting how racist language replicates itself across time. Some might suggest that Rachel's inversion in this scene—referring to an airport in one of the world's financial hubs as equivalent to Mogadishu—puts the United States in its place as a world power already in shambles. Whatever superficial satisfaction that might bring to some, the analogy and comparison's power rely on anti-Black colonial and imperial tropes.

Changi Airport, but all of Singapore being "an upscale tropical resort," as one character amends Rachel's view (Kwan *Crazy* 112)—reveals itself in a conversation between Rachel's college friend Peik Lin; her father, Wye Mun; and Dr. Gu, a local doctor who served in World War II with James Young, Nick's grandfather and husband to matriarch Su Yi.

Dr. Gu's telling of the Young family history foreshadows the Rich trilogy's conclusion, in which the family's fabled home Tyersall Park is turned into a museum and boutique hotel. His evasive mode of storytelling that highlights his admiration for Dr. Young's medical service obfuscates Peik Lin and Wye Mun's interest in the Young family. Dr. Gu praises his former colleague Dr. Young for saving lives as part of an "underground medical corp," and later "set[ting] up his clinic in the old section of Chinatown, specifically to serve the poor and elderly" (Kwan *Crazy* 304–5). But working as a physician, even if it was his heritage, is not how Sir James Young became wealthy (according to Dr. Gu, James would have been able to trace his lineage to the Tang dynasty's royal court physicians). Rather, it was his marriage to Shang Su Yi that secured his wealth, who "comes from a family so unfathomably rich, it would make your eyes water" (Kwan *Crazy* 306). Dr. Gu discloses that the Shang family wealth comes from banking and flourished especially due to an astute decision to move the family's finances to Singapore prior to the fall of the Qing dynasty; the timing permitted Shang Loong Ma, Su Yi's father, to invest in shipping through which he created a monopoly across much of Southeast Asia and consolidated the (Hokkien) banks in the early twentieth century. Through this conversation, an older generation of Youngs, T'siens, and Shangs comes into view; people who "*are* the centers of power" (Kwan *Crazy* 307) but also are clearly hidden in plain sight across the political, financial, and physical landscape of Singapore. What disturbs Dr. Gu as Peik Lin and Wye Mun depart, having succeeded in their fact-finding mission, is that he failed to tell the *real* story of a "man whose greatness had nothing to do with wealth or power" (Kwan *Crazy* 309). Such binaries of "greatness" perpetuate a notion of a moral good that can be accessed and thus reproduced by anyone. It elides the very real material conditions that allow a physician such as Young to be selected as the leader of an underground clinic, or to dispense healthcare without pay to the working poor. It subtly reinforces cultures of saviorism distributed across the infrastructures of philanthropy, charity, and heritage as the foreground and permits for an ongoing consolidation of wealth in the background.

Cheryl Narumi Naruse and Weihsin Gui's assertion that Singapore is a "sunny island set in the sea, its national space is always already transnational, its trajectory of postcolonial development already anticipating the global encroachment of neoliberalization" (481), extends Rachel's characterization of Singapore as a place of leisure, intertwining it with the immense wealth that both is present in Singapore, having been accrued over centuries, and that makes Singapore an attractive place for pleasure and doing business for the global elite. Within this context, they argue that "race is mobilized for optimum natural economic productivity, so too are the built up and lived spaces" (Naruse and Gui 479). While Dr. Gu's frames of reference demonstrate his colleague as "giving back" to "his" community by providing care to the poor and elderly in Chinatown, it clearly demarcates a racialized boundary between a Chinese elite capable of tracing their lineage over centuries against a minoritized laboring Chinese. Following Ruth Wilson Gilmore's articulation of racism—"state-sanctioned and/or legal production and exploitation of group differentiated vulnerabilities to pre-mature death in distinct yet densely interconnected political geographies" (261)—and Shih's assertion that "racialization is relational and global at the same time . . . always already comparative as a historical [and] psychosocial process" (Shih, "Racializing" 58) allows us to read against a homogenizing racialization of Chinese persons. In probing the history of the Chinese in Southeast Asia with their contemporary status, Shih notes that "despite a history of settler colonialism, Chinese Southeast Asians have been increasingly minoritized since the region's independence from European colonialisms. Their political and cultural power is not commensurate with their economic power" (Shih, "Concept" 714). To be sure, economic prosperity does not insulate individuals or communities, for that matter, from structural violence fully; nevertheless, as both contemporary cultural representations of racialized difference and histories of capital and labor mobility across Indian Ocean worlds show, there are significant material differences among populations that in a Euro-American racial imaginary might otherwise be collapsed into a singular racial formation.

Asia Is the Future, Asia Is the Past

Mixing institutions of care (such as medical clinics and hospitals) through practices of settler colonialism are habits, not isolated incidents across these trilogies. In the closing pages of *Flood of Fire*, Shireen, Bahram's wife, who is now engaged to be married to his friend, Zadig Bey, appears at the first land auction in Hong Kong in 1841. We learn that alongside the European and American opium traders, Bahram, too, received a settlement for his opium losses in 1839. With his debts remunerated and "large sums [sent] to his daughters," Shireen—in addition to her Mistrie familial wealth—has received "a sizeable fortune, amounting to tens of thousands of silver dollars" (Ghosh, *Flood* 604). When queried by a fellow Parsi, Seth Hormuzjee Rustomjee, on why she did not make any bids, Shireen discloses that she prefers to bid when "the slopes of 'Peaceful Mountain' [are] made available to buyers [since] the air [is] more salubrious there . . . and it [is] her intention to endow a public hospital in the name of her late husband, Bahram Moddie" (Ghosh, *Flood* 604). One wonders whom she intends the public hospital to serve given that Hong Kong is a newly acquired British possession and remains one until 1997 when the British transfer authority to China; the only exception is imperial Japan's occupation during World War II.

In China to settle the debts—financial and affective—that her family owes, Shireen's attempts at repair for the harm caused by her husband's participation in the opium trade are paltry at best. In addition to her plans for the hospital, when she learns of the death of Ah Fatt, or Freddie, Bahram's "natural child" with the boat woman Chi-mei (Ghosh, *Flood* 565), she chooses to bury him alongside her husband to the chagrin of the local Parsi community. She rationalizes that "in death at least I think [Bahram] would have wanted to give Freddie the acceptance he could not give him in life," with which Zadig Bey, who accompanies her in organizing the burial, agrees: "Bahram-bhai would have wanted it so" (Ghosh, *Flood* 548). This moment recalls Bahram's desire for a future that is "ours" but one that is laced with his abiding commitment as "the most loyal of the Queen's subjects" (Ghosh, *River* 422–23). The future in which the "our" is reconstituted between an elite Parsi subject and a multiply dispossessed boat woman in the waters of Canton's Fanqui-town is only available in death and negotiated, if only for the male subjects in this illicit "family." Chi-mei was murdered under suspicious circumstances by men who were searching for her son and, according to Freddie, remains trapped in the river with her soul refusing to rest (Ghosh, *Flood* 446). Zadig Bey's explanations to Shireen when she learns of Bahram and Chi-mei's deaths— about how Bahram died "haunt[ed]"—attempt to ameliorate the incredible violence inflicted upon scores of colonized Indians and across China, yet the crisis of consciousness that Bahram experienced did not entice him to action against his beloved Queen. Despite being "above all a family man ... [who] fate gave ... two families, one in China and one in India" (Ghosh, *Flood* 452), in Zadig Bey's words, Bahram remains complicit in the machinations of Euro-American colonialisms and imperialisms. Thus, Shireen's efforts to endow a public hospital in his name and to bury his son alongside him provide a sentimental performance of commitment to family and gesture toward the relations possible among differently subjugated persons; yet they do not actually engage in a solidarity among minoritized subjects because of the multiple, overlapping hierarchies that consigned boat people and "Mixed-kind-boy," or "West-ocean-child" like Ah Fatt (Ghosh, *River* 87) to premature deaths. Shireen's benevolence in these moments is a sword that subtly slices toward such structures of violence, but, ultimately, is not invested in dismantling them.

Rich People Problems, the final novel of Kwan's Rich trilogy, similarly seeks to refurbish the facade of the Young, Shang, and T'sien families' history in Singapore when heir Nick Young overcomes myriad obstacles in his path to set the direction for the family home (Tyersall Park) upon his grandmother Su Yi's death (1919–2015). Nick, who has been estranged from his grandmother for five years because of his decision to marry Rachel against Su Yi's will, is galvanized to action when his grandmother is hospitalized due to chest pains. With Dr. Gu's exposition of the Young family in mind, we can re-read the family tree in each book's front matter as not only a recitation of their genealogy but a ledger of how wealth accumulates through inheritance and marriage.

Much of Su Yi's final days are passed with her serenely enclosed in a private room while her extended family frantically debates the contents of her will. While the family frets about their futures—immediate and longer-term—readers experience the family's histories from Su Yi's focalization in short but sustained bursts, a rare point of view in a trilogy where her presence looms large, but where her perspective is most often mediated through others' perceptions of her. Through flashbacks, we travel with Su Yi to her young adulthood: a secret flirtation with an unidentified man at the Mount Mary Church in Bombay (Kwan, *Rich People* 68–71), to a reminiscence of her brother Ah Jit, who was "manag[ing] our family business" in Batavia and is said to have died of cholera[13] during the epidemic in Batavia

---

[13] We learn later via Su Yi's diaries that, in fact, she was with Ah Jit when he died and that his death happened on the family's West Sumatran estate. She writes, "It's not cholera. He's bleeding internally. He was tortured by Japanese agents.... They broke his body, but they couldn't break him" (Kwan, *Rich People* 486).

(Kwan, *Rich People* 75), to the Adinatha Temple, where she speaks about her missing brother Ah Jit with a Jain priest; Ah Jit speaks to Su Yi through the priest Jai's body, instructing her to "Trust [her] instincts. This is the only way we can atone for all that our ancestors have done" (Kwan, *Rich People* 154–56). In yet another memory, we find Su Yi in a shop basement in dialogue with her father, where she is being reprimanded for returning to Singapore from India. They disclose to one another how they transformed their outer appearances to present us as "*an illiterate dockworker*" or "*a lady's maid*" traveling with Princess Narisara Bhanubhakdi who traveled from India to Burma by train and through Thailand to return to Singapore (Kwan, *Rich People* 161, emphasis original). Such recollections and Su Yi's journey to colonial India and back during the mid-twentieth century present a remarkably different view of the lives of her "crazy rich" family than the gossip-filled events and trips by private jets. Whereas Dr. Gu's telling of the Shang, Young, and T'sien family histories focused more narrowly on his colleague Dr. Young, Su Yi's memories reveal the families' business ventures and political alliances across a wider geography, from Bombay to Batavia. That they are presented in glimpses from the point of view of a dying woman might mark them as extraneous details, but they take on a pronounced resonance when thought carefully alongside family arguments about who ought to speak at Su Yi's funeral, which features a number of high profile guests— "You only care about the sultan because of all the Leong plantations in Borneo" (Kwan, *Rich People* 322)— or even private conversations around mundane topics, such as when Astrid discloses to Charlie, while sailing on his restored eighteenth-century junk in Hong Kong's Repulse Bay that "there's a family legend that my great-great-grandfather dealt in opium. . . . In a very big way— that's how part of the family fortune was really made" (Kwan, *Crazy* 490–91). Surfacing disparate and small moments across a loud and vast narrative show the family's imbrication in well-traveled routes across the Indian Ocean and between the ocean and the South China Sea. Piecing them together in the way that I have done here insists, too, on their rootedness, in that these are not only often traveled, even if the mode of travel between them has shifted from waterways to airwaves, but that the traffic across these spaces and through the commodities produced there is the root of the family's diversified wealth portfolio.

The reading of Su Yi's last will and testament—conducted at the headquarters of Singapore's oldest bank, Overseas Chinese Banking Corporation (OCBC), where the exclusive legal firm Tan and Tan has its offices—presents a new conundrum for the families, when they realize that she has refused to pass down the coveted property Tyersall Park to a single heir. Rather, the house is parceled out to each of her children, with her only son receiving the largest sole portion (30 percent) and each of her four daughters receiving an equal portion (12.5 percent), and with the smallest portions divided between two grandsons (10 percent) (Kwan, *Rich People* 351–60). Thus, the male heirs in the family combine to inherit half the property, with the majority of that half isolated—as suspected by the family—to the Young family line; Su Yi's daughters, collectively, inherit half the property. While the novel represents Su Yi as a vanguard who disrupts the structures of (patriarchal) wealth accumulation by ensuring that no single party receives a majority share of the house and that the wealth is divided between her male and female heirs, the trilogy's closing pages reveal her actions to be less radically disruptive to consolidating and ensuring the longevity of the family's wealth.

Su Yi's time in Bombay proves critical to Nick's commitment to keeping the family home from going to the highest bidder. The final chapters re-narrate Su Yi's travels across the Indian Ocean in the form of a more "stable" archive—her diaries—than the fleeting memories transmitted from her sickbed. The figure of her flirtations turns out to be a Thai prince, M. C. Jirasit Sirisindhu, "grandson of King Chulalongkorn of Thailand [and now an] exceedingly reclusive figure but . . . one of the wealthiest individuals in the world" (Kwan, *Rich People* 476). Su Yi and Jirasit met in 1941 at the Bombay branch of the British India Office during the Japanese occupation of Malaya; she worked in "code-breaking" and other "sensitive diplomatic work," whereas he helped cartographers in making "detailed maps of Thailand . . . especially in these northern parts near the border" (Kwan, *Rich People* 480). As we learn through Su Yi's diaries, which have been in Jirasit's possession for safekeeping, her eldest daughter Catherine Young was born of her relationship with the Thai prince, a fact glaringly absent from the simplified family tree that appears in the frontispiece of each novel. As it turns out, Su Yi and Jirasit's relationship is why the Thai court has, for decades, provided lady's maids for Su Yi, and why Cat inherits Su Yi's three-hundred-acre property in Chiang Mai. Unlike the vast majority of the rumors and gossip—relayed to the reader via dialogue between characters, emails, newspaper and magazine excerpts—the contents of Su Yi's diaries are largely for her grandson's eyes alone (only three entries from March 1943 are reproduced for readers). While the secret of Cat's birth remains with Nick, the diaries otherwise enflesh the world of a young woman in the service of British Empire, which the historian grandson uses to repaint the family's image. Yuan Ding calls this resolution of the status of Tyersall Park "the crown jewel of the neoliberal racial uplift narrative of the series" for how it demonstrates "the cultural establishment's capitalizing of history" and how Kwan reifies a "version of Singaporean history from colonial subjugation to capitalist modernization" (77). While I am persuaded by Ding's analysis of neoliberal racial uplift, I hesitate at a periodization that situates families like the Youngs, Shangs, and T'siens within a regional history—and a global capitalist network—as beginning with European colonial subjugation. Certainly the rearticulation of the family home as a museum adjoins the family's history to the nation's history and presents what Brian Bernards has called the "Nanyang trope" as a "national policy of 'multiculturalism' . . . [that] attempts to sanitize, but not eliminate, cultural and linguistic diversity" (27). However, I find more revealing what *else* happens to the vast property on which the historic home sits.

The epilogue, which features yet another wedding (between Rachel's college friend Peik Lin Goh and Nick's cousin Alistair Cheng), reveals that Tyersall Park has not only received landmark status and become a museum, but that the property includes "an incomparably elegant new boutique hotel . . . [featuring] forty guest villas . . . set among nineteen acres of lush gardens" to be run by Nick's childhood best friend Colin Khoo (from an old money family) and his wife Araminta Lee (Kwan, *Rich People* 535). Another forty-five acres on the property are devoted to "sustainable housing specifically designed for artists and middle-income families" by none other than Peik Lin's family business, Goh Developments; all of which "sold on the first day of offering, because for so long no one with less than ten million dollars has been able to afford a house with a garden in Singapore!" (Kwan, *Rich People* 535). Much like the secrecy around these families' finances that pervades the trilogy, the financial specifics remain largely hidden from view. The focus on Tyersall Park and its (re)presentation as a historic home not only enact the kind of sanitization and racial uplift that Bernards and Ding discuss, but they function to obscure how such entanglements between national history and elite families work toward consolidating power and wealth. In other words, the issue is not only of an isolated cultural reframing—or a multicultural inclusion in a representational regime—but how cultural positioning is a critical avenue of entrenching wealth. Indeed, the narrative of "colonial subjugation to capitalist modernization" (Ding 77) is economically useful to an Asian elite whose complicities in global racial capitalism have yet to receive a necessary reckoning.

The Uses of History: Racial Capitalism in Indian Ocean Worlds

If ports like Bombay, Singapore, and Canton have historically entered our narrative frames as critical nodes in transoceanic voyages that produced global capitalism as we know it during an intensification of British colonial occupations across the world, then critics of texts like Ghosh's Ibis and Kwan's Rich trilogies must read these novels in relation to a parallel archive of Asian economic activities and strategic complicities with European colonialisms, as I have done here. While scholars who are trained comparatists, working in multiple languages, can address such Anglo-washing of history with a linguistically robust skill set, which has the capacity to provincialize the Anglophone archive, Anglophone scholars are not to be let off the hook. Reading these texts from Indian Ocean frames wrests us away from a singularizing impulse and insists that we refuse easy binaries that position all colonized figures as subjugated under the same conditions. Contemporary Anglophone literary texts and the critics who study them bear a particular responsibility in short-circuiting the ongoing hegemonic relation of a representational politics that privileges a selective inclusion into an expansive network of global racial capitalism that can be leveraged by differently positioned figures—elite Asians or Westerners—toward a shared investment in perpetuating wide-scale inequities.

In the time of the so-called Asian century, it becomes imperative for us to utilize relational modes of comparison. As Shih argues, such a practice permits "scaling back and forth between the world and the text as well as long the intermediary scales . . . excavating and activating the historically specific set of relationalities across time and space" ("Comparison" 80). Such relations foreground "movement . . . not just a description of the past where Relation did its work, the constantly changing present . . . but also the unforeseeable future" so that we might "arrive at interconnections" rather than the universal (Shih, "Comparison" 84–86). Moving across these scales is a foundational practice of understanding and responding to structures of racial capitalism, because "racial capitalism" as an analytic is "sequentially disruptive" to conventional studies of capitalism; it demands we "rethink the past, present, and futures of capitalism" (Jenkins and Leroy 10). Rather than understand primitive accumulation as a modality that precedes the formation of the capitalism system, racial capitalism focuses on "intertemporalities, residues, and excesses" (Manjapra 8). Through this essay's focus on South Asia, the Malay Archipelago, and China, I argue that Indian Ocean worlds are critical to the study of racial capitalism. In that, I follow Sharad Chari, who—building on Édouard Glissant and Marcus Rediker's scholarship—posits that the "ocean calls for attentiveness to mediation, concealment, and haunting rather than an uncritical affirmation of transparency" (Chari, "Subaltern" 193). Ceding ground that European colonialism obliterated Indian Ocean networks of trade and exchange leads to an uncritical affirmation of colonial histories.

In this essay, I have sought to mediate these relations and focus on how histories of Asian wealth accumulation haunt the contemporary, especially as they are reshaped in the current contestations of power in a global world. By foregrounding the ebbs and flows of millennia-long oceanic relationships when reading across key moments in the nineteenth, twentieth, and twenty-first centuries—we can see multiple histories leveraged to consolidate the position of historically wealthy and elite figures. Lowe teaches us that "in order to account for differentiated yet simultaneous colonial histories and modalities, we must retire the convention of comparison as an operation that presumes equivalences between discrete analogous units, in order to be able to think differently—politically, historically, and ethnically—about the important *asymmetries* of contact, encounter, convergence, and solidarity" ("History" 90; emphasis mine). I suggest that an Indian Ocean orientation toward the Ibis and Rich trilogies provides a much-needed corrective that allows us to hold several asymmetries of contact simultaneously, with the understanding that the nature of these asymmetries were themselves not static. Submerging competing histories in one another "destabilize[s] conventional notions of progressive and coherent time and space," which "through unsettledness and unevenness . . . prompts us to think about storytelling as an oceanic force of reconstitution" (Rodríguez-Silva and Sears 17, 13). Indian Ocean worlds make it possible to know otherwise from the Euro-American hegemonic frames that have come to dominate how and what we learn, from whom, and toward what political horizons. This essay contributes in that effort by holding in tension that although elite Asians were colonial subjects, their experiences of colonial life differ dramatically from figures like lascars, convicts, and the indentured and enslaved. In order to have a meaningful reckoning with the violences that structure contemporary life, we must be attuned to these plural pasts, presents, and the possible futures herein.

University of North Carolina, Greensboro

Works Cited

Amrith, Sunil. *Crossing the Bay of Bengal: The Furies and Fortunes of Migrants in the Bay of Bengal.* Cambridge, MA: Harvard University Press, 2015.

Bernards, Brian. *Writing the South Seas: Imagining the Nanyang in Chinese and Southeast Asian Postcolonial Literature.* Seattle: University of Washington Press, 2015.

Bhutto, Fatima. "Crazy Rich Asians Is No Racial Triumph: It's a Soulless Salute to the One Percent." *Guardian*, September 12, 2018. https://www.theguardian.com/film/2018/sep/12/crazy-rich-asians -racial-triumph.

Bose, Sugata. *A Hundred Horizons: The Indian Ocean in the Global Age of Empire.* Cambridge, MA: Harvard University Press, 2009.

Burton, Antoinette, Madhavi Kale, Isabel Hofmeyr, Clare Anderson, Christopher J. Lee, and Nile Green. "Sea Tracks and Trails: Indian Ocean Worlds as Methods." *History Compass* 11, no. 7 (2013): 497–502.

Bystrom, Kerry, and Isabel Hofmeyr. "Oceanic Routes: (Post-It) Notes on Hydro-colonialism." *Comparative Literature* 69, no. 1 (2017): 1–6.

Chari, Sharad. "Subaltern Sea? Indian Ocean Errantry against Subalterization." In *Subaltern Geographies*, edited by Tariq Jazeel and Stephen Legg, 191–209. Athens: University of Georgia Press, 2019.

Chen, Kuan-Hsing. *Asia as Method: Toward Deimperialization*. Durham, NC: Duke University Press, 2010.

Chen, Tina, and Eric Hayot. "What Does It Mean to Study Global Asias?" *Verge: Studies in Global Asia* 1, no 1 (2015): vi–xv.

Chu, John M, dir. *Crazy Rich Asians*. Burbank, CA: Warner Bros. Pictures, 2018.

Desai, Gaurav. "The Novelist as Linkister." *American Historical Review* 121, no 5 (2016): 1531–36.

Ding, Yuan. "'Asian Pride Porn': Neoliberal Multiculturalism and the Narrative of Asian Racial Uplift in Kevin Kwan's *Crazy Rich Asians* Trilogy." *MELUS* 45, no. 3 (2020): 65–82.

Frost, Mark Ravinder. "Amitav Ghosh and the Art of Thick Description: History in the Ibis Trilogy." *American Historical Review* 121, no. 5 (2016): 1537–44.

Ghosh, Amitav. *Flood of Fire*. New York: Farrar, Straus and Giroux, 2015.

Ghosh, Amitav. *River of Smoke*. New York: Farrar, Straus and Giroux, 2011.

Ghosh, Amitav. *Sea of Poppies*. New York: Farrar, Straus and Giroux, 2008.

Gilmore, Ruth Wilson. "Race and Globalization." In *Geographies of Global Change: Remapping the World*, 2nd ed., edited by R. J. Johnston, Peter J. Taylor, and Michael J. Watts, 261–74. Oxford: Blackwell, 2002.

"History Meets Fiction in the Indian Ocean: On Amitav Ghosh's *Ibis* Trilogy." Introduction to special section. *American Historical Review* 121, no. 5 (2016): 1521–22.

Ho, Eng Seng. *The Graves of Tarim: Genealogy and Mobility across the Indian Ocean*. Berkeley: University of California Press, 2006.

Hong, Grace Kyungwon. "Speculative Surplus: Asian American Racialization and the Neoliberal Shift." *Social Text* 36, no. 2 (2018): 107–22.

Jenkins, Dustin, and Justin Leroy. "Introduction: The Old History of Capitalism." In *Histories of Racial Capitalism*, edited by Dustin Jenkins and Justin Leroy, 1–26. New York: Columbia University Press, 2020.

Kirk, Mimi. "The Selective Singapore of *Crazy Rich Asians*." *Bloomberg CityLab*, August 24, 2018. www.bloomberg.com/news/articles/2018-08-24/the-superficial-singapore-in-crazy-rich-asians.

Kwan, Kevin. *China Rich Girlfriend*. New York: Anchor Books, 2016.

Kwan, Kevin. *Crazy Rich Asians*. New York: Anchor Books, 2014.

Kwan, Kevin. "Meet the Real Family That Inspired Crazy Rich Asians." *Town and Country*, August 9, 2019. https://www.townandcountrymag.com/leisure/arts-and-culture/g22143613/kevin-kwan-interview-family-crazy-rich-asians/.

Kwan, Kevin. *Rich People Problems*. New York: Anchor Books, 2018.

Lowe, Lisa. "History Hesitant." *Social Text* 33, no. 125 (2015): 85–107.

Lowe, Lisa. *The Intimacies of Four Continents*. Durham, NC: Duke University Press, 2015.

Machado, Pedro. "Views from Other Boats: On Amitav Ghosh's Indian Ocean 'Worlds.'" *American Historical Review* 121, no. 5 (2016): 1546–51.

Manjapra, Kris. *Colonialism in Global Perspective*. Cambridge: Cambridge University Press, 2020.

McKeown, Adam. "The Social Life of Chinese Labor." In *Chinese Circulations: Capital, Commodities, and Networks in Southeast Asia*, edited by Eric Tagliacozzo and Wen-Chin Chang, 62–83. Durham, NC: Duke University Press, 2011.

Naruse, Cheryl Narumi, and Weihsin Gui. "Singapore and the Intersections of Neoliberal Globalization and Postcoloniality." *Interventions* 18, no. 4 (2016): 473–82.

Ray, Rajat Kanta. "Asian Capital in the Age of European Domination: The Rise of the Bazaar, 1800–1914." *Modern Asia Studies* 29, no. 3 (1995): 449–554.

Ray, Rajat Kanta. "Chinese Financiers and Chetti Bankers in Southern Waters: Asian Mobile Credit during the Anglo Dutch Competition for the Trade of the Eastern Archipelago in the Nineteenth Century." *Itinerario* 11, no. 1 (1987): 209–34.

Rodríguez-Silva, Ileana M., and Laurie J. Sears. "Thinking Comparison with the Politics of Storytelling." *positions* 29, no 1 (2021): 1–20.

Shih, Shu-mei. "Comparison as Relation." In *Comparison: Theories, Approaches, Uses*, edited by Rita Felski and Susan Stanford Friedman, 79–98. Baltimore, MD: Johns Hopkins University Press, 2013.

Shih, Shu-mei. "The Concept of the Sinophone." *PMLA* 126, no. 3 (2011): 709–18.

Shih, Shu-mei. "Racializing Area Studies, Defetishizing China." *positions* 27, no.1 (2019): 33–65.

Stankiewicz, Damien. "Anthropology and Fiction: An Interview with Amitav Ghosh." *Cultural Anthropology* 27, no. 3 (2012): 535–41.

Thanapal, Sangeetha. "*Crazy Rich Asians* Is Not a Radical Win for Representation." *Wear Your Voice*, May 17, 2018. www.wearyourvoicemag.com/crazy-rich-asians-not-radical-win-representation/.

Trocki, Carl A. "Opium as a Commodity in the Chinese Nanyang Trade." In *Chinese Circulations: Capital, Commodities, and Networks in Southeast Asia*, edited by Eric Tagliacozzo and Wen-Chin Chang, 84–104. Durham, NC: Duke University Press, 2011.

Tseng-Putterman, Mark. "One Way That Crazy Rich Asians Is a Step Backward." *Atlantic*, August 23, 2018. https://www.theatlantic.com/entertainment/archive/2018/08/asian-americas-great-gatsby-moment/568213/.

Yang, Anand. *Empire of Convicts: Indian Penal Labor in Colonial Southeast Asia*. Oakland, CA: University of California Press, 2021.

Yahaya, Nurfadzilah. *Fluid Jurisdictions: Colonial Law and Arabs in Southeast Asia*. Ithaca, NY: Cornell University Press, 2020.

FRANÇOISE LIONNET

Under the Sign of Ariel: Disputed Territories, Rising Tides, and Literary Mauritius

Full fathom five thy father lies,
Of his bones are coral made:
Those are pearls that were his eyes.
Nothing of him that doth fade,
But doth suffer a sea-change
Into something rich and strange . . .
Sea-nymphs hourly ring his knell.

—Shakespeare, *The Tempest*, 1.2.400–406

Then all collapsed, and the great shroud of the sea rolled on as it rolled five thousand years ago.

—Herman Melville, *Moby Dick; or, The Whale*

SEVERAL RECENT MAPS of the Indian Ocean region have the merit of including both the terrestrial and aquatic zones of its island nations and archipelagoes, departing from previous representations of nations as land masses neatly outlined by their coastlines, contained within semi-continental or insular territories. The most recent map from Médecins sans frontières (MSF, also known as Doctors without Borders) landed in my mailbox in August 2021, part of their yearly fundraising efforts to remain independent and, as they explain, "go where we are most needed." It is the first time that such a yearly MSF map shows the Republic of Mauritius as a national body inclusive of its member islands in the Mascarenes (fig. 1): Agalega and Rodrigues are there. But the Chagos Archipelago, currently under UK control and US military occupation, is not. Tromelin Island, administered by France but over which Mauritius claims sovereignty, is also missing. The second map (2013), conceived by Rafi Segal and Yonatan Cohen, similarly indicates that continuing control of the Chagos belongs to the British Indian Ocean Territory or BIOT, as does the third map (2019; see fig. 3), from Marineregions.org, an international partnership managed by the Flanders Marine Institute (figs. 2, 3).

Comparative Literature 74:2
DOI 10.1215/00104124-9594891　© 2022 by University of Oregon

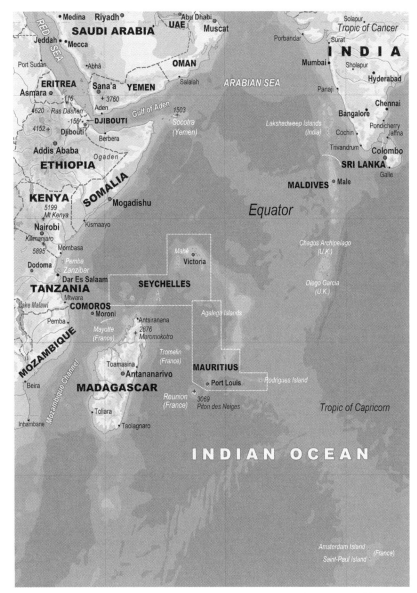

Figure 1. Map by GeoAtlas/GraphiOgre, 2019. Featured in Doctors without Borders' 2021 map and fundraising campaign. Courtesy of Laurent Lafitte-Campagne, CEO of GeoAtlas/GraphiOgre.

None of these organizations concedes the fact that the US presence is in fact unlawful, the consequence of arbitrary negotiations imposed by the UK on the first Mauritian government as a condition of accession to independence in 1968.[1]

---

[1] As the merely advisory ruling of the International Court of Justice in the Hague stated in its declaration of February 25, 2019: "The Court finds that the process of decolonization of Mauritius was not lawfully completed when that country acceded to independence and that the United Kingdom is under an

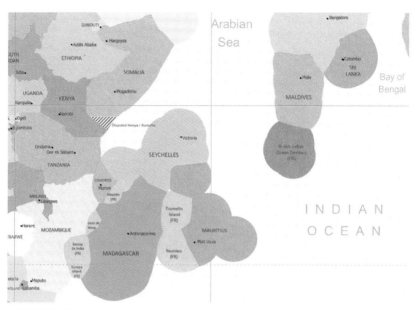

Figure 2. Territorial map of the world by Rafi Segal and Yonatan Cohen, 2013. As the authors explain: "This political map of the world depicts the extent of territories, both on land and at sea (submerged lands), which are under the control of all independent nations. The map incorporates Exclusive Economic Zones (EEZ), which are sea zones whose resources belong to their coastal-lying nations. International law defines these zones as lying within a 200 nautical miles geometrical offsetting of the coast seawards, and, where these geometrical boundaries prove ambiguous, through international treaties" (Segal and Cohen). Courtesy of the authors.

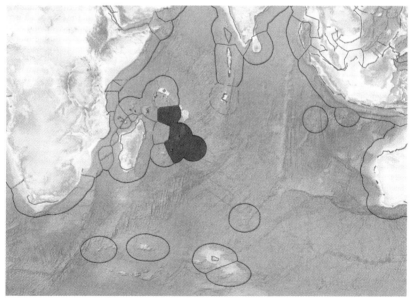

Figure 3. Mauritius Exclusive Economic Zone (EEZ) in solid red, with broken red lines around the Tromelin and Chagos areas, 2019. Courtesy of the Flanders Marine Institute (2021): MarineRegions.org (accessed September 26, 2021).

Even MSF has been blind to the humanitarian crisis that ensued in the early 1970s for some two thousand deported Chagossians exiled to Mauritius, the Seychelles, and the UK, who have never stopped fighting for return to the islands where their ancestors' bones are buried. In a very real sense, the people of this area of the Indian Ocean lived in what Édouard Glissant termed the "hidden face of the earth" (141), and their rich oral culture is all but vanishing.[2] To MSF's credit, its "Missing Maps" project in collaboration with CartONG, a French NGO tasked with providing better maps, encourages the public to provide corrections and new details to their existing information.[3] The two powerful nations' solution to counter the demands of the Chagossian people has been to establish the Chagos Marine Protected Area, an ecological marine reserve of 250,000 square miles comprising the seventy islands and seven atolls of the archipelago. This effectively prevents the return of the original inhabitants, although the presence of the largest US overseas military base on Diego Garcia is known to produce ever more lethal pollution on land and in surrounding waters. The dire consequences of climate crises, rising waters, and fossil fuel disposal are urgent sources of concern for all island nations. Meanwhile, the recent militarization of this area continues apace. India has joined the race and is known to be building an airport and naval military facility on the narrow strip of coral that is the northern Agalega atoll (see Bashfield).

Mauritian writers have been vocal for decades about a situation they have denounced as unacceptable, unfair to the Natives of the Chagos, and detrimental to the protection of the marine environment; but as award-winning author Ananda Devi writes, however loud the people's voice, it is generally met with global indifference. Forbidding distances and cultural headwinds drown almost all efforts: "rien sera entendu sur les terres lointaines que la mer nous interdit" (45; "nothing will be heard of it on those far-away lands that the ocean forbids us" [*Life* 46]), as the young, doomed narrator of *La vie de Joséphin le fou* (*The Life of Madman Joe*) exclaims. An ode to the unforgiving yet nurturing qualities of the ocean, this novella is a reminder of the destructive force of waves and dangerous swells that attack the fragile integrity of the land. Floating in the wide expanse of the Indian Ocean, the Mascarenes are isolated and at risk, coveted by foreign powers who silence and dismiss its inhabitants. In the eighty-page book, drafted with urgency in just three days and completed in under two weeks, Devi stages haunting and fantastic allegorical scenes. We hear the voice of a young boy whose traumatic experiences have made him mute.[4] He escapes his violent home life and

---

obligation to bring to an end its administration of the Chagos Archipelago as rapidly as possible" (International Court of Justice 1).

2 The American anthropologist David Vine has written the authoritative book on the issue, *Island of Shame: The Secret History of the U.S. Military Base on Diego Garcia*, and Mauritian writer Shenaz Patel has written a beautiful historical fiction on the people of the archipelago, *Le silence des Chagos* (*The Silence of the Chagos*).

3 Médecins sans frontières, "Cartographie humanitaire: Chacun peut contribuer!," last updated April 26, 2017, www.msf.fr/actualites/cartographie-humanitaire-chacun-peut-contribuer; Missing Maps, www.missingmaps.org/fr/ (accessed September 26, 2021); CartONG, www.cartong.org/fr (accessed September 26, 2021).

4 "La gifle m'a fendu la lèvre en deux.... J'ai plus jamais reparlé" (17; "The slap busted my lip open.... I never spoke again" [*Life* 24]). "Le silence bleu de la mer ... m'écoute et me dit de me taire: les mots sont inutiles" (19; "The blue silence of the ocean ... listens to me and tells me to hush: words are of no use here" [*Life* 26]).

attempts to survive under the sea rather than on land where his mother and others subject him to constant maltreatments.

Having had to hold his breath as a baby in order not to incur maternal wrath, Joséphin explains that it is now easy for him to do it again "pour rester longtemps sous l'eau. Vivre là, en captant quelques bulles d'air échappées des coquilles" (22; "to stay a long long time under water, to live there, off of a few air bubbles escaped from sea shells" [*Life* 28]). As a more welcoming maternal presence, this mer/mère (sea/mother) gradually embraces him, but in the end his efforts are futile. The destructive power of nature takes over; it literally swallows him as he is eaten alive by the hungry family of migrating eels that had befriended and literally embraced him with their strong slippery bodies.

Joséphin initially develops a supportive relationship with the ocean and its creatures. He insists that our responsibility, as mere humans, is to observe the ocean, its moods and habits; to remember the distinct ways of our island-nation's liquid ground; to adapt as best we can to its unpredictable temper since, try as we might, the awe-inspiring sea can never be "maîtrisée" (tamed). His wise and sardonic interior monologue taunts the reader:

Bien sûr il faut l'apprendre, la mer. Est ami qui la connaît. Il faut la comprendre surtout. On l'a jamais maîtrisée, faut pas croire. On vit sur notre radeau de sable et on se laisse tanguer en lui tournant le dos, remarquant pas les creux et les bosses qui bouleversent nos intestins, en croyant être maître de notre radeau, en croyant décider des choses et des gens, ça la fait bien rire. Surtout nous, sur notre île, à nous démener si fort si inutiles, à crier nos voix sans savoir qu'elles vont pas plus loin que le prochain tournant du vent parce que la voix de la mer, elle est si profonde, si engorgée et si voilée qu'elle avale tout, engloutit le moindre soupir, brume les pensées jusqu'à la folie et on reste là avec notre petitesse, notre mesquinerie, nos petites envies, *rien sera entendu sur les terres lointaines que la mer nous interdit*, et puis la mer, *elle a qu'à sortir la langue un jour, sans trop se fatiguer, elle a qu'à lécher l'île de cette langue paresseuse et en un rien de temps, elle l'aura ramenée là d'où elle vient.* Histoire terminée. (45–46; emphasis mine)

Of course, you'll need to get to know the sea. She is a friend to those that know her. More than anything you must understand her. She's never been tamed, no, far from it. We live on our sand raft here and let her sway us around while we turn our backs to her, not noticing the peaks and dips that unsettle our stomachs, believing ourselves to be the captains of our raft, believing ourselves to be in control of things and of people; it just makes her laugh. Especially us, on our island, trying so hard, so uselessly, yelling our voices out without knowing that they won't go any farther than the next wind gust because the ocean's voice is so deep, so saturated, and so veiled that she absorbs everything, absorbs any small sigh, fogging up our thoughts to the point of insanity, and we stay here with our smallness, our pettiness, our longings—*nothing will be heard of it on those far-away lands that the ocean forbids us*—and one day *the ocean will only have to stick out her tongue, and without exerting any effort, will lick the island with its sluggish tongue, and quickly enough bring it back to where it came from.* End of story. (*Life* 45–46; emphasis mine)

At once frightened and fascinated by the power of the ocean, its currents, and its winds, Joséphin chooses the only survival strategy that can save him from the violent encounters that have marked his short life on land. This necessary, self-imposed watery exile means he must learn to deny himself a necessity of life: air and oxygen.

His situation resonates today with two scenarios of restraint and oppression: not only the now-outlawed chokeholds that were routinely used on suspects by police in France and the United States,[5] but also the historic forms of torture applied to victims of the slave trade forcibly packed into airless dungeons in Ghana's slave castles before being cast into the dark holds of departing slave ships, as Delali Kumavie's important work on airlessness and control, "The Air between Us," demonstrates. In

---

[5] See Amnesty International. One of their case studies is France, where the 2016 killing in custody of Adama Traoré made headlines.

addition, Joséphin's aquatic life echoes the experiences of those who, like the Chagossians, have been evicted from home and deported over the waters. Forced into a face-to-face with the realities of (political and physiological) oppression, they have had to survive by gradually adapting to an economy of scarcity, from lack of oxygen during transport to diminished lives as refugees in Mauritian ghettoes or UK substandard housing estates.

In the end, Joséphin's peaceful yet shocking death occurs precisely where the salty sea meets the freshwater estuary of the river, the eels' breeding ground. It is in this liminal area between land and water that Joséphin meets his fate. His prophetic monologue had already figured the ebb and flow of the tides as a "sluggish tongue" "lazily" licking clean the seashore of all traces of human presence, sending the island "back where it came from" (46) before it emerged from the ocean.

Devi's tale can thus be read as a layered parable of the end of man. It is a brilliant poetic translation of Michel Foucault's view of history careening toward the vanishing point of the human, and of his theory about new epistemes emerging only after man as we know him has been effaced, precisely because his face is but an ephemeral trace drawn in the sand and easily washed away by the sea.[6] The novella, however, is also a powerful echo of traditional Hindu cultural beliefs about the continuum between human and animal life-forms, about rebirth and regeneration, transubstantiation and restoration. As Shakespeare's Ariel sings it, "Of his bones are coral made," and as Melville noted in the last lines of Moby Dick, "the sea rolled on as it rolled five thousand years ago," always sublimely indifferent to the fate of busy humans.

For Édouard Maunick (1931–2021), the revered poet of *métissage*, the island itself is the site of a creative beginning, where new forms of culture and identity are created in the crucibles of colonization and creolization. In his luminous *Ensoleillé vif* (*Sunburnt Alive*), he captures the dance of air and water, the tumultuous marriage of wind and sea forming an inseparable couple intent on destroying everything in the wake of its raging path, without regard for the pettiness of humans:

> désordre des vents
> grimpés de la mer
> (Parole 6 p. 47)

> unpredictable winds
> soaring from the sea

> soumission des vents
> au ventre de la mer
> (Parole 7 p. 50)

> submission of the winds
> to the womb of the sea

> envahi envahi de toutes parts
> la mer dévoyée brûlant ses jupes
> la mer anonyme brûlant ses mats
> (Parole 36 p. 95)

---

6 "L'homme est une invention dont l'archéologie de notre pensée montre aisément la date récente. Et peut-être la fin prochaine. Si ces dispositions venaient à disparaître comme elles sont apparues,...alors on peut bien parier que l'homme s'effacerait, comme à la limite de la mer un visage de sable" (*Les mots* 398; "As the archaeology of our thought easily shows, man is an invention of recent date. And one perhaps nearing its end. If those arrangements were to disappear as they appeared,...then one can certainly wager that man would be erased, like a face drawn in sand at the edge of the sea" [*Order* 422]).

> invaded penetrated from all sides
> the wanton sea burning its skirts
> the nameless sea burning its masts (my translation)

Integral to Maunick's vision is a traditional and grammatically arbitrary gendering of island, land, and wind. His imagination is anchored by his "ILE-Femme-Terre" (41; ISLAND-Woman-Land), three words that are feminine in the French language: une île, une femme, une terre, and that he associates with cultural femininity in general. His ceaselessly creative and wind-like poetic agitation is propelled by these elements. Ariel-like, the poet lives life as a series of buffeting motions in his furious nomadic terrestrial pursuit of the Métis identity bequeathed by his slave and Coolie ancestors—who are now "dans le vent" (78; in the wind). Propelled by their memory and the desire to commemorate lives lost in global racial and ethnic conflicts, he explains that he has searched for and "discovered other insular aberrations. Some like blows to the heart": "J'ai découvert d'autres îles. Certaines sont venues à moi comme des coups au coeur. Pêle-mêle Prague Angola Mozambique Harlem Watts Madagascar Biafra Bangladesh Guinée-Bissau Bolivie Leros Londonderry Québec Palestine Oradour Dachau les Indiens d'Amérique" (89). He feels deep solidarity with all oppressed and marginalized groups as he seeks to understand how, despite the seemingly universal occurrence of the deadly ethnic conflicts he enumerates, by contrast, the mixed nuptials of Creole Mauritians unfolded over time, along unpredictable pathways, but in relative if unquiet peace:

> un lent chemin de sangs fiancés
> de sangs-panique de sangs-cyclone
> (91)
> a slow trail of betrothed bloods
> of panicked bloods of hurricane bloods

This resolutely hopeful vision of the island is also found in Marie-Thérèse Humbert's novels. She embraces Maunick's legacy: for her, *métissage* is the defining characteristic of the same unstable creolized world. In *La Montagne des Signaux* (*Signal Mountain*), a more realist narrative that owes much to Jane Austen and the Brontë sisters, ocean waves are the ambivalent vector of a historical rebirth that returns the island and its occupants—human, animal, vegetal, and elemental—to a utopian state of uneasy equilibrium beyond the lies and vagaries of neocolonial dispossession.

As is the case with Devi and Maunick, Humbert's sea, "La mer," is strongly gendered in an ambiguous way. The narrator's sister April is the Ariel figure of the novel; she exclaims: "Je suis née pour cela, moi: partir" (11; Me, I was born for this: to leave). The ocean is her way out: it figures here as a liquid world onto its own. It exceeds representation and invades the soul, ears, and eyes of the narrator who cannot follow April who abandons her and departs for England. With the cycle of its ebbing tides, the sea is both omnipresent and elusive:

Mais bientôt des vagues étaient venues du large, petites et courtes d'abord, puis plus hautes, plus amples, de véritables houles enfin, lourdes et lisses comme celles de la pleine mer ; elles se suivaient de plus en plus près, elles progressaient avec la silencieuse reptation de *félins en chasse*, avançant, avançant encore, puis, au dernier moment *bondissant* avec bruit sur le rivage, un peu plus haut à chaque *offensive*. Quand elles avaient ainsi *dévoré* toute la plage, ... le lagon débordait d'une eau verte et bleue qui se renflait de partout, une masse, une épaisseur liquide inimaginable.... On aurait juré que la mer allait accoucher d'une autre mer! De partout je pouvais voir et entendre cela ; même si je m'étais bouché les oreilles ... j'entendais, oui, je voyais: ce ruissellement énorme de la mer en travail, et la chaleur qui *casse* tout sur la plage, et le ronflement de forge des récifs. (14; my emphasis)

But soon the waves would arrive from beyond the reefs, small and short at first, then higher, wider, becoming real swells, heavy and smooth like the ones on the open seas; they would advance closer and closer together, progressing like the silent reptation of *hunting felines*, crawling forward and further forward, until finally they would *bound* noisily onto the shore, *attacking* it each time a little bit higher. When the entire beach had been *devoured* . . . the lagoon would overflow with bulging blue-green water everywhere, an unbelievable mass of thick liquid. . . . You could swear that the sea was going to give birth to another sea. I could see and hear it from everywhere; even when I had covered my ears . . . the rumbling flow of the sea in labor, and the oppressive heat *beating down* on the beach, and the forge-like roar of the reefs. (my translation)

The semantic field of Humbert's signature descriptive style is remarkable for the precision with which it conveys the aggressive, military-like encounter between water and earth. To describe the rising tide, she uses the image of an organized hungry pack of wild animals—hunting felines, attacking, bounding, devouring, destroying—in whose presence the fragile shore has no chance and humans are reduced to insignificance, overtaken by events beyond their control.

What emerges from this brief account is the stunning consistency of the aesthetic response of some of the most incisive writers of Mauritius, whose literary imagination is open to global realities, past and present. As this archipelagic area continues to be coveted by strong nations—France, India, the United Kingdom, and the United States—their imperialist geopolitics include demands to position their military arsenal in ever more strategic sites of the Indian Ocean. Writers and artists respond with strong, but eventually futile, pushback against an impossible situation. These responses are mediated by their eloquent poetic attachment to two of the four elements—namely, water and air, which can of course be understood here as the enemies of military fire and terrestrial conquest, and as irresistible cosmic forces that will eventually prevail in the *longue durée* of the planet.

Such creative responses appear to reveal a degree of resignation about the troubling short-term consequences of the violence meted out by the natural world, on the one hand, and the historical power struggles of nations, on the other. These include rising tides and ever-stronger storms, together with foreign encroachments by colonizing entities. But if Devi, Maunick, and Humbert show a marked fatalism about humanity's terrestrial future, they also suggest that it is possible to have unwavering confidence in the destructive and reconstructive resources of our ocean, a force more massive and enduring than any on earth. Rather than merely bemoan its material exploitation, to which they are not blind, these writers' works reveal a deep-seated conviction that the ocean will prevail and "roll on" long after land formations and their occupants have disappeared or undergone "a sea-change / Into something rich and strange."

Works Cited

Amnesty International. "Police Violence around the World." www.amnestyusa.org/issues/deadly-force-police-accountability-police-violence/ (accessed September 26, 2021).

Bashfield, Samuel. "Why Is India Building a Military Base on Agaléga Island?" *Al Jazeera*, August 5, 2021. www.aljazeera.com/opinions/2021/8/5/why-is-india-building-a-military-base-on-agalega-island (accessed September 26, 2021).

Devi, Ananda. *La vie de Joséphin le fou*. Paris: Gallimard, 2003.

Devi, Ananda. *The Life of Madman Joe*. Translated by Heather Suzanne Jones. Unpublished manuscript, PDF. Submitted for the degree of Master of Liberal Arts, Indiana University, May 2007.

Foucault, Michel. *Les mots et les choses*. Paris: Gallimard, 1966.

Foucault, Michel. *The Order of Things: An Archaeology of the Human Sciences*. London: Tavistock, 1970.

Glissant, Édouard. *Le discours antillais*. Paris: Seuil, 1981.

Humbert, Marie-Thérèse. *La Montagne des Signaux*. Paris: Stock, 1994.

International Court of Justice. "Legal Consequences of the Separation of the Chagos Archipelago from Mauritius in 1965." Press release no. 2019/9, February 25, 2019. MarineRegions.org, Flanders Marine Institute. www.marineregions.org/documents/169-20190225-PRE-01-00-EN.pdf (accessed September 26, 2021).

Kumavie, Delali. "The Air between Us: Reading The Poetics of Air in Global Black Literature." Paper presented at the Mellon seminar of the Mahindra Humanities Center, Harvard University, February 25, 2021.

Maunick, Édouard. *Ensoleillé vif*. Paris: Nouvelles éditions africaines, 1976.

Patel, Shenaz. *Le silence des Chagos*. Paris: L'Olivier, 2005.

Patel, Shenaz. *The Silence of the Chagos*, translated by Jeffrey Zuckerman. New York; Restless Books, 2019.

Segal, Rafi, and Yonatan Cohen. "Territorial Map of the World." openDemocracy, October 7, 2013. www.opendemocracy.net/en/territorial-map-of-world/.

Vine, David. *Island of Shame: The Secret History of the U.S. Military Base on Diego Garcia*. Princeton, NJ: Princeton University Press, 2009.